RESILIENT CITY

LANDSCAPE ARCHITECTURE
FOR CLIMATE CHANGE

Elke Mertens

RESILIENT CITY

Elke Mertens
**LANDSCAPE ARCHITECTURE
FOR CLIMATE CHANGE**

BIRKHÄUSER BASEL

RESILIENT CITY

Table of Contents

Foreword	7
RESILIENCE AS A FACTOR OF URBAN DEVELOPMENT	9
TORONTO	17
VANCOUVER	37
NEW YORK CITY	57
DETROIT	83
HOUSTON	95
BOGOTÁ	115
MEDELLÍN	135
RIO DE JANEIRO	161
MANAUS	181
BRASÍLIA	199
MONTEVIDEO	221
LANDSCAPE ARCHITECTURE AND THE RESILIENCE OF CITIES IN TIMES OF CLIMATE CHANGE	235
References/Sources	244
Index	251
Illustration Credits	254
About the Author	255
Thank you!	255
Imprint	255

PROJECTS, INSTITUTIONS, INITIATIVES

Amazonia 186
Botanical Gardens, Manaus 191
Buffalo Bayou Park, Houston 100
CALP—Collaborative for Advanced Landscape Planning, Vancouver 51
Campus Martius Plaza, Detroit 92
La Ciclovía, Bogotá 130
Citizen's Coolkit 53
Civic Center of the Department of Antioquia, Medellín 153
Climate Museum, New York City 68
Complete Streets and Green Streets, Toronto 20
Corredor Verde Recreio, Rio de Janeiro 176
Domino Park, New York City 69

Ecovila Aldeia do Altiplano, Brasília 211
EPM Building, Medellín 156
Evergreen Brick Works, Toronto 24
Future Delta 2.0 52
Governors Island Park, New York City 63
Greenest City, Vancouver 42
Humedal Santa Barbara, Bogotá 124
Hunter's Point South Park, New York City 73
INPA and the ATTO Research Project, Manaus 195
Institute of Design, University of Uruguay, Montevideo 232
Keep Growing Detroit 89
Levy Park, Houston 107
Mauá Square with New Museums, Rio de Janeiro 169
Midtown Park, Houston 111
Millennium Water Olympic Village, False Creek, Vancouver 44

Moravia, Medellín 150
National Resettlement Plan, Montevideo 231
Park Libraries, Medellín 144
Parque 93 and the DEMOS P 93 Master Plan, Bogotá 120
Parque del Río, Medellín 142
Parque de la Imaginación, Medellín 146
Parque de los Deseos, Medellín 147
Parque de los Pies Descalzos, Medellín 148
PICS—Pacific Institute for Climate Solutions, Vancouver 56
Porto Maravilha, Rio de Janeiro 166
Ruta N, Medellín 157
Sidewalk Labs and the Quayside Project, Toronto 32
University of Brasília 214
Tominé Regional Park, Bogotá 131
Wychwood Barns, Toronto 27

FOREWORD

Richard Stiles

Colonial histories record that it was in 1855 that the Scottish explorer David Livingstone "discovered" that massive wonder of nature which he named Victoria Falls. Today, from our somewhat more enlightened perspective, we ask ourselves how it could be that the local native population had for centuries completely failed to notice this spectacle and that they required a foreign explorer to point it out to them!

Such colonial hubris comes to mind when one reflects on the recent rise to prominence of green infrastructure as a potential new savior of our cities and landscapes in the face of today's combined climate and biodiversity crises. The first use of the term "green infrastructure" can be traced back to a 1994 report on land conservation to the governor of Florida,[1] yet what is now being referred to as urban green infrastructure is surely nothing more than the very parks and squares that William Pitt "the Elder," British prime minister during the middle of the 18th century, was already referring to as "the lungs of London."

The fact that the life-enhancing qualities of urban green spaces have long been understood is further reinforced by examples such as the work of the prolific writer on gardens and horticulturalist, John Claudius Loudon, who was instrumental in proposing urban green space planning concepts for London with his *Hints for Breathing Places for the Metropolis,* published in 1829. Understanding parks and green spaces as "lungs" and "breathing spaces" viewed them very much from the perspective of green infrastructure, as did the call for "green rings around cities" in a German publication in 1874 by Adelheid Ponińska, Countess of Dohna-Schlodien, or the promotion of "sanitary greenspace for cities" in the 1915 dissertation of the Berlin city planner, Martin Wagner.

So if green infrastructure, like the Victoria Falls, is not such a new phenomenon after all, but perhaps just a new way of looking at something we have known about all along, then perhaps it is not "foreign" explorers that we need to bring it to our attention, but rather the "local knowledge" of those "natives" who knew it was there all along. As this excellent book wastes no time in reminding us, those "natives" are in fact landscape architects, for whom the planning and design of urban greenspace has long been a major concern. *Resilient City* invites us to view the urban environment from a fresh perspective, drawing attention to the critical relationship between three factors: climate change, green infrastructure, and resilience.

[1] Karen Firehock (2010): A Short History of the Term Green Infrastructure and Selected Literature, January 2010, www.gicinc.org/PDFs/GI%20History.pdf

With the help of eleven city portraits of metropolises located across a wide spectrum of climate zones in the Americas, from Vancouver in Canada to Montevideo in Uruguay, it illustrates the ways in which landscape architecture is seeking to use different forms of green infrastructure to promote resilience to the impacts of climate change. In each case, a general introduction to the conditions in the city together with the challenges posed by the changing urban climate are followed by in-depth examples of landscape policies, plans, and projects which are being developed to strengthen the future resilience of the cities concerned. What these examples also highlight is the fact that, while the amelioration of climate change impacts is a vital function of urban green infrastructure, it is not its only function. As a rule, green infrastructure does not exist independently of traditional parks and urban greenspaces, and thus its role in promoting resilience has to happen alongside their many other time-honored functions, from being urban lungs and breathing spaces, to attractive places for recreation and relaxation, refuges for flora and fauna, as well as being important carriers of meanings and values for the people of the city.

As *Resilient City* convincingly demonstrates, navigating this, at first sight unfamiliar territory of urban green infrastructure does not, after all, call for a new breed of colonial explorer; instead we can put our faith in the tried and tested knowledge and skills of our reliable "native" guides to this terrain, landscape architects.

FOREWORD

RESILIENCE AS A FACTOR OF URBAN DEVELOPMENT

URBAN GREEN INFRASTRUCTURE

Today, more than half the world's population live, work, and spend their time in cities. To lead productive and fulfilling lives, they need healthy environments that allow them to flourish and realize their potential. In this context, green areas and public spaces where people can spend free time, play, exercise, and relax are of vital importance for cities. As experts for the design, construction, and maintenance of outdoor spaces, landscape architects play an important role, and in times of climate change, it is their competence that is especially needed to address the increasingly challenging and important planning and design tasks facing cities.

Green open spaces such as parks and gardens not only provide recreational opportunities for city dwellers but also serve other functions, such as ecological compensation areas for sealed surfaces, fresh air corridors for ventilating the city, and retention, infiltration, and evaporation surfaces for maintaining the water balance. In addition, they are needed as buffers for increasingly recurrent extreme weather events, during either heavy rainfall and storm surges or heat and extended dry periods. These functions, which are vital in all cities, are often referred to as green infrastructure, or, where bodies of water are also involved, as green-blue infrastructure. Like gray infrastructure—the technical facilities and utilities for supply and disposal, and social infrastructure, such as schools, care facilities, hospitals, sports grounds, and cultural facilities—green spaces are equally a form of infrastructure that serves important needs. They are generally accessible to the public as places to meet and are usually provided and looked after by the public sector, even if the land does not always belong to the city.

Any form of infrastructure only functions effectively if well maintained and kept in optimal condition on an ongoing basis. Green infrastructure, when properly managed, even becomes more valuable over time as vegetation grows, because the effect it brings improves as plants mature compared with when they were just planted. A further important quality of infrastructure is flexibility—especially in the context of climate change. Many gray infrastructure assets, such as road and rail structures or canals, flood protection walls or dams, as well as larger buildings, are static and can adapt only slightly to changing conditions. Green infrastructure, on the other hand, has a high degree of spatial and temporal flexibility, and its functions can adapt more quickly to new environmental conditions, such as climate change. In addition, green infrastructure serves multiple functions: alongside being spaces for urban recreation, they help keep cities cool, retain groundwater, and bind and convert CO_2. Unlike gray or social infrastructure, green-blue infrastructure has no standard solutions, and must respond to the specific conditions of each place and be regularly reviewed, adjusted, and redeveloped, especially with regard to climate resilience. Adapting green infrastructure to changing climatic conditions is therefore an iterative process of ongoing development and management. While landscape architecture has increasingly embraced the wider remit of green infrastructure, in practice it still often fails to fully utilize the spectrum of available sustainable opportunities, such as rainwater harvesting, green roofs and facades, natural shading using tree canopies, and urban gardening.

This book looks at eleven cities in North and South America and examples of some of their outstanding projects by landscape architects to show how cities are preparing for climate change and using landscape architecture to mitigate its effects. Each of the cities was visited in 2018 and 2019 as were many remarkable landscape architecture projects and other relevant climate initiatives, and the author met and talked to numerous landscape architects, city administrators, and research institutions. Finally, the projects and lessons learned were evaluated and presented in this book. The approaches and plans described can serve as models for other cities, and the projects likewise as pioneering examples of new landscape architecture that can make a significant contribution to climate adaptation. Together they illustrate the factors that need to be considered in the design and development of climate-resilient open spaces. Of particular importance is collaboration with other disciplines and it is here that landscape architects can play a leading role.

CITIES IN THE CONTEXT OF CLIMATE CHANGE

While cities have been identified as major contributors to pollution and the emission of greenhouse gases in the discourse on climate change, city dwellers are also among those most directly affected by its impacts. Cities, therefore, have a particular responsibility to effectively reduce the causes of climate change and, at the same time, must also ensure that their citizens and urban infrastructure are not harmed by its effects. Many cities are already experiencing the urban heat island effect and accompanying heat stress for its citizens. Clearly, people are less able to adapt to higher temperatures, and young children and the elderly are particularly vulnerable to extreme heat. Climate change is therefore already affecting urban climates and its impacts are likely to be more pronounced in future. Even though the scale of the challenge varies, every city in the world is faced with the task of limiting such impacts and must adopt effective measures based on its size, geographic location, climatic conditions, and social and economic situation, to mitigate the impacts of climate change on economic and political equality, environmental justice, food security, public health, and biodiversity. In particular, the creation of networks between cities can help share knowledge and experience, and contribute to developing concerted action towards more rapid climate resilience, which ultimately benefits urban populations around the world.

Of central importance for research on the causes and consequences of climate change around the world is the Intergovernmental Panel on Climate Change (IPCC). Founded in 1988 by the World Meteorological Organization and the United Nations Environment Programme (UNEP), it is based in Geneva and serves as a source of information on climate change for policymakers, industry, and the general public. All 193 United Nations Member States can participate in the IPCC. It is divided into three Working Groups: the first works on the scientific basis of climate change, the second on the impacts and options for adaptation and vulnerability due to climate change, and the third on mitigating climate change by reducing emissions. The IPCC compiles findings from global research and regularly publishes assessment reports, which undergo a thorough scientific peer review process and are thus highly reputable. Additionally, the IPCC provides a knowledge base for decision-makers and is an important advisor to the UN Framework Convention on Climate Change. The upcoming Sixth Assessment Report will be published in 2021/22. Among the IPCC Special Reports are those on *Global Warming of 1.5 °C* and on *Climate Change and Land*, published in 2018 and 2019, respectively. A working group report on the *Mitigation of Climate Change* was prepared as part of the Fifth Assessment Report in 2014.

The IPCC Reports attribute climate change to the emission of greenhouse gases into the atmosphere from anthropogenic sources. Of these, the most harmful gases are carbon dioxide (CO_2), methane (CH_4), nitrous oxide (N_2O), and man-made fluorinated (F) gases (HFCs, PFCs, and SF_6), with CO_2 accounting for the largest share. The major source of CO_2 is the combustion of fossil fuels in the power conversion systems of electric power plants, aircraft and vehicle engines, cooking, space heating, and industrial manufacturing processes. While these emissions account for the largest share of greenhouse gases, a further third of emissions result from agriculture (mainly CH_4 and N_2O), deforestation (mainly CO_2), fossil fuel production (mainly CH_4), industrial processes (mainly CO_2, N_2O, and F-gases), as well as municipal waste and wastewater (mainly CH_4).

Among the most common impacts of climate change are increasing temperatures and heat stress, rising sea levels with more frequent storm surges and heavy rain events, and flooding. Climate change affects all major climate parameters—temperature, precipitation, wind speed and direction—and the exact impacts of these changes are still unclear. Similarly, it is hard to make accurate predictions about the ramifications that will affect a city, when, or to what extent. What is clear, however, is that if cities evolve sustainably to address climate change, this will benefit climate adaptation around the world.

Although societies and cities are changing greatly as part of the global megatrend of urbanization, it was not until its Fifth Assessment Report in 2014 that the IPCC included a chapter on "Human Settlements, Infrastructure, and Spatial Planning" as part of the Working Group Report on *Mitigation of Climate Change*. By 2050, the urban population is expected to grow by 2.5 to 3 billion and will account for 64 to 69 percent of the world's population. There will also be correspondingly more urban spaces and infrastructure than at present. How cities and urban areas develop in the coming decades will be crucial for global energy consumption and CO_2 emissions.

Already in 2014, cities were estimated to account for between 67 and 76 percent of global energy consumption, and 71 to 76 percent of global energy-related CO_2 emissions. In the context of the urban realm, the factors that contribute most to greenhouse gas emissions include density of development, land use mix, and transportation and accessibility, which strongly determine traffic flows and volumes. Since these aspects interact with each other, they should therefore be considered not as isolated but rather as interdependent factors.

While cities are responsible for a high proportion of global CO_2 emissions, they occupy only 2 to 3 percent of the Earth's land area. Although the growth of conurbations will increase this to 4 to 5 percent by 2050, the ratio will still be disproportionate. Considering that cities are think tanks with the economic, scientific, and political potential to steer climate-sensitive development, and at the same time are major contributors to global warming, they have both the opportunity and a special obligation to positively influence climate change. Their focus must be twofold: on reducing, and ideally avoiding the production of greenhouse gas emissions (mitigation), and on reducing the impact of the changes that are occurring (adaptation).

Since cities are dependent on their hinterland for food production, for parts of their infrastructure, and for recreation, it is also important to establish a climate-respecting connection between the city and its surroundings. As cities grow, they expand into areas formerly used for agriculture and forestry, resulting in land use conflicts. Agricultural land, which currently accounts for 37 percent of the world's land area, has increased over the last three decades, especially in the tropics. To feed the growing world population, even greater areas of agricultural land will be needed. Much of it is converted into large-scale farming of meat and of soybeans, the latter being mostly used as animal feed, and for the extraction of palm oil. This in turn results in a tragic loss of biodiversity and ecosystem capacity, including the sequestering of CO_2. In contrast to the growing consumption of land by cities and for agriculture, forests are dwindling. Currently, forests account for about 29 percent of the world's land area, of which about two-thirds is forested, and only 36 percent is primary forest. Despite large-scale afforestation in various regions around the world, forests are being razed at an alarming rate, contributing to a loss of biodiversity and ecosystem capacity, as well as higher land erosion due to the removal of land cover and lower soil fertility.

The 2019 IPCC *Special Report on Climate Change and Land* points out in its "Summary for Policymakers" that land use actions that help adapt to climate change and mitigate negative impacts also counter desertification and land degradation, and improve food security. It explicitly mentions the mitigation potential of better cropland and livestock management, of agroforestry and systemic improvements to the entire food system from production to consumption, including food loss and waste.

The IPCC proposes Climate-Resilient Development Pathways (CRDPs) that can be used to shape a society-wide desirable future that is both socially equitable and low in carbon dioxide emissions. These correlate to the United Nations Sustainable Development Goals (SDGs) and the statements of the Paris Climate Agreement, in which the implementation of rapid greenhouse gas reductions must be based on equity and take place in the context of sustainable development and efforts to eradicate poverty. The CRDPs combine the near-term implementation of the Sustainable Development Goals with a long-term sustainable strategy for development and reducing emissions to net zero by the middle of the century. To achieve this, urban habitats must become more resilient and able to adapt flexibly. Aside from that, networks are needed to enable and promote exchange when elaborating CRDPs, but each city will still need to develop its own CRDPs.

The 2018 IPCC Special Report on *Global Warming of 1.5°C* stresses the importance of not exceeding the 1.5°C global warming goal agreed at the 2015 Paris Climate Summit, because any effort required to adapt to temperatures beyond that is much greater. It also underlines that adaptation measures must go further than merely responding to specific impacts of climate change, for example building a seawall as a barrier against tidal surges, and instead require profound, systemic change, such as new strategies for responding to storm surges and runoff from rainfall events. This kind of transformative adaptation also involves reshaping social and ecological systems. In this respect, the IPCC's goals to meet the 1.5°C limit overlap to a large extent with the United Nations SDGs, which were also adopted in 2015.

The 17 SDGs are part of the 2030 Agenda, the UN's global plan to promote sustainable peace and prosperity and to protect the planet. To this end, national development plans should address the problems of poverty and social inequality, paying particular attention to the most vulnerable populations so that no one is left out in the effort to achieve the Agenda's goals by 2030. Overall, the SDGs aim to eradicate extreme poverty and hunger; to secure health, education, peace, clean water, and clean energy for all; to promote inclusiveness and sustainability in consumption, cities, infrastructure, and economic growth; to reduce inequalities such as those between genders; to combat climate change; and to protect the oceans and terrestrial ecosystems. *Goal 13: Climate Action* explicitly identifies climate change, its negative impacts on economies and the lives of people, especially the poorest and most vulnerable. Other goals closely linked to climate change include *Goal 3: Good Health and Well-Being*, *Goal 7: Affordable and Clean Energy*, and *Goal 11: Sustainable Cities and Communities*. *Goal 17: Partnerships to achieve the Goals* stresses the need to build networks and many cities have already established very good global connections, for example through the C40 cities and 100 Resilient Cities Network.

At present, C40 brings together 97 of the world's largest cities taking climate action to achieve a healthier and more sustainable future. The mayors of these cities, which together are home to more than 700 million citizens and account for a quarter of the global economy, have pledged to steer development in their cities to meet the climate goals of the 2015 Paris Agreement, and also to substantially improve their city's air quality by combating pollution. Among the cities featured in this book, Toronto, Vancouver, New York City, Houston, Bogotá, Medellín, and Rio de Janeiro belong to the C40.

The 100 Resilient Cities Network (100RC) was established in 2013 by the U.S. Rockefeller Foundation to help cities build resilience to the challenges of the 21st century. Of the more than 1,000 cities that applied, 100 were selected. These received project-based financial support over six years, as well as funding for a resilience manager to steer the city's efforts to become more sustainable and resilient and to assist in developing a resilience strategy. In addition, membership also involved participating in intensive knowledge sharing and collaboration among the cities. The 100 Resilient Cities represent one-fifth of the world's urban population and more than 50 resilience strategies with over 1,800 provisions and initiatives have been written to date. Ultimately the network has led to over 150 collaborations between cities. Although the initiative came to a close on July 31, 2019, the Rockefeller Foundation continues to support the resilience managers to ensure the valuable work done to date can continue. Of the cities described in this book, Toronto, Vancouver, New York City, Houston (as the 101st member, supported by Shell), Medellín, Rio de Janeiro, and Montevideo are all members.

THE RESILIENCE OF CITIES

Climate change is without doubt a significant challenge for cities actively working towards more sustainable development. Therefore, any strategy must ensure that no group of residents is disadvantaged, that public services are safeguarded, and that at least a certain level of prosperity is distributed as evenly as possible. Public green and open spaces are usually sizeable areas in cities that are accessible to all residents as well as visitors. Due to their vegetation, they have a better microclimate than the more built-up neighborhoods around them, but parks and green spaces are often unequally distributed throughout a city. While private green spaces likewise have a positive climatic impact, they are in most cases not accessible to the general public and are often found on the outskirts of cities. Where neighborhoods have comparatively few green spaces but a large number of inhabitants, the pressure on public spaces is correspondingly high. Such spaces must be designed to a particularly high standard and regularly maintained to ensure they retain their character and continue to serve the needs of their neighborhood.

The consequences of climate change, such as extreme weather events, have drawn attention to the fact that open spaces can serve an important buffer function to protect surrounding built-up areas against flooding and landslides. Hence, open spaces in flood risk areas should be designed as water retention areas to limit the extent of flooding, and at the same time also be able to withstand extreme weather events without excessive damage or destruction. Similarly, residential areas built on sloping sites prone to erosion during heavy rain events can be protected from damage by the creation of stabilizing open spaces. In extreme cases where safe housing cannot be ensured in the long term, residents of areas with particularly unstable ground may need to relocate to other, safer urban locations. The impacts and threat of climate change have increasingly refocused attention on the interests of urban communities, such as the development of green-blue infrastructure or building measures aimed at improving the city's climate resilience. Because each city has its own structure, specific location, size, and pattern of development, it is important that it becomes aware of how its climate is changing now and in the future, and of the parallel developments that need to be reconciled with climate change. Needless to say, citizens must be involved in climate change adaptation decisions.

In general, most cities already have plans in place to reduce greenhouse gas emissions, and this is true for nearly all of the cities in North and South America featured in this book. In addition, most cities have developed climate change adaptation plans and, in some cases, also resilience strategies that identify expected impacts—based on data from climate monitoring, aerial or satellite imagery, model simulations, or more usually a combination of these—and elaborate proposals for mitigation action and adaptation strategies.

Only occasionally is green infrastructure explicitly outlined as a means of mitigating climate change impacts and improving resilience. By contrast, investments in technical infrastructure are mentioned very frequently. Community participation and involvement in adaptation is sometimes also mentioned as an important factor. The fact that green infrastructure and landscape architecture are rarely brought up is especially surprising given the widely documented climatic benefits of green spaces, and especially of trees and various other accompanying solutions for increasing urban resilience. In fact, green spaces, when robustly designed, can absorb large amounts of rainfall during severe precipitation events and pass it on in a controlled manner without incurring permanent damage. Plus, rain gardens are being integrated into the design of new parks and street spaces as temporary water reservoirs during heavy rains, and at the same time help raise awareness of water cycles and climate change in the population, and especially among children. Improved tree planting is a further area where landscape architecture can benefit cities: it significantly increases the lifespan of urban trees and their ecosystem capacity, and it is well known that plants, and especially trees, act as carbon sinks as they store CO_2 and through photosynthesis release oxygen into the air. In addition, adequate planting can lower the ambient temperature through moisture evaporation and by providing shade, so that urban environments heat up less dramatically. In essence, the more vegetation there is, the more effective its ability to sequester carbon and the better its cooling effect through shading and evaporation for the local microclimate. It is, of course, essential that plants have an adequate supply of water and any necessary nutrients so that they can grow appropriately, live to a mature age, and contribute effectively to mitigating climate change. As such, the IPCC's goal to limit global warming to no more than 1.5° C, as well as other sustainability aspects such as food security, healthy ecosystems and, to some extent, reducing poverty, must be seen in direct relation to green infrastructure.

Cities in general are considered particularly vulnerable to the effects of climate change due to their high population density, important economic relevance, and predominance of gray infrastructure. While extreme weather events themselves do not automatically pose a risk, their consequences, such as heat stress or flooding, do when they endanger people's lives or health, or cause damage to the fabric of the city. The risk therefore depends on the kind of weather events that may be expected and the degree of vulnerability where they occur. It is, therefore, particularly important to conduct a risk assessment of the damage that may arise as a consequence of climate change, as a basis for identifying appropriate measures to take, especially in the most vulnerable parts of a city.

Making cities more resilient means equipping them so that extreme climatic and weather events do not have a lasting impact on the inhabitants and infrastructure of a city, but that urban functions can be resumed or at least rapidly restored without permanent impairment. Ideally, solutions should act at multiple levels and combine various measures, leading to a broader transformation of cities. Landscape architects are absolutely imperative for this process, yet it is also increasingly clear that in order to improve the resilience of cities to climate change, landscape architecture must in this context reexamine its priorities. Site-specific adaptations to climate change must be a central consideration of designs for open spaces; collaborations with planners and professionals from other disciplines must be strengthened; and landscape architects should ideally lead planning processes to coordinate the climate resilience of the various design aspects.

TORONTO

TORONTO

"Diversity Our Strength" is the motto of the city of Toronto, Canada's largest metropolis with almost 3 million inhabitants. Together with the Greater Toronto Area, the population figure doubles to 6.2 million. Situated on Lake Ontario, it is part of the so-called Golden Horseshoe, a densely populated, economically prosperous region that encircles the western end of the lake. The region has experienced significant growth in recent decades, and indeed nearly a quarter of Canada's population live there. Both socially and architecturally progressive, Toronto boasts modern buildings in the downtown and more recent waterfront areas, as well as extensive districts of terraces and houses, a multicultural community, and vibrant neighborhoods. The city's residents come from many different ethnic backgrounds and nearly half were born abroad. After Miami, Toronto has the second-highest proportion of foreign-born residents in North America—but unlike Miami, Toronto's immigrant population is not dominated by just a few ethnic groups; instead, it comprises a broad range of diverse minorities seen in few other cities of the world. The city's diversity motto therefore attests to its social and cultural self-image.

Toronto owes its byname *City of Ravines* to a distinct topographical feature that formed after the last ice age: the ravines and rivers flowing through the city area towards Lake Ontario. These densely forested areas, which make up 20 percent of the urban territory, serve several vital ecological functions, the most important of which is to collect water from the adjacent urban areas during rainfall and drain it into Lake Ontario. To this day, all urban planning considerations and initiatives are subject to the ravines' crucial role in channeling the flow of water in the city.

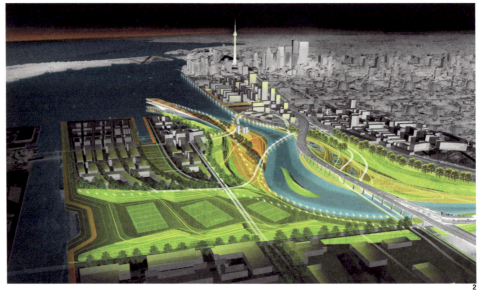

1 (previous page)
Downtown Toronto on Lake Ontario.

2
Design for the mouth of the Don River into Lake Ontario. New retention areas at the mouth of the river help regulate the flow rate of swelling waters after heavy rainfall. The new hydrological and green infrastructure proposed as part of this competition entry creates new ecosystems, recreational spaces, and a residential environment with cultural offerings.

Toronto's climate is cold and temperate. The mean annual temperature is 8.7 °C, with the lowest monthly average in February, -4.4 °C, and the highest in July, at 21.9 °C. The highest daytime temperatures of the year are usually measured in August, reaching around 25 °C. While the mean total precipitation is 845 millimeters per year, monthly rainfall ranges from 50 to 85 millimeters across the year.

Temperatures differ significantly between the seasons. In winter, they can dip temporarily to -10 °C, and seem even colder due to the winds blowing in from the lake. From November to April, precipitation falls mainly as snow; relative humidity in winter is 80 percent, sunshine duration is two hours. In spring and summer, the sun shines on average up to seven hours a day.

EFFECTS OF CLIMATE CHANGE

Toronto is among the "100 Resilient Cities" selected as part of the Rockefeller Foundation's competition in 2013. Within the framework of this program, the city developed both a *Resilience Strategy* and a *Climate Action Strategy*, called *TransformTO*. In 2015, these plans were further supplemented by a *Climate Change and Health Strategy*.

The *Resilience Strategy*, a quite comprehensive document, outlines the specific expected impacts of climate change on the city: Toronto expects to become hotter, wetter, and stormier. This implies significant changes for the individual climate parameters: from 1976 to 2005, an average of 12.2 hot days with temperatures above 30 °C were recorded per year; from 2021 to 2050, 30.7 such days are expected, and in the period from 2051 to 2080, this number is again expected to rise, to 54.9 days. While the average mean precipitation between 1976 and 2005 was 786 millimeters, it is projected to increase to 817 millimeters by 2050 and 854 millimeters by 2080. Prior to 2005, heavy precipitation days—where more than 20 millimeters of rain or snow fall in a single day—occurred on average 6.6 days per year; by 2050 this is expected to rise to 6.9 days, and by 2080 to 7.8 days annually.

In 2017, the City Council unanimously approved *TransformTO*, Toronto's strategy paper for tackling climate change. Setting out long-term goals for the transformation of the city, it includes reducing greenhouse gas emissions, promoting public health, economic growth, as well as improving social equity. In this vein, targets for reducing greenhouse gas emissions are a 30 percent reduction by 2020, 65 percent by 2030, and zero energy consumption by 2050 or sooner. The paper also identifies buildings, transportation, and waste management as the main sources of greenhouse gas emissions.

The *Climate Change and Health Strategy* provides an overview of the anticipated negative impacts on the health of the city's population. These include an increased incidence of heat-/cold-related illness and premature death, a rise in direct and indirect injuries and disease resulting from severe weather (including water-borne and vector-borne diseases), disruptions to food supply (including food insecurity and food-borne illnesses), and degraded air quality, increasing cardiovascular and respiratory illnesses.

Weather events that cause large-scale damage are typically strong motivators for raising awareness of climate change among a city's population. For Toronto, Hurricane Hazel on October 15, 1954, was such a landmark event: 121.4 millimeters of precipitation fell during that hurricane, causing significant damage that many older residents still recall today. Even though climate change is not expected to cause stronger and more frequent storms for the Toronto region, the example does show that such natural disasters remain anchored in the collective memory of a population for a long time. Tapping into this memory can help raise awareness of the frequency of other weather extremes that Toronto is expected to experience.

COMPLETE STREETS AND GREEN STREETS

To prepare for the consequences of climate change, the City of Toronto has developed two street renewal programs specifically designed to contribute to environmental quality, as well as to the social and economic development of streets. The two programs categorize streets into so-called *Complete Streets* and *Green Streets* and aim to combine their positive aspects with a view to improving Toronto's streetscapes.

The Toronto metropolitan area encompasses some 5,600 kilometers of streets and paved surfaces, typically contributing to climate change by heating up in summer and discharging surface runoff directly into the sewer system. Road surfaces account for about a quarter of the area of the city of Toronto. Only in New York do streets comprise a larger share of the total urban area, as comparisons with cities in Europe, North America, and Oceania have shown.

The *Complete Streets* program focuses on streets that are designed for all users: people who walk, cycle, use public transportation, or drive, as well as people of varying ages and degrees of ability. They also consider other uses like sidewalk cafés, so-called street furniture (e.g., benches, kiosks, and planters), street trees, utilities, and stormwater management. While *Complete Streets* aims to create street spaces that can accommodate multiple functions and seeks to improve their quality for all users, the *Green Streets* program, developed a few years later, focuses more on the ecological effectiveness of streets through the incorporation of green infrastructure. Accordingly, Green Streets are roads or streets that feature natural and human-made elements such as trees, green walls, and low-impact stormwater infrastructure providing ecological and hydrological functions and processes. Unlike traditional streets where rainwater is discharged directly into sewers and drains along with any pollution that collects on sealed surfaces, "green" streets capture rainwater and make it available to plants. In this context, the soil acts as a natural filter to clean the water before it soaks into the ground or makes its way into local waterways. Urban vegetation can therefore benefit from rainwater for longer, helping it grow better, and more water is available for evapotranspiration, in turn reducing the heat island effect.

Permeable infiltration areas can help replenish groundwater levels by taking up stormwater, especially after heavy rain events, while improving air quality and increasing humidity levels. As examples of possible approaches, the program cites the walkable green roof on Toronto City Hall, the greening of streets and parking lots, and roadside greenery that can retain and cleanse water in its soil.

The *Green Streets* program compiles technical guidance for planners, project developers, and local government to assist in planning sustainable stormwater management solutions. In doing so, it details a selection of appropriate green infrastructure measures that can be incorporated into street redesign or reconstruction. Particular emphasis is placed on the design of systems for soils and substrates that can absorb large amounts of precipitation to assist in meeting runoff requirements. Not only must green streets be attractive and functional, they must also fit in with their urban surroundings. By prioritizing *Green Streets* over traditional, less multifunctional streets, the aim is for their diverse forms of green infrastructure to promote effective stormwater management at the point where it occurs.

3
Example of a "complete street" at West Donlands, where the Athletes' Village was built for the XVII Pan American Games in 2015.

STREET TREES

Planting, maintaining, and caring for trees along streets is already a particularly important aspect in Toronto, as it is in most cities. Climate change has made it even more challenging.

Of Toronto's roughly 10.2 million trees, 60 percent are privately owned. The remaining 4.1 million trees grow on public land. Six percent of all trees in Toronto, or about 600,000, are street trees, and only 1.5 percent of all trees, 150,000 specimens in absolute numbers, have a trunk diameter over 30 centimeters, measured at chest height.

Trees, and especially street trees, play an important role in mitigating the negative effects of climate change in cities: evapotranspiration through the leaves of trees helps cool urban areas where heat builds up through buildings and sealed roadways. At the same time shade from the trees cools the ground, reducing heat build-up from exposure to the sun. Trees counteract the warming of their immediate surroundings and create a more pleasant microclimate for people outdoors. In addition, they also sequester CO_2 and bind pollutants.

But trees, and again especially those street trees in urban centers, are also particularly vulnerable to the impacts of climate change. They must adapt to the higher temperatures in cities, cope with more irregular precipitation, withstand more frequent storms at unusual times of the year, adjust to longer growing seasons, and possibly resist new kinds of pests. Since not all trees adapt equally well, reliable guidance on how these new challenges are best addressed at the selection and planting stage is still lacking. Current research is wide-ranging and covers topics such as the suitability of different tree species and varieties, and of substrates and soils, or the water and maintenance requirements of specific trees, their watering frequencies and fertilizer duration. The results depend heavily on where the data are recorded, and the findings must be adapted to the existing species of trees in a city as well as the new tree species to be planted.

The goal is—and must be—to allow street trees to develop over a long period of time in a manner appropriate to the species, as it can take decades for trees to mature and develop their full potential. Therefore, not only the number of trees, but also their size and health are of great importance for their climatic effectiveness. Research into the life expectancy of street trees has been contradictory, and the findings do not apply equally to every location anyway. In a study from the end of the last century, for example, Gary Moll came to the startling conclusion that a tree in the center of an American city survives on average for only seven years.

Another study by Lara A. Roman et al. from 2001 compiled and compared several existing American studies on the survival rate of street trees along with one study from Belgium, England, and China respectively. In addition, the authors undertook their own research on field maple (*Acer campestre*) trees in Philadelphia, PA, USA, planted over a ten-year period. They concluded that these studies do not corroborate the very low life expectancy of street trees in Moll's study. In view of this, the annual survival rate was between 94.9 and 96.5 percent, i.e., only about 5 percent of newly planted trees die within the first year after planting.

A field maple's estimated average life expectancy was found to be between 19 and 28 years. Since this refers to the period after planting—trees are planted after 12 or more years' growth in a tree nursery—their average life expectancy is about 35 years. While significantly longer than Moll's claim, it is still cause for concern as most trees do not develop their specific form and full ecological potential until they reach this age. Many trees never make it to this stage because they do not grow healthily or are removed. If half of the trees are indeed removed, or ideally replaced, in such young "tree years," they never reach their full ecological potential. The overall ecological effect actually sinks because older trees naturally reach the end of their lifetime and can only be replaced by young trees. A way out of this dilemma could be to plant significantly more trees in cities, and especially in the central districts—but there is often not enough space to plant sufficient trees and allow them to develop in a species-appropriate way. In any case, trees need intensive care and support to grow as much as possible—and the money is well spent, since planting new young trees at ever shorter intervals is certainly more expensive than the proper, regular care and upkeep of trees.

Overall, the general condition of existing street trees in large cities is moderate and often poor, although these findings refer to trees planted in the past. Regulations on suitable substrates and maintenance patterns during their initial growth and later maturing phases have not always existed. Many cities, including Toronto, have since developed guidelines for planting and maintenance, as well as for species and cultivar selections for street trees. The target is typically a life expectancy of 40 years and a mature trunk diameter of 40 centimeters at chest height.

In Toronto, trees were previously planted in 6 to 10 cubic meters of soil or substrate per tree at 6-meter spacings. Today, 20 to 30 cubic meters and 10-meter spacings are recommended. Planting fewer trees with wider spacing improves the chance that trees will grow to their full size. Since tree grates have so far been very small at 1.25 square meters, new guidelines specify at least 1.5 square meters or larger open planting areas with a greater capacity to absorb rainwater in the root zone. Also, tree grates should be covered with mulch and the root areas irrigated with collected rainwater. According to the current guidelines, 30 native and non-native tree species are being recommended for new tree planting. If, as predicted, climate change causes a general rise in temperatures and decrease in regular rainfall, the recommended tree species may need to be adjusted in future.

The following two projects are examples of the sustainable development of former commercial sites in Toronto as described by Joe Lobko, partner in the landscape architecture and urban design firm DTAH. In both projects, building structures as well as outdoor areas were defined by their respective original use and transformed as part of an intensive design process to serve their new purposes. With sustainability as a core principle, they are now vibrant amenities for their respective neighborhoods and for the city. Both projects were developed by non-profit organizations with committed civic involvement from the local communities in raising funding, determining the usage profile, and undertaking administrative tasks.

EVERGREEN BRICK WORKS

The former brick works is situated in the Don Valley, one of Toronto's typical ravines, which is part of the Don River and Mud Creek floodplain. Founded in 1889, it remained in operation for nearly 100 years, producing bricks for the construction of the many single-family homes so characteristic of Toronto. After the natural resources were largely depleted and clay mining ceased in the 1980s, the site was sold. It was initially offered to the local authorities, because its location in an ecologically sensitive ravine implied a potential for development as part of the river valley parkland. However, due to the economic recession in the early 1980s and the complex task of redeveloping a clay quarry and brick plant, the city declined the offer. Instead, a private developer took on the property with the intention of building an extensive residential project. After the site was partially filled and building permission was granted, local residents became aware of the project and opposition to the development in the sensitive, flood-prone river valley grew. The protests eventually led to the city reclaiming and buying back the 5-hectare site, which includes 16 historically listed buildings.

The Conservation Authority began converting the clay pit into a recreational area called a "quarry garden." Measures included daylighting Mud Creek, creating ponds and meadows, and planting native trees, shrubs, and wildflowers. Before long the park had become a popular local amenity and is now considered a model example of the successful ecological development of a river valley. It was only later that the non-profit organization Evergreen Canada embarked on the development of the landmarked buildings on the site. In fact, its mission is to bring nature back into the cities of Canada and to promote environmentally sound, socially progressive urban development. Further areas of focus include environmental education and schoolyard greening. The extensive planting work in the lower Don River water catchment area caught the attention of the organization's founding director, Geoff Cape. He immediately saw the potential of developing the clay quarry and buildings as a community environmental center that could house his own organization and others with a similar focus. His vision is that of a hub for people to explore the relationship between nature, culture, and society, and to plan a green future for Toronto and other cities. Since diversity is a key aspect of Evergreen Canada's philosophy, both in terms of healthy ecosystems and an open, sustainable society, it likewise informed the organizational, architectural and landscaping realization of the project. Working with a variety of partners—three architecture offices, two landscape architecture firms, plus engineers, ecologists, hydrologists, environmental educators, and other professionals—Evergreen was able to consider and incorporate many different perspectives throughout the project planning process.

The most important elements of the development and design of this landscape were both its natural features and the anthropogenic alterations it had experienced. The design encompasses waterways, slopes and edges, planting schemes and wooded areas as well as bike lanes, a road, an expressway, two railroad lines and a power line fed by a hydroelectric plant.

4
Just how deep the pit was when still in operation can be seen on a photographic mural on the wall of one of the old buildings in the brick works.

5
Entire neighborhoods of Toronto were built from bricks sourced from this clay pit.

6
The site of the former clay pit was partially filled in and turned into a park with paths through the natural vegetation.

7
The combination of natural vegetation and water creates a special habitat for animals and plants and a tranquil amenity for local residents.

8
The height difference is considerable despite partial filling of the terrain, resulting in a variety of biotopes with their own microclimate in the valley.

EVERGREEN BRICK WORKS

After completion of the park, Evergreen embarked on reuse concepts for the existing buildings, recognizing that repurposing existing structures is the "greenest" approach. At the heart of the brick works site is the Centre for Green Cities, a new building with LEED Platinum certification grafted onto an existing structure. Besides serving as a visitor center and presenting green technologies, it also houses exhibitions and conferences. Accessibility to the somewhat outlying site has been improved, with cycle paths and pedestrian connections to the city, as well as a car-sharing service and the provision of a shuttle bus service to and from the nearest subway station.

Since its completion in 2010, Evergreen Brick Works has certainly lived up to the hopes and expectations of the project and has become an ecological hub for the entire city. This involves a weekly farmers' market, a comprehensive program of environmental activities for children, and a variety of events showcasing local foods. In addition to these local activities, it also hosts conferences and workshops on topics ranging from the future of cities to the development of a green economy.

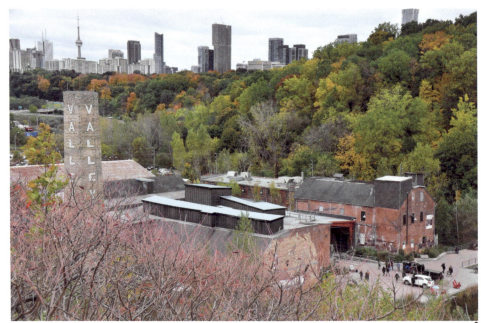

WYCHWOOD BARNS

The Wychwood Barns streetcar depot and accompanying repair barn were built between 1913 and 1921 on the west side of downtown to provide public transportation for the growing population. The five barns, each 12 meters wide and 60 meters long, were built directly next to each other, two as steel frame structures, three with concrete frames. Up to 167 streetcars ran from here on ten lines; however, as the city expanded at the end of the 20th century, the location of the depot proved increasingly inconvenient. Less and less used after 1980, operations ceased altogether in the mid-1990s. The site subsequently lay derelict. A plan proposed by the city to demolish the barns and redevelop the site for housing and businesses was opposed by local citizens who pointed to a lack of local parks and green space.

Eventually a heritage study concluded that the structures are of historical significance, and soon after, in 2001, the non-profit urban development agency Artscape was selected to initiate a public consultation process with the goal of identifying possible future uses for the halls and the development of a new park. Alongside civic organizations, architects and engineers were involved in the project, and local residents were invited to voice their ideas and interests. One suggestion came from The Stop Community Food Centre, an organization that works to increase access to healthy food for disadvantaged segments of the population. They proposed using an entire barn for the activities of a food network that would benefit especially the residents of the surrounding neighborhood. This implied using the building to produce food, to offer training on nutrition, cooking classes, and community meals, and to host a farmers' market. Their proposal placed the emphasis on developing a diverse neighborhood center with sustainability as the central unifying theme for further development. After much discussion and rounds of participation, Artscape ultimately proposed that four barns be retained in their entirety and that one be partially retained as an element of the forthcoming park. Using these existing resilient structures as the basis for the site's future development was seen as a special opportunity.

The final concept envisaged establishing artists' studios and living accommodation as well as a gallery in the first barn, which adjoined the street. The second barn, by contrast, was to be open for various uses as a kind of "covered street" that can be both a passageway and marketplace. While the third barn was designated as an events space for the neighborhood, the fourth was the "Green Hall" with a greenhouse for growing vegetables, a sheltered garden area, and space for cooking, learning, and community meetings. Finally, the fifth barn was to be used as a farmers' market and as an extension of the park that stretches to the west, south, and east of the barns.

9
The old brick works in the Don Valley, now Evergreen Brick Works, with the silhouette of the city center in the distance.

10
Making learning about gardening fun for children at one of the gardens at the Evergreen Brick Works.

11
Wychwood Barns, the former streetcar depot, is now a neighborhood center with a market, fruit and vegetable greenhouse, as well as an arts space.

12
Market day between the sheds of the streetcar depots.

13
Various neighborhood groups grow vegetables alongside the market stalls.

14
Fully equipped greenhouses are also available for growing produce.

TORONTO

The sustainable measures employed include energy conservation methods, reduced water consumption, the appropriate use of existing building structures, and comprehensive green planning. A geothermal system with 50 well points, 120 meters deep at 6-meter intervals, was installed in the park to meet a large part of the heating and cooling needs. Rainwater collected on the roof's roughly 0.4-hectare surface is recycled for flushing toilets and irrigating the park, gardens, and greenhouse. In addition, the designers carefully considered where it would be most sensible to insulate the building walls.

Since it opened in the fall of 2008, Wychwood Barns has become a vibrant community center whose impact extends far beyond the immediate neighborhood. In particular, the weekly farmers' market with homegrown food has met with great interest in multicultural Toronto, stimulating conversations on the health, wellness, and overall quality of life in Canada's largest urban agglomeration. Other uses have also emerged that could not have been foreseen during planning. Artscape writes in that regard that the project has given rise to animated debate on the roles of an urban park and the potential for reusing existing structures. In 2010, the redevelopment site received the first LEED Gold certification in Canada awarded to a heritage building.

URBAN AGRICULTURE

Our visit to the Wychwood Barns coincided with a presentation by Joe Nasr, in which several urban agriculture projects were described and presented, some by the respective local protagonists. Alongside the project at Wychwood Barns, we learned about the garden of the Regent Park Community Food Centre and Black Creek Community Farm in Toronto. Although Canada is a rich country, access to good quality food is not guaranteed and affordable for everyone, and these facilities are of great importance to many citizens. Joe Nasr, along with June Komisar and Mark Gorgolewski, co-authored the acclaimed book *Carrot City*, which was published in 2011 and has since also become well known outside Canada. Conceived as a collection of ideas and projects on how to reintegrate sustainable food production into cities, the book presents 40 groundbreaking examples of how urban planning, landscaping, and architecture can enable and promote ecological urban agriculture in visually and artistically interesting ways. While a website accompanying the book maintained an open access database of other projects around the world, the authors also produced a traveling exhibition that was shown in Europe and North Africa. The success of *Carrot City* was so great that the database now only includes new projects in Toronto.

15
Joe Nasr, founder of the Carrot City project, and Ashrafi Ahmed, urban gardening representative for the newly built Regent Park neighborhood, describe their project.

16
Community gardens and Community Food Centre, in Regent Park.

17
Raised beds for seniors at Black Creek Community Farm.

18
Fall harvest ready to distribute to people in the neighborhood.

19
Cultivating mushrooms. The farm teaches people how to grow all kinds of food.

TORONTO

20

The project shows that urban agriculture not only helps improve the supply of fruit, vegetables, and other healthy foods to the population—often in a spirit of solidarity—but also makes an important contribution to counteracting the negative effects of climate change: additional plants are cultivated (and also watered, especially during drought periods), resulting in more evapotranspiration, surfaces are unsealed or planting containers are placed on sealed surfaces to trap water, while people, especially those directly involved, develop a better understanding and awareness of plants and their needs.

20
Greenhouses at Black Creek Community Farm.

SIDEWALK LABS AND THE QUAYSIDE PROJECT

To revitalize the long-neglected former industrial areas along the shores of Lake Ontario, the City of Toronto established Waterfront Toronto as a development agency in 2000. Its objective is to sustainably develop an 800-hectare abandoned site into a vibrant urban neighborhood with a mixed social structure, a variety of different uses, and a high proportion of public spaces. In addition, a new Quayside district will be built on a stretch of the waterfront.

The tender for the design of the new urban neighborhood was won in 2017 by the startup Sidewalk Labs, a subsidiary of Google's parent company Alphabet, who proposed a "smart city" neighborhood. Though the project began promisingly in 2017, it was abandoned in May 2020 due to the impact of the COVID-19 pandemic and the accompanying economic uncertainties. Sidewalk Labs had however already begun addressing important current issues in urban design, particularly housing affordability and sustainability, and the firm plans to continue its work on these despite the cancellation.

Plans for the 5-hectare area included new buildings with new mass timber construction techniques, autonomous driving transportation, smart garbage collection using a pneumatic system, air quality monitoring, heated streets lit at ground level, and public Wi-Fi, as well as numerous cameras and sensors to monitor traffic and public spaces. The latter, however, proved to be particularly contentious, triggering data privacy concerns from citizens' interest groups. While intelligent systems leverage user data, how these data are used is not always sufficiently transparent.

Sidewalk Labs' work on novel solutions for affordable housing, improved mobility, and strategies for addressing the impacts of climate change are applicable not just to the Quayside Project but also to much of Toronto as well as other cities around the world. Based on its own research into sustainable city concepts (currently at a relatively small scale), Sidewalk Labs organized an exhibition and series of talks and events. The exhibition explains their research with the help of display panels, visuals, and three-dimensional videos. In addition, Sidewalk created a computer-aided visualization that shows the real world enhanced with further virtual information (augmented reality) as an immersive demonstration of the concept.

Of particular interest from a climate-protection perspective is their concept for building with timber. The ability to use timber as a construction material becomes particularly relevant when new techniques make it possible to build multistory and high-rise buildings. Because conventional materials such as steel and concrete are energy-intensive to manufacture, they have a significant negative impact on the climate. Solid wood, by contrast, acts as a pure carbon sink. According to a study published in *Nature* in May 2018, the construction industry could reduce its global carbon emissions by up to 31 percent if concrete and steel were replaced with wood from sustainably managed forests.

Sidewalk Labs also developed a concept for more affordable housing using a modular concept that can adapt to the changing needs of residents and society. This approach should make construction faster and significantly cheaper than

21
Part of the Sidewalk Labs Toronto exhibition showing possible future urban development options.

22
Virtual Reality vision for a sidewalk patio heater for being outdoors at comfortable temperatures in winter.

SIDEWALK LABS AND THE QUAYSIDE PROJECT

34

23
Plan of the Quayside site by Sidewalk Labs.

24
The Quayside site on the Toronto waterfront overlooks Lake Ontario and lies west of Downtown Toronto near the mouth of the Don River.

TORONTO

25, 26

27

26, 25
Visualizations of the center of the Quayside area in summer and winter.

27
Unusual visualization of the development area on a rainy day. The project has since been abandoned.

SIDEWALK LABS AND THE QUAYSIDE PROJECT

conventional construction, while still permitting architectural variation and creativity. Without any need for extensive preparation, the modules—prefabricated sections—are assembled on site. The floor plan designs are also flexible: by installing or removing walls, the modules can be used for various purposes—such as in apartments, offices, or stores. Several smaller units can be combined into one larger apartment allowing expanding families to continue living in the same neighborhood. A local quarter can therefore develop and evolve naturally. At the same time, it increases the likelihood that neighborhoods can remain diverse, as factors such as different household incomes, size of housing, or types of use can be accommodated within the same neighborhood. In addition, daily amenities are also within walking distance. The overall goal of the urban design project is to create an integrated urban community.

The streets in Sidewalk Labs' concept are termed "people-first streets." All users, regardless of whether pedestrians or drivers, should feel safe on urban streets. Among the technological innovations featured were camera-equipped traffic lights that extend the green phase when a person is slow to cross the street, or road surfaces that can be heated in winter to keep them free of snow and ice for safe driving. For public transport, Sidewalk proposes autonomous vehicles that either provide a shuttle service or are for shared use. Naturally, it is imperative to overcome the current challenges of autonomous driving, and to ensure a high safety standard. By eliminating the need for parking private cars, the use of road space can essentially change. Parking lanes along streets can become sidewalk space, and be used for creating outdoor restaurant space, markets, and other public uses on current sidewalks.

Despite the cancellation of the Quayside project, Sidewalk Labs continues to work on its plans for an innovative city that opens the doors to a new future of urban mobility, community-based health care, and next-generation infrastructure.

Up to now, Toronto has largely lived up to the expectations and hopes that many associate with social diversity and the active promotion and implementation of sustainability strategies. Canada's largest city has already demonstrated many interesting ways in which an open, multicultural, and democratic society can address climate change with joy, creativity, verve, and mindfulness. Whether in its strategic plans for adapting to and mitigating the negative impact of climate change, or in its support for promoting public health and neighborhood initiatives for healthy food production, Toronto continues to demonstrate that it is not afraid to tackle the challenges it faces. Now more than ever it is attaching great importance to environmental and climate protection, as well as to a socially sustainable, solidarity-based urban society.

VANCOUVER

"By Sea, Land, and Air We Prosper" is the motto of Vancouver. Founded on April 6, 1886 on Canada's west coast, this port city was named in honor of George Vancouver, a British Royal Navy officer who explored and surveyed the east coast of what is now the USA and Canada, in the late 18th century. The city lies in the very southwest corner of the province of British Columbia, on the Strait of Georgia, an inlet shielded from the Pacific Ocean by the offshore land mass of Vancouver Island. The Rocky Mountains rise to the north and east of Vancouver, and to the south the city extends up to the border between Canada and the United States. Approximately 630,000 people live in the metropolitan area, while Greater Vancouver, Canada's third-largest metropolitan region, has a population of 2.65 million.

Waterways play a central role in Vancouver's economy, and also contribute to the health and well-being of its residents. Right through the center of the metropolitan area runs False Creek, a 2-kilometer-long inlet. Besides, Vancouver's numerous parks and gardens together total 1,300 hectares and account for about 11 percent of its urban area. The largest of these, Stanley Park, covers 404 hectares, making it one of the largest municipal parks in North America. That many of these green spaces have been preserved as the city has expanded into a large metropolis can be attributed to its traditionally progressive political outlook. Civic initiatives and political movements campaign often on topics ranging from environmental protection and nature conservation to community-oriented urban planning, poverty reduction, and local democratic participation. It is probably no coincidence that the now internationally active and world-renowned environmental organization Greenpeace was founded by peace and environmental activists in Vancouver in 1971.

The World Expo in 1986 marked the beginning of intensified construction activity in the city that has continued almost without interruption to this day. The highly successful, and also last North American World Expo to date, was sited on a former industrial wasteland on the north bank of False Creek. After the Expo, the area around it became one of the largest urban development zones in North America and later a popular and high-density residential area on the edge of downtown. Furthermore, the Olympic Village for the 2010 Winter Games was built on the south bank of False Creek.

Canada's immigrant community is also a visible characteristic of Vancouver. After immigrants from Europe and their descendants, people of Chinese origin make up the second-largest ethnic group and represent nearly 30 percent of the population. While the first Chinese immigrants arrived during the gold rush and for the construction of the transcontinental railroad in the 19th century, a second wave came in the 1980s and 1990s before the handover of Hong Kong to China. Today, 20 percent of farmers in the Vancouver region are immigrants from China and produce a wide range of typical Chinese foods. Other ethnic groups in Vancouver also grow vegetables in their own gardens, and Chinese Canadians sometimes use their front gardens and even public verges along the sidewalk. Then there are also other private front gardens that feature more unusual plants complementing and augmenting public urban green planting. Because private green spaces and those close to homes tend to be better maintained and watered, they are an important part of the green infrastructure.

1 (previous page)
The center of Vancouver with waterfront marina.

2
Bean racks and beds extend the front garden onto the sidewalk.

3
Vegetable beds on the sidewalk in front of the dooryard.

4
Ornamental plants flanking the sidewalk also provide shade and a pleasant climate for passing pedestrians.

5
The snowcapped mountains in the hinterland provide a picturesque backdrop for the city.

VANCOUVER

Alongside the city's predominantly environmentally sensitive urban development and its overall liberal citizenry, Vancouver's geographic location and climate make it one of the cities with the highest quality of life in the world. Surrounded by imposing and unspoiled natural landscapes, the city boasts both beaches and nearby mountains, and enjoys a year-round climate that is mild by Canadian standards. Unlike Canada's other major cities with continental climates—cold and snowy winters and hot summers—Vancouver's maritime situation results in comparatively balanced seasons. Due to its location in a humid temperate zone, there are neither long dry periods nor pronounced periods of snow cover. Mean temperatures range from 6 to 8 °C in winter and from 21 to 23 °C in summer, with an annual average of about six hours of sunshine. The annual average humidity is 80 percent. The mean water temperature of the sea is only 11.1 °C, and rarely rises to more than 18 °C.

Precipitation falls as rain throughout the year with an annual total of 1,580 millimeters: from May to August, monthly precipitation is low at under 25 millimeters; from October to February, it is over 75 millimeters. It rains on average 13.4 days per month over the year, in winter rising to an average of 20 days, in summer 6 to 10—which amounts to almost three more rainy days than other cities in Canada. In winter, precipitation falls as snow in the nearby mountains, allowing residents to enjoy winter sports. Snowmelt in spring is rather slow and also provides Vancouver with drinking water.

EFFECTS OF CLIMATE CHANGE

In January 2019, Vancouver City Council adopted a motion acknowledging the global climate crisis and the need for the city to do more in response to this impending crisis. As a coastal city, rising sea levels and flooding are two of the greatest challenges Vancouver faces through global warming. Changes in the climate have been monitored and forecast for Vancouver and the surrounding area for many years. The first *Climate Change Adaptation Strategy* was adopted in 2012 and revised again in 2020. Practical information on the physical impacts of climate variability and changes in the Pacific region of Canada is provided primarily by the Pacific Climate Impacts Consortium (PCIC), a regional climate data information center located at the University of Victoria. It collaborates with climate researchers and regional stakeholders and uses its results to support long-term planning.

The data published by the PCIC on its website (PCIC Climate Explorer) use global, standardized climate simulations under broadly standardized conditions (CMIP5). Climate scenarios calculated daily have a resolution of about 10 kilometers for the period from 1950 to 2100 (BCCAQv2). In addition, indices of climate extremes are calculated based on annual or monthly statistics (CLIMDEX), which can be visualized and downloaded as maps or graphs. Long-term climate change assessments are based on a standard reference period from 1961 to 1990. (Thirty-year periods are a common climatological benchmark. The above period was usually used as a reference when climate change was not yet regarded as being particularly relevant, and the following period from 1991 to 2020 has not yet been fully evaluated.) Changes in temperature values, precipitation, and other derived climate values are calculated relative to the reference period for specific time horizons, for example the 2050s as the midpoint of the next 30-year period from 2040 to 2069, and for the 2080s for the British Columbia region. In this context, mean values are indicated along with upper and lower variations. The Plan2Adapt website also uses the PCIC database but to generate maps, charts, and data that describe future regional climate conditions in British Columbia. Using these data, climate change can be assessed on the same basis and with the same criteria. Its simpler user interface is geared towards the needs of those working in local and regional community planning.

Based on this climate change impact modeling, the 2012 *Climate Change Adaptation Strategy* found that in the Vancouver area changes will remain moderate through the 2050s, but will increase to have a major impact around the 2080s. By the 2050s, the projections foresee an increase in temperatures, a 15 percent longer growing season, and a 72 percent decrease in the number of frost days. Snowmelt is also forecast to begin earlier in the year, and average rainfall in April is projected to be 20 percent higher. In line with this trend, maximum temperatures will be higher in summer and heat waves will occur more frequently. The number of days with temperatures above 25 °C will double, resulting in, among other things, greater health risks for vulnerable individuals. Because rainfall is also predicted to decrease by 20 percent during the summer period, water use restrictions can be expected in the longer term. In the fall, heavy rainfall events are predicted to occur 35 percent more frequently, and an overall 21 percent increase in rainfall is anticipated. Ultimately, this would increase the risk of flooding.

Winters are forecast to be warmer and there will be a 58 percent decrease in snow cover in the region. As most of the region's drinking water comes from snowmelt from the surrounding mountains, a decrease in snow depth—and faster melting due to higher temperatures—indicate a significant increase in the risk of summer droughts. Minimum temperatures will rise by 4.8 °C, reducing the need for heating by 29 percent. Higher tides and storms will increase the degree of coastal flooding. As the West Antarctic Ice Sheet melts by an estimated thickness of 0.5 meters, sea levels are predicted to rise for Vancouver, further heightening the risk of flooding. This will affect not only residential areas but also the sensitive coastal habitats of certain birds and fish.

The *Climate Change Adaptation Strategy* of 2012 is an example of how political decisions are effectively implemented in a democracy with functioning institutions. Since 2012, more than 50 actions have been initiated, including coastal flood risk assessments, plans and pilot projects for adapting drainage strategies, an urban forest action plan, and tree planting in those urban areas most affected by heat build-up.

Revised and expanded in 2018, the *Climate Change Adaptation Strategy* now includes new measures, many of which will require the expertise and input of landscape architects. Key aspects involve creating more climate-resilient frameworks, including stormwater management and green infrastructure.

In terms of green and natural spaces, this means a shift towards a more proactive and less reactive approach when it comes to managing urban forest resources as well as soil and water preservation. Coastal protection is a further important aspect.

Just two years later, in 2020, the strategy measures were updated once again to include additional projects to improve resilience to climate events. One example is street renewal using permeable surfacing materials, underground water retention and special tree planting initiatives. Already, 150,000 trees have been planted since 2011, and this will be expanded for green and natural spaces. The measures also include the implementation of a biodiversity strategy, precautionary actions to prevent forest fires in Stanley Park, a strategy for planting street trees, as well as for promoting natural forest development.

For the False Creek area, which is particularly at risk, a new so-called coastal design challenge, called Sea2City, is being initiated. Starting in 2021, the city will work with citizens to develop a vision for the future in 2050, as well as a pathway to achieving the goals, culminating in the *False Creek Coastal Adaptation Plan*. The results will then be incorporated into the broader Vancouver Plan for 2050.

VANCOUVER—THE GREENEST CITY

In 2009, Vancouver City Council announced the ambitious goal to become the greenest city in the world by 2020. Two years later, the *Greenest City Action Plan* was put into effect. As a good vehicle for achieving climate goals, the program also supports climate change adaptation efforts. For example, the plan aims to reduce the city's greenhouse gas emissions by 5 percent below 1990 levels, despite the population growing by more than 27 percent and the number of jobs increasing by more than 18 percent in the last 30 years. In construction, CO_2 emissions are to fall 20 percent below 2007 levels, and all buildings constructed after 2020 must be carbon neutral in operation. Since the residents of Vancouver spend nearly 90 percent of their time indoors, heating is an important consideration for reducing emissions. With regard to generating electricity,

6
Progress notice for the *Greenest City Action Plan 2018* posted on a notice board at City Hall.

7 (opposite page)
Urban gardening in front of Vancouver City Hall. The beds are allotted but the gardens are open to everyone to visit and enjoy.

93 percent of energy in British Columbia already comes from renewable sources, and this sector will be expanded further, creating new jobs. Transportation and mobility are also to become more environmentally friendly. This can be achieved by building denser neighborhoods and creating a mix of housing, workplaces, retail, and recreational facilities. Rather than building new roads, infrastructure for pedestrians and cyclists as well as mass transit will be prioritized. The plan includes numerous other goals that address various aspects contributing to a "Green City": minimizing waste, access to nature, clean water, increasing locally produced food by 50 percent compared to 2010, clean air, a "green" economy, and reducing the ecological footprint by 33 percent compared to 2006.

While the aim of creating the "greenest city" is both an attractive slogan and a bold goal, the inclusion of such a wide range of goals under the "green" heading can lead to the overall objective becoming all too vague. A "Green City" usually implies improving the green infrastructure and its interplay with gray infrastructure, as well as creating public access to these natural and semi-natural areas. Other aspects include reducing the high consumption of resources for new buildings, the provision of climate-compensating green spaces, especially in densely built-up urban areas, and the creation of relevant infrastructure for bicycle use.

MILLENNIUM WATER OLYMPIC VILLAGE, FALSE CREEK

Sustainability played a central role in the Vancouver Organizing Committee's decision to host the 2010 Winter Olympics. The Games were intended not just to be of economic benefit to the city but also to be socially and environmentally responsible. An example of this approach, which remains a model for urban planners and landscape architects today, is the specifications for the Olympic Village in False Creek, which was designed to become a residential area after the Games. At the time the planners specified that no drinking water should be used to irrigate plants in the outdoor areas, only collected rainwater. The result is a rainwater retention system fed by the outdoor areas and the architecture. This means that rainwater from all the residential rooftops as well as all paved surfaces is stored in large cisterns located beneath the underground garages. The rainwater is used to feed water features in the outdoor areas such as ponds, fountains, etc., for watering the plants and green areas, and for flushing toilets in the apartments. Some buildings were also equipped with an enlarged roof area similar to an inverted umbrella to collect additional water.

Engineers and planners had to consider seasonal variations in rainfall, especially since much more rain occurs in the winter months (October to March) than in the summer months (March to October). The system regulates use of the collected rainwater so that when precipitation is frequent in winter, the cistern contents are used predominantly for flushing toilets in the apartments, there being little need to irrigate the plants or operate water features in the outdoor areas. In summer, by contrast, water from the cisterns is used to irrigate planting in the green areas and for the water features, and here the system forms a loop, with most of the water returning to the cisterns. Circulating the water from the cisterns keeps it oxygenated and maintains its good quality. Collecting rainwater from roof surfaces and outdoor areas for toilet flushing during periods of

8
Plan of the Olympic Village.

9–12
Top left: Interplay of intensively and extensively greened roof areas with gardens and amenity areas on the roofs, which are staggered at different heights.

Middle left: Entrance to the underground car park with water basin and sculptural artwork (in 2009 soon after completion).

Middle right: Wide roof canopies and symbols of the Olympic disciplines (in 2009 soon after completion).

Below: The Creekside Community Centre.

MILLENNIUM WATER OLYMPIC VILLAGE

13, 14
Illuminated water features at night.

15
The water basin at night with sculptural artwork above the entrance to the underground car park.

VANCOUVER

16
Outdoor lounge areas alongside the water pool in the green inner courtyard.

17
Green courtyard with axial water pool, fountain, and waterfall circulating water from the cisterns. Trees grow on the balconies of the upper floors (in 2012).

MILLENNIUM WATER OLYMPIC VILLAGE

ample rainfall reduces the demand for drinking water in the urban neighborhood by 40 percent. This effectively halves the water demand compared with conventional toilet flushing. In addition, each apartment was equipped with its own water meter to display water consumption and encourage residents to use water carefully.

In modern housing, toilet flushing consumes a significant proportion of a household's water demand but is rarely called into question. At Millennium Water Olympic Village, the city provides drinking water credits for every cubic meter of rainwater collected. When rainfall is scarce, these credits can then be used to water the green spaces in summer. This system works because, in contrast to traditional urban neighborhoods, no drinking water is used for flushing toilets in seasons with greater rainfall.

The Olympic Village has many green spaces that rely on irrigation during periods of low rainfall. To minimize the amount of water needed, an automatic irrigation system is used, coupled with a weather station and sensors in the ground. While the system can be configured to meet the respective needs of plants and their soil conditions, it can also detect that beds do not need watering if rainfall has already sufficiently soaked the soil. This intelligent technology reduces water consumption by nearly 50 percent compared to one programmed to water at regular intervals.

Although significant parts of the innovative rainwater management system in the Olympic Village are invisible to the outside world, such as the cisterns beneath the underground garages, the "green" roofs for storing rainwater are a visible piece of sustainability. They show how valuable rainwater—and water in general—is as a resource, and how important it is to plan its use carefully and economically. The Millennium Water Olympic Village can therefore serve as a model for cities elsewhere and inspire them to make similar facilities for sustainably using rainwater and drinking water a fundamental requirement for new construction projects.

Alongside the requirement to conserve water, the City of Vancouver also stipulated that 50 percent of the roof areas be greened. The planners were initially concerned because a lot of roofs are visible from many residential units. When planted roofs are not well maintained and/or dry out, they are not always seen as beneficial, since they can look unsightly. Through a combination of intensive and extensive green roofs, the required 50 percent was ultimately achieved. Landscape architects Durante Kreuk, who designed the outdoor areas throughout the Olympic Village, created a range of sustainable, attractive, and diverse open spaces. On some of the roofs, they created motifs of the Olympic disciplines using a variety of plants (sedum species) that can be seen from above and from taller buildings. Likewise, vegetation mats with drought-tolerant vegetation covered these extensively landscaped roof areas. Open spaces on the roofs as well as terraces and balconies were equipped with larger plants, and what's more, the residents enlisted in the continued maintenance of these intensive green roof areas.

Urban open spaces in built-up areas are often conceived as decorative green spaces to complement the buildings. In that regard, planters, green roofs, and terrace plantings are typical. Spaces around the buildings in the Vancouver Olympic Village were developed specifically to provide outdoor recreation and to promote the social dimension of sustainability. Designed for social interaction, neighbors can get to know each other and develop a sense of community. Also, indoor spaces open directly onto communal outdoor areas, and public areas are interconnected horizontally and vertically. In one example, a courtyard on an upper floor is connected to a garden on the ground floor via a waterfall. Outdoor areas adjoining individual units are designed to provide residents with private space outside while also enabling as many communal uses as possible. Many public spaces have playgrounds, and each courtyard is equipped with a water feature fed by rainwater from the cisterns. Ultimately, these neighborhood-enhancing outdoor places and facilities complement communal spaces inside the buildings, such as a community kitchen or a games and gymnastics room.

As Peter Kreuk, one of Durante Kreuk's two partners, explains, the combination of green roofs and stormwater management has long been standard practice. What is new in this project is the synchronization of the building infrastructure and the green infrastructure of the outdoor spaces. The goal was to circulate and use rainwater to irrigate the green spaces, for toilet flushing, and rain gardens. Kreuk is convinced that it is possible to incorporate sustainable systems into aesthetically pleasing designs that also meet the environmental and social needs of residents. Clearly, the high quality of the open spaces at the Olympic Village is primarily a product of the landscape architects' careful and skilled planning. Their design ensures, for example, that plants are watered and continue to thrive in drought conditions. To this end, native and adaptable plant species were selected—a necessary condition for the buildings' LEED certification.

Land has also been set aside for urban agriculture in the new Olympic Village development, particularly for schools, neighborhood centers, and interested groups of residents. The fact that roof gardens are also used for gardening is further evidence of the positive impact of the 50 percent green roof requirement. With a soil cover of about 45 centimeters, the roof gardens are suitable for growing vegetables and other crops. Producing food in urban areas for personal consumption has multiple benefits. Firstly, people generally become more aware of the importance of producing healthy food, and secondly, working in community gardens can promote integration and social solidarity, in addition to the economic effects.

GREEN ROOFS IN WEST VANCOUVER

In the suburb of West Vancouver is another notable example of a green roof as a climate-resilient addition to buildings for human occupation. The private residence sits on a hillside above the Strait of Georgia, the waterway that borders the northwest edge of the city. Staggered on a slope, it comprises three sections, each with an extensively greened roof. The planting helps the house blend in with the landscape of its surroundings, and the roofs, which slope between 1 and 7 degrees, together provide 180 square meters of greened surfaces.

18
Extensive roof greening of a private house with sedum.

19
Green roof for a private house with a broad selection of sedum species.

The vegetation comprises mainly low-growing sedum species such as white and Mongolian stonecrop or *Pachysandra terminalis* (Japanese spurge), which not only make the view over the roofs of the water more attractive but also serve to retain rainwater. The roof structure includes a drainage and water retention layer that can store up to 20 to 40 liters per square meter, providing the plants with a ready supply of water on dry days while also reducing water runoff during heavy rainfall. Unlike green roofs on high-rise buildings, this roof has a cooling effect, because moisture evapotranspiration from vegetation occurs at a height that adjoins the living areas of the residents. Compared with a dark, flat roof, the green roof also heats up less. Finally, because green roofs can store a significant amount of water, they also mitigate soil erosion from precipitation. Heavy rainfall in steeper urban areas can lead to landslides where mature vegetation that holds the soil in place is lacking. Consequently, greening buildings and retaining water from rainfall in the roof structure reduces the risk of soil erosion.

CALP—COLLABORATIVE FOR ADVANCED LANDSCAPE PLANNING

CALP is an interdisciplinary research group at the University of British Columbia that connects research and practice, focusing especially on the fields of landscape planning, landscape visualization, environmental perception, public land management processes, and sustainable landscape development. It is led by Professor Stephen Sheppard, who has spent many years researching the impacts of climate change, and specializes in its visualization. Together with his colleagues, he creates visual representations of specific landscapes and places threatened by climate change that are both fictional, because they are future projections, but also realistic: for example, images of potential flooding in the city of Delta south of Vancouver; images showing the progressively receding snow-line at ski resorts in the Swiss Alps; or photorealistic images of changing land use as climate change progresses. Using these visualizations Sheppard presents climate change and its impacts as a means of communicating the urgency of the situation. He stresses that the works have been produced in accordance with ethical standards of transparency and truthfulness and are based on scientific analysis. The dramatic images are not sensationalist depictions but the result of calculations, extrapolations, and realistic forecasts.

These kinds of creative and interactive forms of presentation bring home very vividly the possible consequences of climate change for people's places of living and their own lives. Alongside these visualizations and accompanying lectures, other educational and didactic materials are currently being developed to encourage people to get involved in the climate-friendly transformation of their region. CALP also collaborates with other institutions, including the Pacific Institute of Climate Solutions (PICS), which is presented below.

FUTURE DELTA 2.0

Future Delta 2.0 is a place-based educational video game developed by CALP to explore upcoming climate change challenges and potential solutions. Those who take part find themselves in the city of Delta in the year 2100, which has made no previous effort to prepare for climate change. Participants are faced with an almost dystopian situation: threatened by rising sea levels, the city must deal with frequent storm surges, heat waves and fires; there are food shortages, prices have risen, and traffic and pollution have increased. As the game progresses, participants return to the starting point, allowing them to see the potential impact of inaction and what needs to be done now to prepare for climate change and create a better future.

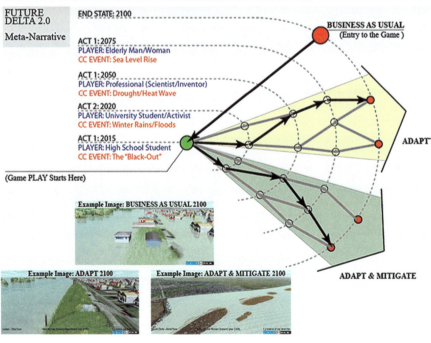

20, 21
Future Delta 2.0: The game depicts the lifetime and possible courses of action for a 15-year-old student at game start for the years 2015, 2020, 2050, and 2075 for three different scenarios:

1. Business as usual (no change from the current situation).
2. Adapted behavior.
3. Adapted behavior and mitigation of climate-damaging behavior.

22, 23 (opposite page)
Questionnaire with instructions and notes on the importance of urban trees (left).

Instructions for mapping one's local block and determining the importance of urban trees (right).

VANCOUVER

The particular value of this video game is that it shows the consequences of climate change in a way that the general public—from retirees to schoolchildren—can understand, encouraging them to see what they can do for their own environment. Accordingly, it combines commercial computer game technology with scientific research to create a participatory tool that can be very useful for social education and political decision-making. With the help of students and school teachers, the game sequences were developed in order to find out how simulated future scenarios of local environments can influence the interest and willingness of people to learn about what they can do in their region, and whether they can bring about behavioral change and motivate civic engagement. The game makes it possible to show changes to the environment in real time and to employ appropriate adaptation and avoidance strategies to directly address the problems that arise. At the same time it communicates scientific findings and proposed solutions in a way that makes them accessible to a potentially broad audience, which conventional climate science teaching methods often fail to achieve. An analysis of the game examined both the game experience and the impact it had on the users' knowledge, attitudes, familiarity with the immediate environment, and their levels of concern about global and local climate change.

CITIZEN'S COOLKIT

The Citizen's Coolkit is another communication tool developed by CALP, this time in the form of a neighborhood simulation game. It aims to bridge the gap between people's knowledge about climate change and the necessary actions that follow from it for their neighborhoods. Ideally, as many local stakeholders as possible should participate in decision-making and action as they know their environment best and in turn the possibilities for adaptation. Coolkit helps them

FUTURE DELTA 2.0

learn how climate change affects their region and encourages them to talk about it with their neighbors. In the process they learn how they can work together to improve their environment and make their homes and neighborhoods more climate-resilient. They also learn about ways in which they can jointly reduce their CO_2 emissions. At the same time—and this is an important point—Coolkit is designed to be fun to use.

Coolkit is designed as a four-week project and is structured so that it begins by providing information about the tool and on climate change. A typical project might begin with a local neighborhood party to introduce the process and jointly embark on first steps. First, there are conversations to get to know one another. Then, photos are used to analyze the neighborhood, and with a quiz participants can test their knowledge about climate change. The photos mark potential ways of avoiding climate change, for example identifying existing green spaces and possible locations for new trees or vegetable beds, as well as possible contributors to climate change such as sealed surfaces and heavy traffic.

24, 25
Comparison of a street
in a residential area:
a) in its actual state and
b) if the trees were removed.

VANCOUVER

In the next step, citizens are shown how to map their living environment. For this purpose, Coolkit provides aerial photos with instructions on how to create mappings—using various freely available software tools such as Google Earth, i-Tree, or Vanmaps—along with how to use GIMP to add or clarify information on the maps. An example might be to map the extents of tree canopies as "squirrel habitats" along with tree heights and trunk diameters. Locations that are particularly sensitive to climate change, or that exacerbate its effects can equally be mapped, for example sealed surfaces, dark roofs, or poor stormwater drainage on the one hand, and white roofs, water-permeable surfaces, and ample tree shade on the other. The main risks that apply to Vancouver are the urban heat island effect, droughts in the summer months, and flooding. Therefore, potential measures to address climate change include cooling by vegetation, water infiltration and controlled stormwater runoff, and vegetable gardens and solar panels.

Participants are then encouraged to determine their own carbon footprint. By using a website and with the help of a questionnaire they can review what to do as a household to avoid climate-damaging behavior and ways in which to adapt to the effects of climate change.

Afterwards, the participants are invited to suggest possible improvements: How could they change their own properties and neighborhoods to be more climate-friendly? Tips on how to visualize these changes using software such as GIMP or Photoshop are also given, enabling residents to take their future into their own hands and make it more climate neutral. Alongside possible measures in the public realm, alterations to buildings are also discussed, such as insulating roofs and basements to save energy.

The final step is to implement the plans. Coolkit also contains several suggestions ranging from climate-tolerant woody plants, rainwater harvesting containers and composting to replacing monoculture lawns with diverse meadows with clover and herbs, and natural pest control methods. In addition to strategies for private properties, Coolkit also aims to transform public spaces, for example turning roadside greenery into "street gardens." Aside from encouraging action on climate protection, Coolkit seeks to strengthen social interaction in the community, and to stimulate better awareness among participants. That way they may undertake steps to modify their own behavior with a view to reducing their carbon footprint, for example by moderating car use, avoiding waste, and changing their consumption patterns.

PICS—PACIFIC INSTITUTE FOR CLIMATE SOLUTIONS

PICS is an independent knowledge network for evaluating, developing, and promoting innovative approaches to mitigating and adapting to climate change. Formed in 2008, it is a collaboration between four universities in the province of British Columbia: the University of Victoria (UVic), Simon Fraser University (SFU), the University of British Columbia (UBC), and the University of Northern British Columbia (UNBC). The Institute's aim is to close gaps between research projects and programs conducted at individual universities on the one hand and programs by cities and municipalities designed to counter the negative impacts of climate change on the other. Finally, it seeks to develop projects for involving communities in the necessary processes of change.

In a special report, for example, PICS identified ways in which people can be motivated to act on climate change. Seven research projects were examined that explore innovative tools and multiple ways to mobilize the public to engage with climate change issues with a focus on reducing energy use and carbon footprints. It found that most British Columbians were unaware of the link between CO_2 emissions and climate change even if they had heard that the province had set targets to reduce greenhouse gas (GHG) emissions to 80 percent of 2007 levels by the year 2050.

The report provides extensive advice and guidance for government agencies and public administrators, non-governmental organizations, and community-led groups on effectively mobilizing workforces, members, and communities on climate change. Related recommendations range from methods for strengthening social engagement, the use of digital, visual, and social media, the benefits of neighborhood initiatives, and the need for open exchanges between citizens and government.

PICS plays a special role in connecting scientists and engaged citizens with appropriate funding programs. In order to bring about climate protection, research has to be put into practice and actions have to adequately address research findings. Thus, promising individual initiatives need to be networked with other research findings and stakeholders, as well as with new developments.

NEW YORK CITY

With 8.3 million inhabitants, New York City is not only the most populous city in the United States, but also the most densely populated and most economically and culturally significant. Its extensive metropolitan area, home to nearly 20 million people, is likewise one of the most populous in the world. Though New York—*The City That Never Sleeps!*—is not just famous as a financial and economic capital and for its rich cultural life, it also boasts several exceptional parks and green spaces, first and foremost Central Park. What is more, a series of sensational new parks have more recently been created in the city that are the product of ongoing efforts by public institutions and civic agencies to improve the resilience of the global metropolis to the effects of climate change.

The city lies on the Hudson River, a comparatively short river that flows into New York Bay and on into the Atlantic Ocean. Its situation somewhat removed from the ocean means the city is protected against direct impact from the open seas, but it is still affected by rising sea levels and other effects of climate change.

Undeniably the most well-known of New York's five boroughs, and the center of the city, is Manhattan, named after the island on which it stands. Bordered by the Hudson River and the strait of the East River, Manhattan's importance is in part a product of its prominent position in the middle of a natural harbor. Due to its desirable location, Manhattan was subject to increasingly intensive and ever denser development that continues to this day. Few metropolises in the world can boast a similar or greater number of high-rise buildings. While in the 2010s, several large building projects were completed in both Manhattan and the other boroughs, more are currently under construction or in planning, including several supertall skyscrapers over 300 meters high. Unlike many other cities, New York earmarked a substantial green space in the middle of the city for preservation as early as the mid-19th century. This went on to become the now world-famous Central Park, designed by the renowned landscape architect Frederick Law Olmsted.

Nevertheless, New York's need for more green space and parks is ongoing. Under Mayor Michael Bloomberg (2002–2013), a number of public green spaces were redesigned on a large scale and the conditions and requirements for planning new parks were also significantly revised. In that respect, the construction of the High Line, a 2.3-kilometer-long park on a defunct former elevated railroad line, marked the beginning of this new phase. Originally the product of a citizens' initiative protesting against the demolition of the abandoned railroad, the project has since become a popular landmark and is now a global attraction. Subsequently, the High Line's success has improved awareness of the potential that lies in reutilizing decommissioned urban infrastructure and former industrial sites for the creation of centrally located parks—also beyond New York! More recently, other criteria have likewise begun to influence the design of outdoor spaces: Governors Island, just south of Manhattan, has been redesigned by landscape architects and engineers as a new climate-resilient park offering ample greenery, relative tranquility, and excellent views of the Statue of Liberty, as well as Lower Manhattan, and Brooklyn.

1 (previous page)
View from Brooklyn to Manhattan.

Arguably the most important new parks recently completed or in planning in New York are those that respond to and are designed to withstand the anticipated effects of climate change. These include two parks that are located on the East River alongside newly revitalized neighborhoods. Firstly, there is Domino Park in the Williamsburg neighborhood of Brooklyn, just north of the Williamsburg Bridge, which crosses over to the Lower East Side of Manhattan. And a few miles further north, where the mouth of Newtown Creek divides Brooklyn from Queens, is Hunter's Point South Park. These two parks represent different responses to the problem of rising sea levels and storm surge events, which the city is increasingly facing.

New York City's temperate climate with a mean annual temperature of 11.9 °C varies significantly between over 30 °C in summer and well below 0 °C in winter. Due to its island situation and proximity to the Atlantic Ocean the weather is often changeable and windy. On hot, windless days in summer, 70 percent relative humidity and six to seven hours of sunshine can cause the city to feel hot and sweltering, while in January, the coldest month, it can well be freezing and windy. Beyond that, heavy snowfalls and hurricanes occur frequently and vary considerably in strength and impact. While annual precipitation totals 1,139 millimeters, monthly precipitation does not vary significantly.

EFFECTS OF CLIMATE CHANGE

The single most dramatic weather event that brought home the tangible threat of climate change to the people of New York was Hurricane Sandy, which wreaked havoc across much of the city on October 29, 2012, killing 43 people. It undeniably marked a new scale of the impact of climate change, especially for the upper East Coast of North America. With a diameter of nearly 1,800 kilometers, Sandy was the most extensive storm ever measured in the Atlantic, and nearly a decade on it still serves as a stark reminder of the increasing severity of future extreme weather scenarios in the minds of New Yorkers. Since then, scientists' predictions have been heeded more seriously, and the city's vulnerability has become a political issue. With this region's sea level rise being unusually high by global standards, flooding poses a particularly urgent problem for New York's future. In addition, the city's dense urban development results in heat waves that will become more frequent and intense in the coming decades as a result of global warming.

According to the New York City Panel on Climate Change (NPCC), an independent panel founded in 2009 to advise city policymakers on preparing for climate change, the climate in the New York area will become more variable, and extreme weather events can be expected to be more severe and frequent. Along these lines, New York's *Climate Resiliency Design Guidelines* published in 2019 confirms their findings. Already, unusually severe storms with accompanying heavy downpours are becoming more pronounced: Sandy, for instance, caused widespread flooding, power outages for hundreds of thousands of people, and interruptions to much of the mass transit system.

According to projections, mean annual temperatures will increase by 2 to 3.6 °C by 2050, and by 3 to 5.7 °C by 2080. While the frequency of heat waves will triple to five to seven times per year by 2050, it is expected to increase further to five to eight times per year by the 2080s. Mean annual precipitation is projected to go up by 4 to 13 percent by the 2050s, and by 5 to 19 percent by the 2080s. In addition to climate change, the coast of the Northeastern United States is subsiding due to natural geological processes that will cause extreme sea level rises of 28 to 53 centimeters in the 2050s and 45 to 99 centimeters in the 2080s. At the southern tip of Manhattan, for example, tidal effects are twice as pronounced as the global average. With New York's more than 900 kilometers of coastline, the rising sea level poses a challenge of almost immeasurable proportions for the city. After a proposal to build a flood barrier south of the tip of Manhattan in New York Bay was briefly discussed, it was eventually discounted as the flood barrier would only have temporarily prevented a storm surge but would not have been able to avert the adverse consequences of a gradual rise in sea level.

One institutional consequence of climate change is that the New York City government established a dedicated department for green infrastructure, which now employs about 120 staff. Subsequently, a *Green Infrastructure Plan* was ratified and implemented from 2011 onwards. Since then, green roofs have been promoted and numerous so-called *Rain Gardens* have been created, along with greened areas around trees and urban planting that can absorb rainwater, retaining it temporarily for the plants before allowing it to dissipate. Rain gardens in particular perform an important function by retaining and storing rainfall during incidences of heavy rain. In the course of gradual infiltration or slowed drainage, the plants and substrate cleanse stormwater runoff from the street. At the same time standardized designs have been developed for these rain gardens, or *bioswales* as they are often called elsewhere. Studies have shown that streetside trees planted in such rain gardens have a longer life expectancy than trees planted and maintained in the usual way.

What is striking about the *Climate Resiliency Design Guidelines* is the attention given to climate change in the design of new large urban projects, whether for infrastructure, green spaces, or buildings, and also for associated building services. Going forward, utilities and plant technology are to be installed above predicted flood levels to protect them from getting damaged in the event of flooding. Just how relevant these specifications are becomes clear when one considers that an 80-centimeter sea level rise will cause almost a quarter of the city to lie under water. And according to NPCC predictions, a water event of such proportions will most likely occur by 2050. What the forecast also shows is that a number of urban development areas along the waterfront of the Hudson River, East River, and New York Bay will be affected, all of which are currently highly desirable locations.

Last but not least, New York City has committed to reducing greenhouse gas emissions by 40 percent by 2030 and 80 percent by 2050. That implies new bike lanes—1,800 kilometers have been built since 2010—and increased street space for pedestrians, as seen for example in the reconstruction of Times Square, should help to reduce car traffic. Nevertheless, much more needs to be done, and at a faster pace, to achieve the goals.

2
A rain garden collects rainwater runoff from the street to supply the tree and planting.

3
An elongated sidewalk rain garden using stormwater to water street greenery.

EFFECTS OF CLIMATE CHANGE

4, 5
Furniture at Times Square (by Vestre) in bold colors and eye-catching designs creates points of interaction and communication in the city.

6
Pedestrians at Times Square in the evening enjoy the urban space gained by removing the roadway.

NEW YORK CITY

GOVERNORS ISLAND PARK

Governors Island is an island south of Manhattan and west of Brooklyn within sight of the Statue of Liberty, and is part of the New York City metropolitan area. Originally inhabited by Native Americans, then by immigrants from the Netherlands, it fell under British control in 1674, like the rest of the city before it. Due to its prominent location, the island was always used for military purposes from 1755 onwards and was not publicly accessible for hundreds of years. Over time, the area of the island more than doubled as fill material was dumped there in an effort to cope with the huge amounts of excavated material originating from rapid building development in the city. The island's largest expansion was the result of excavations for the subway line under Lexington Avenue, which increased the island's area from 28 to 70 hectares.

In 2004, the island opened to the public as Governors Island Park. From the outset, the new landscape architecture concept focused specifically on aspects of sustainability and resilience. The park aims to be an example of how cities can adapt to climate change and rising water levels without compromising access to shorelines and its amenity qualities for residents. A regenerative design concept was developed that emphasizes sustainability and longevity and claims to be highly resilient in the face of climate change. In other words, the intent is to mitigate the impact of climate change by accommodating both temporary flooding and gradually rising water levels as well as counteracting the urban heat island effect. At the same time, the design encompassed everything from the topography, plants and soil to rainwater and groundwater management, air quality, and habitat areas.

7
Governors Island lies south of Manhattan and west of Brooklyn.

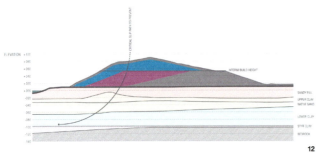
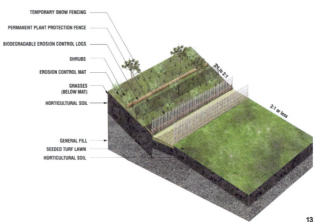

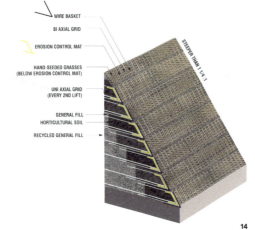

64

8, 9
Development of the island:
Phase one: Conversion of the central area to a park and southern tip as a picnic point.
Phase two: Development of the hills and shoreline reinforcement with riprap.

10, 11
Schematic drawings of the hill construction.

12
Diagram of a hill showing height, construction of a particularly critical section, and the layering of materials.

13
Long-term growth of vegetation on a steep section of a hill.

14
Sectional diagram showing erosion control measures and planting of a hill.

15, 16
Structure and planting of vegetation on a steep slope of a hill.

NEW YORK CITY

While the southwest end of the island is exposed to more rapid weather changes and stronger winds and currents, the northeast side is much calmer. The starting point for the resilient park design concept was the 100-year high water line of the pre-existing topography, which was then modified so that most of the island and, more importantly, most of the root zones of the perennial planting lie above the water level of a 100-year flood event. Hence, the intention is to ensure the park has a life expectancy of 100 years or more.

To raise the level of the terrain, four mounds were created, with heights of 7.5, 11, 12, and over 21 meters. They consist of material derived from the demolition of existing buildings on the site and from breaking up no longer needed sealed asphalt and paved parking areas. By reusing this material, the project minimizes impact on the climate caused by the transportation of soil, debris, and other materials. Consequently, building measures take into account the environmental consequences of the construction process itself.

The hills are used in different ways, for example as a vista point, or as a base for several slides, including the longest slide in the city. The hills also offer unprecedented new views, among them a 360° panorama of Manhattan and Brooklyn, and of the southern perimeter of the island. These vistas make connections between the park and its immediate surroundings as well as with the city as a whole, establishing the park as a place of special significance.

The new skyline of Governors Island is that of a green island. Most of the pre-existing surfaces were unsealed and replaced with new lawns, gardens, wetlands, and wooded areas. As part of this, some 3,000 trees were planted throughout the island, effectively doubling their number. The shade they provide helps protect the ground against overheating and also creates pleasant conditions for people on hot days. At the same time it benefits the microclimate for flora and fauna and can help reduce heat build-up and moisture evaporation in green areas.

Almost 43,000 shrubs were planted on the hills. Of the 54 plant species deployed, most were selected to withstand harsh weather conditions and to have suitably salt-tolerant root systems. As temperatures rise as a consequence of climate change, the more long-lived plants must be able to cope with a more southerly climate. One species that has proved particularly resilient to future climate conditions is *Rhus aromatica*, a plant from the sumac family commonly known as fragrant sumac. This woody plant is native to North America, and the use of native plants was an explicit goal of the planting design. Moreover, the choice of plants was tailored to the respective local microclimate created by the topography, and the planting substrate was adapted to the needs of the plants and their roots. In those elevated planting areas that are not subject to flooding with saltwater, a soil was chosen that enables the woody plants to thrive in the long term. Here, the intention is to create plant communities that can provide long-lasting healthy habitats for birds so that over time Governors Island Park will play a role in the regional network of habitats.

In addition to breaking up large asphalted surfaces and extensive planting, the designers improved the infiltration capacity of the soil and reduced runoff by specifying water-permeable surfaces for the paved areas. Rainwater is collected and used on-site for watering plants and maintaining the various habitats, rather than allowing it to flow into the harbor or discharging it in the city sewer system. Furthermore, the white concrete edging around lawns and planting areas has both formal and functional purposes: it serves on the one hand as seating and on the other as a protective barrier against erosion through wave action for the mounds in the case of storm surges or flooding.

17
Edging of the lawn and planting areas is both a design element and a means of channeling water flow after heavy rains.

18
The teardrop-shaped hill.

Conveniently accessibly by ferry from the southern tip of Manhattan, Governors Island is car-free and thus ideal for cyclists and pedestrians alike. With its many different open spaces, the park provides places for a wide variety of activities, from sports and games to artistic pursuits and urban gardening. The extensive transformation of Governors Island makes it not only an interesting example of climate change preparedness, but beyond that, a place that captures the imagination.

19
The long slides at Slide Hill.

20
Seawall blocks and alternative "scramble" pathway up the tallest hill, Outlook Hill.

21
The lawns and park planting looking towards Brooklyn.

GOVERNORS ISLAND PARK

CLIMATE MUSEUM

As the first American museum dedicated to the climate crisis, the Climate Museum uses art and science to highlight and address the challenges and opportunities presented by climate change for public health and safety. Moreover, it explores the future of urban design and other issues such as social justice. Founded in the aftermath of Hurricane Sandy the museum aims to improve awareness and deepen understanding of climate change, and inspire action in the community to address the challenges it poses. Its starting point was the realization that most people in the United States are worried about the climate crisis while mostly remaining inactive. By building on the popularity of museums and the trust accorded to them as reliable sources of information, it invites people to acquire in-depth knowledge, learn about solutions, and join the fight for a safer and brighter future.

In 2018, the museum used Governors Island and other locations to stage *Climate Signals*, an outdoor multisite installation conceived by the artist Justin Brice Guariglia. Consisting of ten large, mobile, solar-powered highway traffic signs installed in parks and public spaces, which display provocative statements, the show sparks dialogue and draws passers-by into the climate conversation. Modeled on illuminated highway warning signs, they demand attention and evoke a sense of urgency. The Climate Museum used these as a medium to place

22
Logo of the Climate Museum, which ran a hub on Governors Island in 2018.

23
One of the *Climate Signals* on Governors Island that flashed alerts about the impacts of climate change.

NEW YORK CITY

"climate warnings" on sites on Governors Island and in other parks throughout the city, and in some of the neighborhoods most affected by climate change. These warnings are flashed out as food for thought for passers-by in English as well as in several other languages spoken across New York including Chinese, French, Russian, and Spanish.

DOMINO PARK

Domino Park, which opened in 2018, is a 2.4-hectare narrow strip of waterfront, 400 meters long and 30 meters wide. It covers some of the grounds of the former Domino Sugar Refinery, which closed in 2004 and once refined up to 98 percent of the sugar consumed in the United States, while the entire site of the former sugar refinery is currently being developed by the local family-owned company Two Trees Management. Next to the park is a new mixed-use development that will provide 2,800 rental apartments, 700 of which will be affordable housing, along with an office complex in the historic factory building.

The design of the park explicitly incorporates remnants of the iconic industrial plant that defined the waterfront at this spot: four 11-meter-high cylindrical tanks that once stored syrup for sugar production, 21 columns of the raw sugar warehouse, various screw conveyors, and some 180 meters of crane guide rails including the original gantry cranes were not demolished and removed but incorporated into the design of the new park. As artifacts of the original facilities, they testify to the history of the place and sugar trade in New York and lend the park a unique character.

24
Another *Climate Signal*
against the backdrop of Manhattan
on Governors Island.

NEW YORK CITY

25–30
Domino Park is a long and narrow park along the East River with a waterfront promenade linking all its parts. Situated on the site of a former sugar refinery, it fronts a new urban neighborhood. Its hallmark are the repainted gantry cranes from the former factory. The Fog Bridge in front of the Syrup Tanks is a signature water feature that emits clouds of wafting fog at regular intervals and showcases water in a new context, helping to create a cool microclimate for visitors to the park in summer.

With a variety of spaces and activities for all age groups and diverse needs, the park has quickly been embraced by local residents and is already a popular place to go. Thanks to Domino Park, this previously inaccessible stretch of the East River waterfront became a public amenity with direct access to the water and stunning views of Manhattan and the Williamsburg Bridge. A 360-meter-long footpath runs along the waterfront, which is bordered by a variety of different activity zones and attractions: from north to south a dog run, a bocce court, a multipurpose play area, a volleyball court, a water and light installation with "fog bridge" that showcases the four Syrup Tanks, a central seating area with stepped seating facing onto a fountain plaza, a taco bar, a refinery-themed children's playground, a stretch of lawn, and finally, sets of lounge chairs for relaxing alongside the river. Next to the fountain plaza, the path drops down to provide an unhindered view of Manhattan across the East River. Both the repurposing of parts of the industrial facility as components of the park as well as its walkways and lookout points, and the up-beat color scheme (the cranes and other elements are bright turquoise) give the park a distinct and unique charm. Moreover, the northern third of the park is dominated by the eye-catching cranes and the so-called "Artifact Walk," an elevated walkway attached to the columns of the former factory that offers spectacular views of Manhattan.

The resilient design approach of the landscape architects at James Corner Field Operations is reflected in the site's design as both a sponge that "soaks up" water and as a front line against storm surges. To achieve this dual function, the design eschews the usual high protective walls in favor of raising the entire park between 60 centimeters and 2 meters above the 100-year flood line, reducing the risk of flooding and allowing water to drain into the river. Almost half of the park consists of vegetation, and the plants are predominantly native species selected for their resilience to splashing water and flooding. Apart from that, some 175 trees were planted. No pesticides or herbicides are used in park maintenance, and plant waste is composted and used to enrich the planting areas. The use of LED lights reduces both energy consumption and light pollution, and the water for the central fountain plaza with its 21 nozzles is regulated by a pump and water retention system and filtered with UV light.

HUNTER'S POINT SOUTH PARK

Two boat stops north of Domino Park, Hunter's Point South Park extends into the East River on a human-made promontory at the mouth of Newtown Creek. This 4.5-hectare park contains children's playgrounds, a sports field also used by the nearby school, a café, boat rentals, a dog run, and a lookout point in the form of a "ship's prow" with views of Manhattan and across the park. Conceived as a public recreational area within a development area that will provide 5,000 apartments, 60 percent of which are for low- and medium-income households, the park also serves as a protective buffer for the residential area in the event of storm surges. Accordingly, the design concept combines strategies for adapting to changing climatic conditions with recreational facilities such as a floating dock or a "rail garden" that pays homage to the area's industrial past.

A first 2.2-hectare section opened at the end of August 2013 and included a dog run, a perennial garden between the old railroad tracks, a playground, a waterfront terrace, a beach, and a canopy that provides both a shaded seating area as well as photovoltaic power for the café. Of particular relevance for the park's climate resilience is the green and oval-shaped 90 × 70 meter sports and play area. There, a central section for ball games covered with artificial turf for extensive use is bordered by a sloping natural grass lawn. Running around most of the perimeter is a tiered, 80-centimeter-high concrete wall that acts as a flood

31
View of the park, with the East River on the left of the headland and Newtown Creek on the right. In front is the second phase of the park's development; behind it on the East River is the first phase.

retaining wall, rising at the back to create an edge but lying flush with the path on the riverward side. In the event of high water, the oval can flood and then later drain back into the East River. The combination of artificial turf and natural lawn is likewise a response to flood control: artificial turf surfaces are soon reusable after flooding, whereas grass suffers, especially after exposure to saltwater. Furthermore, the lawns around the oval are above the flood line and protected from saltwater infiltration.

While still under construction, the first section of the park was put to the test by Hurricane Sandy in October 2012. Stormwater from the record-breaking hurricane flooded precisely the areas designed to accommodate a 100-year flood. Eventually, the waves in the East River resulted in flood levels of 1.20 meters, which the oval play area was able to contain, preventing the adjacent streets from flooding. The water then drained back into the East River as designed. Similarly, the streets leading to the park held back water before it could flow into the park. Equipped with water-retaining planted areas and tree grates, these roadways collect and hold water before slowly releasing it, allowing it to gradually cascade into lower-lying areas before draining into the river. While these bioswales capture and filter stormwater runoff, they also contribute to improving the water quality of the river by cleansing water from streets and sidewalks before it enters the river.

Another flood control measure is the use of gabions—wire cages filled with stones and gravel—set some 15 centimeters into the ground. A total of 230 meters of such gabions were installed along the eastern edge of the park, visible as stripes in the planted beds of perennials and grasses. They hold back excess water before it enters the sewer, alleviating pressure on the sewage system while also pre-cleansing the water. As a result, construction of the first section of the park was able to resume just a few days after Sandy had subsided, since all structures and planted areas withstood the storm and floodwaters well.

The second section of the park that extends south towards the headland at the mouth of Newton Creek opened in June 2017. Also encompassing an area of about 2.2 hectares, the second section is likewise designed for resilience but is more natural in character, featuring an eco-peninsula, marshy wetland areas, an elevated "Overlook" that rises 7 meters above the river, meadow areas, running trails, and a kayak dock. The paths here are also more winding and varied, and the entire peninsula is designed to accommodate flooding in the event of a storm surge without sustaining damage. Additionally, a sculpture by Nobuho Nagasawa of seven curved and etched concrete domes that depict the seven phases of the moon can already be seen from afar. Their surfaces have a phosphorescent coating that stores sunlight during the day and causes the sculpture to shimmer blue at night. Beneath the cantilevered Overlook, tidal salt marshes form a grassy fringe that is flooded twice daily by the East River tide. Grasses were selected that thrive in the brackish water. Banks of riprap—an edging of large angular boulders—and accompanying planting help improve the water quality and prevent erosion of the shoreline. The park also creates natural habitats for fauna, and fish in particular. To allow this to develop, small pink flags were placed to keep geese away. The system of paths, some leading down to the water's edge, others up to the Overlook, offers a surprising variety of impressions given the comparatively small size of the park.

Other elements of Hunter's Point South Park's sustainability strategy include the use of locally produced steel for the canopy, as well as the solar panels that feed electricity back into the city's electricity grid. It produces enough energy to provide year-round lighting for the park without the need for a battery. The café likewise minimizes its environmental footprint by various means: its orientation avoids excess heat build-up from the sun, obviating the need for cooling, and off-set roof elements provide indirect natural lighting. Made of native pine timber planks sourced from the southern United States, the park's sundeck is treated with Kebony technology, a process that gives sustainable softwoods a durability similar to that of tropical hardwoods. Impregnating the wood with a natural by-product of sugar cane processing avoids the use of toxic chemicals such as copper arsenite, and also avoids further destruction of the already endangered tropical rainforests.

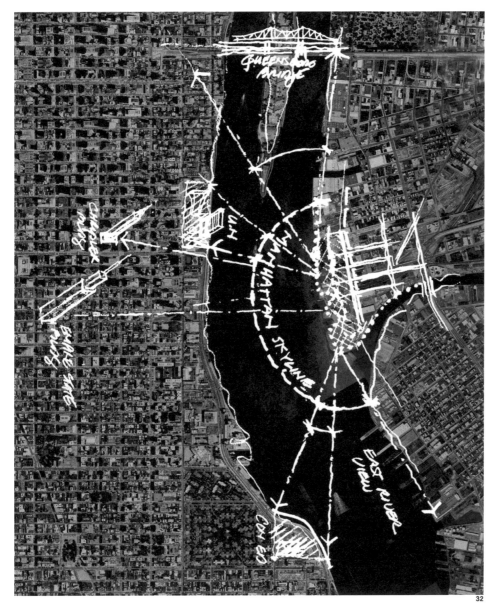

32
The various views across the East River to Manhattan determined the position and design of the Overlook.

HUNTER'S POINT SOUTH PARK

33
The riverside location of the park in the city means that it must fulfill many different functions and demands. The three separate graphics show how the park contains flooding at normal high water levels, and during a 10-year and a 100-year flood event.

34
Not only the vegetation and paved areas need to withstand the effects of flooding but also the fauna in aquatic habitats, the soil, and the air.

NEW YORK CITY

35
The lawn area at normal high water levels.

36
The lawn area during flooding.

HUNTER'S POINT SOUTH PARK

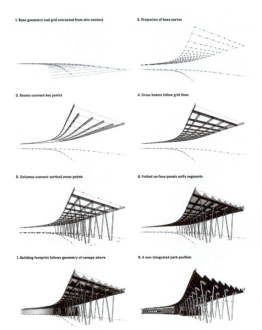

37
The popular lawn area in 2018 with more mature vegetation and building development in the background.

38
The lower ball games area of the central lawn is made of resilient artificial turf while the natural grasses in the higher-lying areas are not affected by floods.

39
An overview of the first phase of the park.

40
Concept and composition of the pleated steel shade canopy.

41
The shade canopy with pavilion and café is an ecologically sustainable construction that echoes the sweep of the Overlook.

NEW YORK CITY

42
Atmospheric view over Nobuho Nagasawa's artwork at dusk against the backdrop of Manhattan.

43
The viewing terrace of the Overlook has stunning views of Manhattan and is itself a striking feature of the park.

HUNTER'S POINT SOUTH PARK

80

44, 45
The vegetation of the floodable wetland areas has developed well, suggesting that the concept has been successful.

NEW YORK CITY

Due to good mass transit connections, visitors do not need a car to reach the park. While a ferry stop and a nearby subway station link it to the wider city, it can also be accessed through the urban network of bike lanes, and there are numerous points of entry for pedestrians and joggers. To minimize the water requirement for irrigation and ongoing maintenance, native and regionally adapted plant species have been selected for their resilience to drought on the one hand and flood resistance on the other. The water permeable path surfaces, shoreline riprap and sandy beach are light-colored reflective surfaces that can absorb storm- and floodwater while reducing runoff. Beyond that, the wetland marshes also respond to tidal fluctuations by restoring natural conditions.

An article in the *New York Times* from 2013 succinctly summarized the key lessons derived from the design of the park: 1. Build higher than you think the water could possibly come. 2. Make it tough, but not impossible, for surging water to get in. 3. Make it easy for water to flow back into the river, but not into sewers.

The underlying principle of foregoing concrete walling to shield the park from water but instead to design "with" the river and its changing water levels can also be understood as a homage to the landscape that once existed here 200 years ago before it was urbanized by European immigrants. At that time much of what is now the park didn't even exist: not just the riparian zones but also the promontory itself are human-made areas first created by tipping fill material into the East River. Today the park is fully integrated into the organism of the city. However, it must function not just above ground but also in the subsoil, the depth of water and strength of the underlying layer, not to mention the urban infrastructure beneath. That includes two parallel tunnels running beneath the East River and the park, which are part of the nearly 2-kilometer-long Queens-Midtown Tunnel connecting the boroughs of Queens and Manhattan as part of Interstate 495. Next to them are four 1,800-meter-long East River tunnels for the regional and intercity railroad lines. During Hurricane Sandy, these all filled with saltwater and, although still functional, have been damaged by the corrosive salts that remained after the water was pumped out. In addition, important power lines also run both through the rail tunnels and through a further underground conduit. As such, the design of the park focuses alongside its own resilience on preserving the quality of "gray" infrastructure.

These examples show that the idea of resilient design is not to prevent flooding at all costs, although it should ideally be avoided. Rather, designing for resilience means firstly that when and if a park does flood, it can drain quickly and at a pace that the river and sewers can handle, and secondly that important urban functions and facilities are better able to withstand the effects of extreme climate events. From today's viewpoint, the new parks in New York are exemplary in both respects and can therefore serve as models for the design of modern, resilient green spaces.

46 The Overlook in the evening.

DE
TROIT

As one of those cities to have experienced dramatic upswings and downswings over their history, Detroit is nowadays perhaps best known as an example of a metropolis in decline. Because its growth as a city was largely dependent on a single industry, automobile manufacturing, Detroit was hit extremely hard by changes in the sector. The past decades have been very difficult for the city, and it is still not clear when its fortunes will change. While the motto on its flag, "Speramus Meliora; Resurget Cineribus"—in English, "We hope for better things; it will rise from the ashes"—was chosen in 1805 after the city was devastated by fire, 200 years on it is once again uncannily relevant.

Founded by Frenchmen at the beginning of the 17th century, the name of the city was originally "D'Etroit" meaning "at the narrows," an allusion to its location on the river of the same name that, together with St. Clair River and Lake St. Clair, forms a strait between two of the five Great Lakes, Lake Huron, and Lake Erie. Due to its favorable location on transportation routes for materials and finished products, Detroit soon became a center of the Manufacturing Belt, the industrial conurbation that developed on the Great Lakes in the northern United States in the late 19th and early 20th centuries. After Henry Ford founded the Ford Motor Company in Detroit in 1903, the city soon benefited from the rapid economic success of the American automotive industry, which expanded to include other vehicle manufacturers and continued into the 1950s. The enormous demand for labor attracted people to Detroit, especially from the southern United States, many of whom were able to fulfill the American dream of a permanent job and a home of their own for their family. In 1950, the city's population peaked at over 1.8 million and Detroit was by then the fourth-largest and wealthiest city in the United States.

1 (previous page)
Large empty lots right on the edge of Downtown Detroit.

2
Abandoned houses and empty lots in large parts of the city, even close to downtown, do not create the impression of a vibrant city.

DETROIT

But with market saturation and increasing competition from abroad, the automotive industry was forced to cut many jobs in the decades that followed, and the impact on the Motor City was particularly severe. This was further compounded by the phenomenon of suburbanization, itself largely a product of mass motorization. Hence, many families and businesses moved to the suburbs, and between 1950 and 2000, the urban region expanded by 30 percent. Over a period of decades, the heart of the city lost jobs and people on a grand scale, so that the current population numbers only about 650,000. As a result of this exodus more than 80,000 houses stand vacant in the inner urban area, or have been torn down, and around 100,000 plots of land are unused. Detroit therefore has an unusually large amount of open space. For the car-oriented city, this poses major challenges: many roads and gray infrastructure need maintaining and the cost of providing water, gas, electricity, and other public utilities is prohibitive. Even the supply of food had become a problem, as there were few regularly stocked supermarkets. Most everyday goods such as milk and bread are sold at gas stations. However, in the context of addressing climate change, the abundance of open space presents opportunities for creating green infrastructure, but also particular challenges given the sparse density of the 360 km² city.

While the city has since begun demolishing vacant and dilapidated houses and putting the land to new use, it has also been actively seeking solutions to preventing further decay and addressing its enormous debt. In 2010, the Detroit Future City organization launched as a non-profit think tank dedicated to creating a strategic framework for the next 50 years to make the city more economically stable and sustainable, and to improve the quality of life. Priorities include economic growth, new land uses, more sustainable and densely populated neighborhoods, reformed (gray) infrastructure and improved public services, and productive and sustainable uses of vacant land. In addition to growing food, open space and vacant lots will be used for stormwater management through

3
Abandoned lots no longer burden the city's utilities. Street lighting, drinking water supplies, and sewer systems were originally built to serve a much larger population.

the creation of surface water and retention ponds, and as areas for research projects or energy production.

After it was destroyed in the Great Fire of 1805, Detroit was rebuilt along the lines of the capital Washington, D.C., with a radial system of axes. Three major radial avenues convene at Campus Martius, an urban space that since that time has marked the city's center and was recently redesigned at the beginning of this millennium. New recreational facilities and green areas give it a pleasant atmosphere, and its role as Detroit's physical center and focal point strengthens the relationship the residents have with their city. Most buildings in the city center have now been renovated and create an attractive context, and an elevated railroad line has been supplemented by a modern streetcar line.

Detroit has a humid continental climate with an annual mean temperature of 14.5 °C. Based on the period from 1961 to 1990, maximum temperatures in summer, from June to September, averaged above 20 °C, while minimum temperatures in winter, from December to February, fell below 0 °C. The mean total annual precipitation during this period was 780 millimeters.

EFFECTS OF CLIMATE CHANGE

Monitoring of the climate of Detroit and the surrounding region began in 1951 and has been conducted by the Great Lakes Integrated Sciences and Assessments Center (GLISA), a facility jointly run by the University of Michigan and Michigan State University. Their findings show a 10.7 percent increase in precipitation from 1951 to 2014. While annual precipitation increased 25.2 percent, the largest increase occurred in the fall months (40 percent) and the smallest in summer (9.4 percent). Most modeling scenarios predict a trend toward more frequent and heavier precipitation in the future, and as temperatures grow warmer, winters will have more rain than snow. The mean temperature went up by 1.5 °C from 1951 to 2014, with nighttime temperatures increasing 1.9 °C and daytime temperatures 1.1 °C. The temperature increase was most pronounced in spring at 1.7 °C, and least pronounced in fall at 1.0 °C. Also, the ice-free period extended by 15 days during the same period.

These trends look set to continue or intensify in the future: average temperatures are expected to increase by 4 to 5 °C by the middle of this century, with more hot days. Accordingly, the growing season—days without frost—will increase by between one to two months, depending on future emissions levels. In addition, the number of days on which buildings will need to be heated (days with outdoor temperatures of 18 °C or lower) will decrease as the climate grows warmer, however, the number of days on which cooling will be required (days with outdoor temperatures above 18 °C) will increase. Between 1951 and 2014, the number of warm days requiring air-conditioning rose considerably by 40 percent, while heating days decreased by 11 percent. As such, the additional energy required to cool buildings offsets the cost savings of the reduced heating requirement. A further problem in this context is the growing short-term demand for energy, for example to cool homes during heat waves. To cover peak demand, further energy is required from electrical power plants in the region, most of which are fired by coal or other fossil fuels, causing additional greenhouse gas and pollutant emissions.

Based on these observations and calculations, a *Climate Action Plan for Detroit* was adopted in 2017. Interestingly, this plan was not imposed "top down" by the city's government but arose as a bottom-up initiative driven by a coalition of city organizations, businesses, municipal agencies, educational institutions, and non-profit groups who lobbied the political leadership. While the plan focuses on tackling climate change, it also considers how people live and work in the city and how the city should be governed.

Based on scientific research, the statements on climate change discussed in the *Climate Action Plan* primarily encompass general recommendations for stormwater management, reducing the heat island effect, and improving air quality. Also taken into consideration are social aspects such as the provision of and access to green spaces for city residents, as is the networking of habitats for wildlife as an ecological goal. Other key points include inventories for greenhouse gas emissions, and environmental justice and vulnerability. This term covers the extent to which communities will be exposed to weather events triggered by climate change as well as the sensitivity of individuals or communities to be impacted by climate change and their capacity to anticipate and adapt to them. People of different ages and constitutions respond differently to climate change, and the effects on their health and well-being can vary widely. Likewise, communities are varyingly well equipped to absorb or mitigate the specific impacts of climate change.

4
The new Ford Rouge Factory in Dearborn, Henry Ford's birthplace near Detroit, has green facades and roofs as well as extensive grounds that are home to bee colonies. A sign at the site says that the green roof was the largest "living" roof in the world at the time of its creation.

The primary topics outlined in the *Climate Action Plan* are waste management, public health, businesses and institutions, with green-blue infrastructure such as parks, public spaces, and water infrastructure in fourth place, and homes and neighborhoods last in the list.

Of particular note is the importance that the *Climate Action Plan* accords to green-blue infrastructure across the entire urban area, especially in the context of water management and water and air pollution control. Through strategic placement and maintenance, these can contribute to reducing the heat island effect and significantly benefit stormwater management. Heavy rainfall often overloads the sewer system, allowing untreated water to flow directly into local rivers. Plants and especially rain gardens, however, mitigate water runoff, filter polluted water, and also promote infiltration and evaporation, relieving pressure on wastewater infrastructure. As alternatives to a costly, traditional "gray" infrastructure these and other stormwater management measures are to be implemented across the city.

What's more, the planting of vegetation as green buffers can filter and clean the air between streets or between industrial and residential areas, reduce noise and light pollution, and serve as carbon sinks. To this end, vacant lots can be planted with prairie vegetation and forests. A citywide green infrastructure plan proposes that the redesign of green infrastructure should also address their functional potential as carbon sinks, for example by including a high proportion of woody vegetation, through incorporating water storage features such as rain gardens, bioswales, or retention ponds, and through appropriate provisions for recreation, and improved maintenance. Quite a few of these measures directly benefit public health.

Due to the backlog of extensive and expensive water infrastructure repairs, drinking water in Detroit is more expensive than in other, comparable cities. As a result, a large number of households have been unable to pay their bills and have faced water shutoffs. The plan therefore proposes that investment in technologies such as green infrastructure will enable the water utility companies to drive down their costs and reduce supply losses due to leaks in the dilapidated water supply infrastructure.

Last but not least, the expansion of green-blue infrastructure is explicitly intended to increase the resilience of the city's ecosystems. To that effect, the plan identifies a significant number of large open spaces within the city limits—totaling some 100 square kilometers—that can be used for recreational opportunities for residents and also as natural habitats for wildlife. A citywide ecosystem services inventory is meant to categorize these vacant sites, identify ecologically valuable areas and wildlife corridors, and implement measures for their protection and enhancement.

KEEP GROWING DETROIT

Vacant lots are not necessarily only a problem for cities; they can also offer opportunities for potentially productive alternative uses, whether economically, for public health, or for social cohesion in the community. One such alternative use that is being practiced at a comparatively large scale in Detroit, so much so that it has made a name for itself, is new urban agriculture.

Since the 1970s the concept of using vacant lots in urban areas for agriculture or gardening is a trend that has existed across much of America and Europe. In Detroit, however, its history reaches much further back, originating in an economic crisis that lasted for about three years in the 1890s. Then, many people were out of work and hungry but had time and labor on their hands. The city, on the other hand, lacked the resources to provide financial support but had large tracts of open land inside and beyond the city limits. The mayor, Hazen Pingree, parceled up the land and made it available to needy citizens to grow potatoes, beans, and other vegetables. Thus, the townspeople turned their hand to farming and helped one another, achieving good harvests that helped them survive the economic crisis and overcome food shortages. At the time, the entire country looked to Pingree and his city, and the "Detroit Model" was soon copied in many other American cities.

5
Volunteers at work on vegetable plots between former factory buildings.

6
The large vegetable beds have professional irrigation and provide abundant yields.

7
A large greenhouse under construction.

8
Keep Growing Detroit supports urban gardening and also owns farms in which volunteers help to grow vegetables.

9
Locally produced fruit and vegetables are sold regularly at the Eastern Market. The area is not very busy when it's not market day.

DETROIT

When the economy collapsed again during the far more serious Great Depression of the 1930s, Detroit's administration had a model to turn to. Again, it was the mayor, Frank Murphy, who took the initiative. Recalling the success of Pingree's earlier model, and convinced that those unemployed were motivated and willing to work, Murphy initiated the so-called Detroit Thrift Gardens program. Needy households could apply to participate in the program and were allocated a plot of land by the public authorities, along with fertilizer, tomato and cabbage plants, and seeds for various kinds of vegetables. Again, the citizens helped each other, with the more experienced gardeners teaching their neighbors to plant their gardens. This program, too, was a success. While distributing produce among neighbors was allowed, selling them was not. The Detroit Thrift Gardens continued until 1936 when the economy began to recover.

As a third program to promote urban agriculture, "Farm-A-Lot" was established by Detroit's first African American mayor, Coleman A. Young, in 1974. Its purpose was to tackle the social problems caused by the city's ongoing economic decline, including poverty, high crime rates, and widespread drug use by motivating the population to grow their own fruit and vegetables. Once more, the city provided plots and seeds, but few of the 3,000 available plots were taken up and the program was eventually discontinued in 2002. Despite its limited impact, it did succeed in igniting a passion among some citizens, showing them what it meant to produce good-quality food of their own. In the 1990s, several initiatives formed to promote the benefits of urban agriculture, which eventually joined forces to become the Detroit Agriculture Network (DAN). With the help of state funding the network formed an organization called the Garden Resource Program (GRP), ultimately the "mother" of many other garden programs. It is now run by Keep Growing Detroit (KGD), another non-profit organization that aims to "cultivate a food-sovereign Detroit in which the majority of fruit and vegetables consumed in Detroit is produced by residents living within the city." The organization runs numerous gardens on large sites, working together with volunteers, children, and all who want to learn about urban gardening, or just want to contribute. The vegetables are not just sold at farmers' markets, they are also used by restaurants and catering providers throughout the city.

Keep Growing Detroit is a success story for the city at multiple levels: while it engages citizens and builds a sense of community, it also provides them with healthy food, and maintains green spaces around the city that contribute to improving the climate. And the numbers speak for themselves: in 2019, the organization helped 25,491 citizens to cultivate 1,589 farms and gardens, integrating the support of 2,650 volunteers. Of the gardens, 983 were family-run, 141 were school gardens, 374 community gardens and 91 farms and markets. Fifty-eight gardeners sold their produce at farmers' markets, generating $51,190 in proceeds. Half of the gardens supported in 2019 had been with KGD for more than three years. In addition, the organization distributed 53,596 packs of seed and 204,015 seedlings from 95 varieties of vegetables and donated 967 fruit trees and shrubs and 10,620 native plants to 150 partners. Seven rainwater harvesting systems retained over 50,300 liters of rainwater, 59 beekeepers kept 55 bee colonies, 16 young people were trained, and 552 people participated in some 80 events.

Among the goals the KGD has laid down in its statutes are promoting the health of neighborhood residents through high-quality food, building resilient local economies, and protecting or preserving soil, water, and biodiversity for future generations.

CAMPUS MARTIUS PLAZA

In cities suffering major economic and social problems, parks and green spaces are often low on the list of priorities, and Detroit is no exception. The problem was further exacerbated by the exodus of families and businesses to the suburbs over the course of several decades. In this context, the redevelopment of Campus Martius Park on the occasion of the city's 300th anniversary was of special significance, not just for the city's urban design but also symbolically and culturally. Although Detroit celebrated its 300th birthday in 2001, the major renewal of the plaza by Rundell Ernstberger Associates was not completed until 2003–2004.

Campus Martius was originally a parade ground. After the Great Fire of 1805, a large stone was placed in the marshy ground as the basis for accurately mapping the cardinal points and planning the city. The stone still exists today and is considered the origin of new Detroit and the center of its coordinate system. In order to stabilize the subsoil for construction purposes, more than 30 meters of fill material was heaped on the swampy marshlands in the mid-19th century.

The 21st-century redesign encompassed not just the park but also the streetscape of the five main boulevards that radiate from this point. It also included the design of fountains, public gardens, lighting, sound and art installations,

10
A circle of granite paving marks the point of origin of the city on the Campus Martius Plaza.

11

14

12

13

15

11
The pedestrian areas continue on to the river and are linked by crosswalks where they pass over roadways. Attractive light installations encourage their use in the evening.

12
Large trees in the greened area create an inviting place for people to meet in the center of the city.

13
Different forms of greened areas and vegetation help muffle the sound of traffic and create a better sense of enclosure and shelter.

14
A sandy beach with palm trees as a relaxed lounge and play area.

15
A lawn invites people to take a seat. Freely arrangeable chairs can accommodate groups of different sizes.

CAMPUS MARTIUS PLAZA

signage, as well as information panels at historically significant points. Since then, the park has won several awards, including the Urban Land Institute's Amanda Burden Urban Open Space Award in 2010. The judges described the park as an outstanding example of a public space that acts as a catalyst for the development of adjacent neighborhoods.

The design provides a range of spaces for different uses and events throughout the year. Of particular note are the many different ways in which people can use the space, the high-quality and well-maintained planting, as well as the lawns and their freely arrangeable seating, and the imaginative lighting scheme that attracts people to gather there in the evening. Although high-rise buildings predominate in the city center, the amount of green space and the amenities overall are surprisingly good. Trees, for instance, provide shade in the recreational areas, and a large sandy beach in the center rounds off the many different invitations to use the space.

Climate change comes at a time when Detroit is still dealing with the aftermath of 50 years of massive economic decline. Clearly, the city has in many ways made a virtue out of the twin challenges of decline and building resilience: it has been able to draw on its experiences of overcoming hardship in the past, especially when it comes to repurposing vacant land. In recent years, urban development has focused on strengthening and regenerating its rich green-blue infrastructure, improving the supply of healthy foods to the population, and revitalizing its urban identity. The redesign of the green spaces in the city center and the use of vacant lots in Detroit's central areas for *urban gardening* and *urban agriculture* represent exemplary models for other cities.

HOUSTON

Houston lies in the east of the U.S. state of Texas, about 60 kilometers from the coast of the Gulf of Mexico, on a low coastal plain only 15 meters above sea level. Colloquially known as "Space City," it has, since 1961, been home to the Johnson Space Center, NASA's astronaut training and spaceflight control hub, and, since 1992 to the Space Center Houston, a visitor and learning center for science and space exploration. Houston is the largest city in the Southern states and the fourth-largest city in the entire country, with 2.3 million residents within its city limits and 7 million in the wider metropolitan region, which now extends as far as the Gulf Coast and is one of the fastest growing metropolitan areas in the USA.

It was founded in 1836 on the banks of the Buffalo Bayou, a barely 100-kilometer stretch of water, following General Sam Houston's defeat of Mexican troops in the decisive Battle of San Jacinto east of the city during the Texas War of Independence in 1835–1836. Today, Buffalo Bayou is still the most important river in Houston, flowing through the city from west to east.

In the southern United States, the word *bayou* denotes a slow-moving lowland river, usually in marshland areas, as is the case in Houston. Since ten such watercourses wind their way through Houston and the surrounding area, the city is also known as "The Bayou City." In fact, these marshy rivers serve as drainage for the developed urban areas. East of the city, Buffalo Bayou continues as the Houston Ship Channel, which opens onto the Gulf of Mexico some 60 kilometers to the south. A 40-kilometer stretch of this is occupied by the Port of Houston, which is the second-largest port in the USA. Built in the more sheltered inland area of the county to reduce its exposure to hurricanes, it is most well known as a port for the shipment of oil and oil-based products. Additionally, the metropolitan area is also home to several of Texas' largest refineries. Due to the region's particular vulnerability to weather extremes and its role as a valuable habitat for a variety of flora and fauna, the large-scale storage and processing of petroleum products is highly problematic from an ecological perspective. Galveston Bay, located between the Houston metropolitan area and the Gulf, as well as the adjacent coastal strip to the east are home to three major bird sanctuaries, the Anahuac National Wildlife Refuge, the McFaddin National Wildlife Refuge and Sea Rim State Park, and the Texas Point National Wildlife Refuge.

Houston lies in a subtropical climate zone with tropical temperatures and high rainfall. The climate is influenced by its location near the Gulf Coast, and it is particularly suitable for agriculture.

While the mean daytime temperature over the year is 26.1 °C, above-average temperatures of up to 34.2 °C are reached in summer between April and October. Temperatures rise above 25 °C in seven months of the year, whereas the mean minimum temperature is 14.1 °C. Annual precipitation totals 1,242 millimeters a year, and it rains all months of the year with monthly rainfalls ranging between 60 and 130 millimeters, less in winter than in summer. Muggy conditions—temperatures above 25 °C and relative humidity greater than 75 percent—are common for more than half the year.

Tropical storms are frequent in the wider Houston region, with the hurricane season lasting from June 1 to November 30. While Houston lies on the edge of the main hurricane zone, in recent years it has experienced an increase in varying

1 (previous page)
Buffalo Bayou Park against the backdrop of Downtown Houston.

weather extremes. For example, in 2011 Houston was exposed to a 24-day summer heat wave of extreme temperatures in excess of 38 °C. A third of its citizens were unable to adequately cool their homes due to a lack of air-conditioning or the prohibitive cost of running the units. In Texas, 301 million trees withered and in Houston alone, some 1,000 water mains burst as the clayey soil dried and shrunk. In the following years, Houston was hit by devastating storms with heavy rainfall. Then, in late May 2015, a large part of the city was flooded in the wake of the heaviest rainfall since weather records began, and two years later, in late August 2017, Hurricane Harvey, then still at Category 4, passed over Houston at a very slow pace. Forty-two fatalities were recorded, and its effect on homes, infrastructure, and green spaces was still evident a year later. Harvey was the rainiest storm ever to hit the United States, bringing 60 to 80 liters of precipitation per square meter within a few hours. Some 1,000 liters per square meter fell during the days of continuous rain. Only two years later, Hurricane Imelda hit Houston, again depositing a vast amount of rain on the city, causing five fatalities and further immense damage to properties. As a result, Houston experienced one 500-year and two 100-year weather events in the space of only a few years. While unusual in such short succession, it is no longer entirely unexpected. It appears that climate change is not only resulting in a higher frequency of such storms but is also decreasing their speed, in turn increasing the amount of water the hurricanes pick up over the ocean and deposit on the land.

EFFECTS OF CLIMATE CHANGE

Houston's particularly drastic experience of ever shorter intervals between extreme weather events highlights how there is only limited time left to repair damage and establish more resilient structures. Following Hurricane Harvey, the local administration formed an Office of Sustainability and developed a *Climate Action Plan*, which came into effect in 2020. This plan calls for massive reductions in greenhouse gas emissions in order to achieve the climate neutrality goals set out in the Paris Agreement by 2050. Despite the U.S. Federal Government's temporary withdrawal from the climate agreement, the mayor of Houston—along with 425 other mayors of American cities in 49 states—committed to meeting the goals of the accord. Less than a year after Hurricane Harvey, Houston became the 101st city to join the Resilient Cities Network. While the first 100 cities received support from the Rockefeller Foundation, which launched the initiative, Houston received $1.8 million from the Shell Oil Company.

The *Climate Action Plan* for the City of Houston describes climate change as an unpredictable challenge to the city's safety and prosperity. In response to the experience of Hurricane Harvey and its disastrous consequences for the people, infrastructures, and properties, the *Climate Action Plan* prioritizes improving flood protection. It also highlights the need for better preparedness to brave major heat waves and droughts, as well as the need to improve air and water quality. Other issues mentioned include the threat to food security and the spread of disease, although these remain general statements with no specific recommendations for the City of Houston.

Further potential threats discussed involve the erosion of the coastline of the Gulf of Mexico and changes to natural habitats caused by saltwater intrusion into freshwater areas as a result of rising sea levels. In fact, Galveston Island off the Gulf Coast has already recorded a 60-centimeter rise in mean sea level. There, houses are generally built on stilts to improve their chances of surviving high water events unscathed. While the ecosystems of the many extensive wildlife conservation areas along the Gulf Coast are already well-adapted to regular flooding, they are sensitive to changes in the salinity of the water, to erosion, and to other effects of storm surges.

The *Climate Action Plan* is divided into four areas—transportation, energy, building optimization, and waste disposal and use—and offers three proposals for reducing greenhouse gas emissions for each of these areas. Under energy, the plan outlines the goal to plant 4.6 million native trees by 2030 to sequester CO_2. It is the only goal in the *Climate Action Plan* that addresses vegetation or green infrastructure.

Shell has shown support for membership in the global Resilient Cities Network by funding the development of a resilience strategy, which aims to enable the city to become considerably more resistant to the impacts of climate change. Particularly illuminating are the climate projections outlined in the strategy document should the city fail to act. Subsequently, the number of days in which temperatures rise above 40 °C would then increase from around 10 at present to 74 per year by 2050. Continuing urbanization, population growth, and the accompanying increased sealing of land surfaces would lead to longer and hotter summers. The forecasts also project a rise in the frequency and severity of storms and heavy rain events. What's more, sea levels along the Gulf Coast of Texas are expected to rise at twice the global average. If these projections come to pass, it would have disastrous implications for coastal habitats, and not just homes on stilts would be at risk but also the numerous industrial facilities, power plants and oil refineries along the Texas coast.

2
The houses of Galveston on the Gulf Coast are already raised on stilts to protect them against flooding.

One of the initiatives established by the city to address the impacts of climate change is the Green Building Resource Center. The facility, which opened on World Earth Day (April 22) in 2009 and resides in a LEED Gold-certified building, offers a mine of information and inspiration on sustainable building. Using diagrams, models, and display panels, it presents more than 50 examples of how buildings and open spaces can be ecologically designed and built for resilience. Included in the exhibits are demonstrations of a green roof irrigated with air-conditioning condensate, a photovoltaic system, and four wind turbines. Overall, the center provides an extremely diverse range of information and expert guides can assist visitors on specific topics.

Alongside detailing practical applications, the Green Building Resource Center also establishes connections to other initiatives and networks such as Project Drawdown, a climate protection initiative. Its name refers to the point at which levels of greenhouse gases in the atmosphere have decreased to such an extent that its harmful anthropogenic impact on the climate is stopped. Project Drawdown identifies three connected areas of action for mitigating climate change: Reduce Sources, Support Sinks, and Improve Society. Drawdown divides the main greenhouse gas emitters into five sectors—electricity; food, agriculture, and land use; industry; transportation; and buildings—and looks at their potential for reduction based on currently available measures and opportunities. Greenhouse gas sinks are found on land, on the banks of bodies of waters, in oceans, or are human-made. While landscape architecture contributes mainly to the sectors of land use and food production, it does so also in transportation and buildings. The project presents a range of concrete measures and evaluates them in terms of their impact on reducing climate gas emissions. Since the list is constantly being reviewed and updated, it is thus considered a living project.

Two differently projected scenarios—a temperature rise of approximately either 2 °C or 1.5 °C by 2100—bring about different priorities on the list of proposed measures. For example, in the first scenario, reducing food waste is considered to have the greatest potential for reducing climate gases, since a third of the food produced worldwide is not currently consumed. As a result, many other resources such as seeds, water, energy, land, fertilizer, labor, and financial capital virtually go to waste and/or cause entirely unnecessary greenhouse gas emissions. Wasted food currently accounts for about 8 percent of global emissions. In low-income countries such wastage is often unintentional, occurring in supply chains, on farms, and during storage or distribution. In higher-income countries, on the other hand, food wastage can be seen as systematic and even deliberate, for example food is rejected because it is unsightly, irregular, or discolored, or wasted because too much is purchased due to its low price. Starting with the areas in which food waste is greatest, the researchers outline solutions to prevent food being thrown away or going to waste, thus reducing greenhouse gases. In conjunction with this, the distribution of the food produced should be organized in such a way that no one goes hungry, and everyone has access to good nutrition. This is not just a prerequisite for ensuring children can develop properly, and for healthy populations—it is the minimum we should be striving for. Beyond national targets, Drawdown argues that there must be an international effort to provide adequate and healthy food for all, and to minimize food waste.

Another solution that Drawdown outlines as having great potential to reduce greenhouse gas emissions is the better management of chemical refrigerants. Those used in refrigerators and air conditioners produce a cooling effect by absorbing and releasing heat. The active agents, particularly chlorofluorocarbons (CFCs) and hydrofluorocarbons (HFCs), are extremely harmful to the climate, by a factor of 1,000 to 9,000 times more than CO_2. Thankfully, efforts to switch to alternative means of refrigeration, for example using propane or ammonia, have been boosted by the 2016 Kigali Accord, signed by all 197 United Nations countries. Thus, industrialized countries are scheduled to reduce HFC consumption by 85 percent by 2036, while developing and emerging economies are committed to reducing HFC consumption by 80 or 85 percent, respectively, for the period from 2024 to 2047. Nevertheless, as long as refrigerants with high global warming potential continue to be used around the world, the amount of HFCs will continue to rise and their appropriate end-of-life disposal will likewise be critical. According to Drawdown's estimates, the impact of the Kigali Accord has the potential to reduce global warming by nearly 1 °C.

As far as resilience-building measures for Houston are concerned, landscape architecture can offer relevant strategies. The Houston Parks and Recreation Department currently manages 370 parks and 200 other green spaces and promenades. Of the three urban parks featured below, Buffalo Bayou Park is the largest and most centrally situated, recently designed as a resilient park. The two other parks incorporate rain gardens as a strategy for stormwater retention and are both located in densely developed downtown areas southwest of the city center.

BUFFALO BAYOU PARK

Buffalo Bayou Park opened in 2015 as a 64-hectare linear park stretching for 3.7 kilometers west of Downtown Houston along the river of the same name. The importance of Buffalo Bayou and other bayou rivers for draining the city after heavy rains was recognized right from the beginning. As mentioned, Houston was founded some distance inland from the Gulf Coast to reduce its vulnerability to flooding. For the same reason, the area that is now the park was already declared parkland in the early 1900s. But for decades, the city authorities showed little interest in preserving the downtown lowland river system—of which Buffalo Bayou is the largest and most central artery—as a potential retention zone in the event of major flooding. On the contrary, stretches of Buffalo Bayou were even straightened in the 1950s and there were plans to channel it with concrete walls in order to dispel floodwaters more quickly. Although these plans, which are now held to be counterproductive, never came to pass, the flood-prone terrain around the bayou and the watercourse itself continued to be neglected. For a while, Buffalo Bayou was even reputedly the most polluted river in Texas. However, that did not stop predominantly affluent neighborhoods springing up along the river and its bank zones.

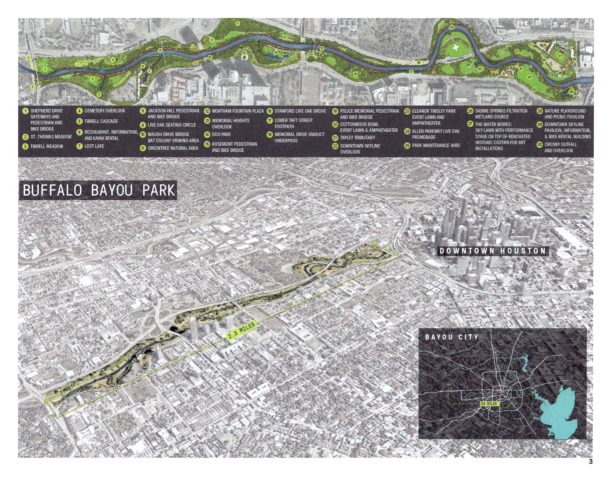

In 1986, a citizens' group formed to address the development of the area and to coordinate planning efforts. Still active 35 years on, the Buffalo Bayou Partnership (BBP) focuses on environmental justice, public participation in design and planning, and commemorating the history of the site through display boards, monuments, and artistic interventions and installations.

The initial plan for Buffalo Bayou Park from 2002 aimed to restore the river's ecosystem where necessary, increasing its water capacity and enhancing the public experience of the river, in turn upgrading adjacent neighborhoods in the process. While flood protection was the primary concern, BBP also wanted to create a riverfront promenade and a proper park as a public amenity. As a public-private partnership, BBP secured significant project funding, including a generous private donation, enabling it to both build the park and finance its continued maintenance. SWA Group, a landscape architecture firm with decades of experience in ecology restoration, stormwater management, and flood control, undertook the design.

Almost the entire park lies below the level of the streets and bridges that connect the surrounding urban districts. Four new pedestrian bridges were added to create different circuits of varying lengths, suitable for walking as well as biking. After the bridges improved access to the park from adjacent neighborhoods, some 44,000 households are now less than a ten-minute walk away, and half a

3
The length and central location of Buffalo Bayou Park means that it serves many different functions for the city.

BUFFALO BAYOU PARK

4
Photos of the park before the flood and one year later show that it was possible to restore most structures. Some gaps in the vegetation along the banks can still be seen and parts of the pathways have been secured.

5
Pedestrian bridges over the river connect adjacent neighborhoods.

million no more than 30 minutes away by bike. Furthermore, the park features a variety of recreational amenities including two visitor centers, a bike hire center, works of art, and gardens. The higher-lying areas also have spaces for sports and ball games, a boathouse, skatepark, and a large dog run.

The park's design prioritizes views of the water in both dry periods and flood situations—two extremes that occur in the park. Eventually, the previous streamlining of the river was reversed and meanders and flood benches were introduced instead to reduce the flow and force of floodwater runoff, causing it to deposit silt and debris. After high water events, these areas are then specifically cleaned.

6, 7
Photos of the park under normal conditions and when flooded makes the extent of the water masses that flow into the park very apparent.

8

9

10

104

8
One year after the flood, minor damage is still visible, but the park is functional again.

9
Flotsam indicates the height of the water level at the time.

10
The signature oaks, *Quercus virginiana*, in the upper portion of the park were not damaged by the flood.

HOUSTON

Sunken oxbows were restored as wetlands, and small tributaries lost to urbanization were restored as pumped-flow waterfalls, providing additional habitat and flood capacity. In addition, steep slopes were regraded, improving conveyance and in turn capacity while also opening up views into the valley. Working together with local conservation organizations, extensive native planting was introduced, including 14,000 native trees and a total of 5 hectares of prairie planting.

Structurally the park is designed to withstand both the force of water and the impact of any debris it may transport. All buildings, park furniture, and other elements have deep foundations to prevent them from being washed away and are made of particularly robust and resistant materials: for example, concrete slabs for the pavilions for shade, precast concrete light poles, deliberately oversized handrails, and concrete-filled galvanized steel bridge abutments that rise above the height of the 100-year flood line. The concrete piles of the new pedestrian bridges are sunk more than 20 meters into the ground and elements that may be exposed to water have rounded corners to help protect bridge piers, benches, and even trash cans from being eroded away during floods. Retaining walls slope downwards to allow silt to drain off, and buildings have ground floor zones that can withstand flooding without permanent damage. In the end, these stronger specifications increase costs by 15 to 20 percent compared with conventional constructions or prefabricated components.

After completion in 2015, the park quickly gained popularity. New paths along the bayou for pedestrians and cyclists run east towards downtown and west towards the popular hiking and bridle trails in Memorial Park. The park also links previously disparate neighborhoods on either side of Buffalo Bayou, creating a common ground for sometimes quite different social and cultural milieus. Beyond that, numerous events add to the attraction of the park. At the same time, however, real estate prices in the vicinity of the park have risen significantly.

The success of the design approach and construction methods became particularly evident after Hurricane Harvey in 2017. Although floodwaters rose by 13 meters at the park's western end, the upper third of the park was not submerged for long, and the trails in that area were usable again shortly after. However, the sheer volume of water that had to drain away down the bayou along with additional overflow from higher-lying reservoirs as well as the mud that washed through or settled in the valley caused considerable damage to vegetation and to the bat colonies in the lower two-thirds of the park. After the water had drained, the riverbanks were eroded, and some 4,000 truckloads of silt and plant debris had to be removed. As part of the restoration works, riprap was added to improve resistance to erosion and gabions filled with recycled concrete as well as coir were added to stabilize the slopes. Among the areas most affected by prolonged flooding were zones under bridges and opposite outfalls, and these have required additional stabilization. Plant debris hanging from the bridges a year later testified to the great height of the floodwaters, and stretches of eroded banks were still visible in some places. Overall, however, the park was fully functional and well-frequented one year after the disaster. Fortunately, financial reserves had been proactively set aside at the beginning of the process for such repair work.

The lessons learned from designing Buffalo Bayou Park will inform the planned reconfiguration of the river further eastwards. Even though the valley is not as narrow, it runs through an area previously used for heavy industry, so that contamination issues will first need to be resolved. BBP has already been purchasing land in preparation for creating new park areas and trails.

The long genesis of Buffalo Bayou Park shows once more just how important green-blue infrastructure can be for a city's viability and quality of life. As climate change accelerates, this becomes ever more urgent. For a long time Houston had neglected its green-blue infrastructure, and the pattern of green spaces and waterways that crisscrossed the city was predominantly defined by technocratic and economic interests that paid little heed to nature and natural conditions. Since the change in thinking brought on by mounting weather disasters, a resilient park with exemplary qualities has emerged in this wealthy Texas metropolis. In this sense, Buffalo Bayou Park demonstrates that when the available technical and design knowledge of landscape architecture is used wisely and skillfully, it can significantly mitigate the threats posed by climate change, even for a city as large as Houston. The park's success also shows that it can unlock entirely new potential for the urban landscape—and perhaps for urban society as well.

LEVY PARK

Just west of Downtown Houston in the Upper Kirby District, this 2-hectare park was originally created back in the 1940s but had been long neglected over the years, to the point where it was rarely used. In 2015, after an extensive planning process spanning several years, the landscape architects OJB Landscape Architecture embarked on the comprehensive redevelopment of the site, and the park eventually reopened in 2017. What is immediately apparent is the wide range of different amenities provided on a comparatively small site: a non-traditional play area for children, interactive water features, a pavilion with a large canopy for shade, various eateries, as well as paved plazas with different kinds of seating, plus lawns for activities, and a dog park.

A characteristic aspect of OJB's renewal concept, alongside the density and variety of activities on offer, is its climate-resilient design, which is configured to cope with both extreme heat and heavy rainfall. Especially notable are two key elements: the Rain Garden and the Community Garden, both of which collect and use rainwater. The Rain Garden on the south edge of the park alongside a broad pathway is planted with native shrubs and flowers. Signs and information panels explain its function to visitors so that all are aware of its important purpose, even if only in passing. The Community Garden, on the other hand, encompasses 27 planting beds separated by narrow paths that aside from growing crops helps people learn about gardening and reusing resources through composting.

Even the hard surfaces are made entirely of regionally available water-permeable materials and together amount to more than 1 hectare, almost half of the total area. Plant species were specifically selected for their resistance to drought and pest infestation. 138 native trees were also planted, which sequester CO_2 and can hold over 20,000 liters of water in their root space. Finally, eight large old oaks were carefully relocated to a new position in the park where they provide

11
Levy Park is open on all sides and, as a neighborhood park, provides a range of amenities for visitors of all ages.

108

12
The inclined areas of the park help direct water for drainage, irrigation, and collection so that it can be used for other purposes such as watering the beds in the community garden.

13
Water flowing towards the pavilion is channeled onwards to the rain garden where it is cleansed by the plants.

14
Levy Park is designed for all kinds of weather conditions. Stormwater collection and utilization is an integral part of the park's design.

15
The design of the entire park is geared towards capturing stormwater runoff.

16
The rain garden in the foreground and the community gardens to the right are both watered by collected rainwater, as is the rest of the vegetation.

HOUSTON

shade for the playground and along the formerly treeless east side of the park, while also reducing temperatures. In conclusion, the redevelopment of Levy Park not only improves quality of life for the surrounding neighborhoods but is also an important part of the city's climate adaptation plan, contributing to stormwater management and temperature reduction. Before its redesign, the park had around 75 visitors per week; after, between 5,000 and 10,000.

17
Cooling down in the play area in summer.

18
A bench in the shade of the large oak tree next to the rain garden provides a cool and pleasant place to while away time in summer.

19
The rain garden is planted with a lush variety of plants.

HOUSTON

MIDTOWN PARK

Midtown Park is of a similar size to Levy Park, but is an entirely new development in the Midtown district near Downtown Houston. Previously a vacant area in an otherwise densely built-up part of the city, the site has been transformed into a new park that likewise opened in 2017. The project, conceived by the office Design Workshop, also includes underground parking under a section of the park and an eight-story residential tower.

Like Levy Park, Midtown Park makes maximum use of the available space, providing a wide range of different activities for its visitors. There is a convertible pavilion with stage, a large lawn area, various artworks, a playground, and a dog run. Beyond that, several elements are designed specifically with climate adaptation in mind, including a rain garden and the adjacent interactive water feature as well as the "Wild Wonderland" mural by the artist Dixie Friend Gay at the south entrance to the park. This 6-meter-wide artwork presents a close-up view of Houston's flora and fauna in the form of a mosaic. All these elements of the park in a playful way raise awareness of the importance of water and bodies of water for the city's natural environment and the specific climatic challenges that Houston faces through storms and heavy rains. They communicate valuable knowledge on water management and wetlands, and about plants that occur naturally in the region.

At the western entrance area, visitors are immediately drawn towards a small-scale artificial bayou. Here, a waterfall muffles the sound of traffic while contributing to a cooler microclimate. Modeled on natural bayous, the rain garden serves as a water retention basin and plays an important role in the sustainable concept of the park's climate-responsive design. Stormwater runoff collects in the rain garden and is filtered by the plants and soil, cleansing it of contaminants before it flows into the sewer system and from there via drainage basins into the Gulf of Mexico. A further feature of this section of the park is an artificial water-circulating wetland environment covered with shrubs and hardwood trees—both native to the local landscape. Information panels explain these relationships to interested visitors.

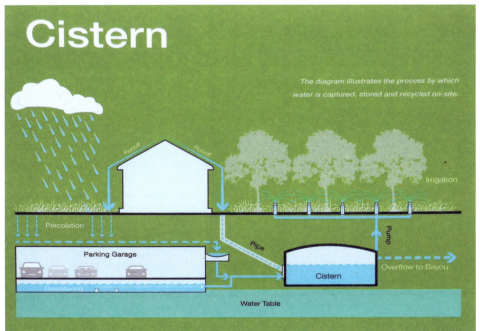

20
An information panel explains the principle of rainwater collection, purification, and reutilization.

112

21
A large lawn in the middle of the park can be used for all kinds of activities. The grass sprinkler is fed by collected rainwater.

22
Water can also spray from jets in the paving that visitors can turn on when they want to cool down.

HOUSTON

23
Large oak trees line the edge of Midtown Park and provide a canopy for the weekend market.

24
The children's play area and rain garden are cleverly interconnected.

25
The volume of water is sufficient to muffle the sound of street traffic.

26
A waterscape at the edge of the park recreates in miniature the natural environment of the bayous and of the city of Houston.

27
Evaporating moisture from the lush, natural vegetation cools its surroundings in warm weather.

MIDTOWN PARK

The natural marshes of south Texas are shallow, permanently flooded freshwater wetlands with a high proportion of shrub cover and herbaceous plants with few trees. In addition to providing habitat for numerous bird species, they also provide other ecosystem services such as erosion control and water quality improvement. The predominant plant species in this environment are red maple (*Acer rubrum*), palm, and sedge (*Carex*). All these can also be found in Midtown Park.

Hardwood forests occur in the riparian floodplains alongside river systems. These ecologically rich alluvial wetlands have alternating periods of drought and flooding after large rain events. Accordingly, the artificial bayou in the park creates similar conditions for the hardwoods planted there. The planting therefore includes species such as oak, bald cypress (*Taxodium distichum*), sycamore (*Platanus occidentalis*), and palm. A garden path explains the native plants and is flanked by a small stream with interactive water jets that children can trigger.

While the water fountains directly in front of the pavilion stage can mimic a cloudburst, they also serve as an interactive water feature: for one thing, they cool the air, and they also invite visitors to play with the water. A thin sheet of water passes over the granite paving, allowing people to cool their feet.

Along Main Street, which borders the park running from southwest to northeast, are shaded areas under imposing oaks of the *Quercus virginiana* species, native to the region. On weekends, this area is home to a weekly market.

Hidden from view is a large cistern that collects rainwater runoff from the roofs and paved areas for using to water plants and lawns. Indeed, the only indication of its existence to visitors is a display panel explaining its function: once the cistern is full, any excess water is directed to the rain garden.

Such green-blue infrastructure like the artificial bayou in Houston's Midtown Park not only helps regulate rainfall and relieve the burden on "gray" stormwater management, but also creates habitats for birds, butterflies, and many other animals. The illustrated display panels, which are designed to be understood by adults and children alike, explain not just the human-made system in the park but also examples in the broader natural environment.

The success of Houston's new climate-resilient parks and green spaces has since inspired other initiatives, such as the *Bayou Greenways 2020* plan, which is a proposal by the ten-year-old Bayou Greenways Initiative. On the one hand, the project envisions transforming bayou waterways on a regional scale into protected greenways and waterfronts that are primarily recreational, while also helping to better withstand future floods and droughts in the greater Houston area. It additionally proposes a network of parks that together encompass more than 1,000 hectares and extend along 240 kilometers of river. Also included are a further 120 kilometers of walking and biking trails. The plan's total investment is estimated at $220 million. Since a large part of the sum has already been pledged by a foundation and a further portion was raised through the sale of park bonds, it clearly indicates the project's popular support. If *Bayou Greenways 2020* is put into practice, 60 percent of Houston's residents will have a park within 2 kilometers of their homes—which is certainly a significant step towards a climate-resilient, green city.

BO
GOTÁ

"Bogotá, 2,600 metros más cerca de las estrellas"—"2,600 meters closer to the stars"—is the motto of Bogotá, the capital and the largest city of Colombia. The slogan refers to its location on a plateau of the Andes at the foot of two mountains of the Cordilleras, which are between 2,640 and 4,000 meters high. With its 7.8 million inhabitants Bogotá is the largest city in the world at this altitude, and the metropolitan region is home to 10.7 million people. As a result of poverty and armed conflict, migration to the city from rural areas has been ongoing for decades, making Bogotá one of the fastest-growing cities in South America. The city's expansion is, however, limited by the mountains to the east and the Bogotá River to the west, and it has therefore extended in a north-south direction.

Although Bogotá lies in a tropical climatic zone close to the equator, the altitude of the city means that temperatures are moderate, even cool, and remain relatively constant throughout the year. With a mean annual temperature of about 14 °C, neither heating nor cooling is needed, or indeed common in many households. Solar radiation is very high in the city due to its proximity to the equator and its altitude. In contrast to the uniform year-round temperatures, the total annual 1,100 millimeters of precipitation are spread unevenly over the year: rainfall is highest in April at 150 millimeters, and lowest in August at 30 millimeters. This is because Colombia has only two seasons, summer and winter, or dry (*sequía*) and rainy seasons (*temporada de lluvias*).

In some years, the pattern of the seasons has begun to vary due to the influence of the El Niño and La Niña weather phenomena. Both represent anomalies in the circulation of the trade winds and water currents. Normally, in the neutral months of the year, the surface waters of the Pacific Ocean flow in a westerly direction towards Australia, Indonesia, and other areas of Southeast Asia, making the climate there rainy and humid. Consequently, the climate in the coastal regions of South America is dry, and the fish-rich deep waters of the Humboldt Current upwell towards the surface. El Niño, however, reverses this pattern: the clouds that normally bring rain to the east coasts of Asia and Australia are driven in the opposite direction and rain down on the normally dry west coast of the Americas.

El Niño originally only occurred on the west coast of South America and was thus named after the Spanish word for the Baby Jesus by Peruvian fishermen, as it frequently begins at Christmas after the tropical trade winds from the East die down. According to recent studies it may have quite a global impact, and its unpredictability and the large volume of water it brings make it a force to be reckoned with. Currently it recurs approximately every three to four years.

El Niño is a "warm" phase that deposits considerable rain on the American west coasts and is often followed by La Niña, a corresponding "cold" phase. During this phase, the upper layers of water in the tropical eastern Pacific cool abnormally and the weather pattern reverses: tropical trade winds increase to the east and low pressure intensifies over the Indonesian archipelago. Once again the Humboldt Current brings fish-rich water to the surface along the coast of South America, and the heavy rains and resulting flooding come to an end. In the past, this alternating pattern had a compensating climatic effect but more recently La Niña has been too short and too weak to ensure a balanced climate. The causes for these changes are still unclear, as are the implications for the global impact of El Niño.

1 (previous page)
View of the vast expanse of Bogotá spread across the plateau.

The relationship between the anomaly in the distribution of water temperatures in the tropical Pacific Ocean and the pattern of atmospheric pressure from the west coasts of the Americas to the east coasts of Australia and Asia is known as ENSO: the El Niño Southern Oscillation.

El Niño has the potential to cause extreme flooding due to saturation of the soil, in turn causing landslides and the flooding of cities and countryside, especially in the western countries or regions of South, Central, and North America. As a consequence, the countries on the other side of the Pacific then suffer from drought to the extent that some cities experience water shortages. This affects not only Australia and Southeast Asia but sometimes also southeast Africa. Both extremes—excessive rainfall and drought—bring an increased risk of disease for humans as well as the animal and plant world. For example, seabirds and seals that rely on the fish-rich cool waters of the Humboldt Current are dying in large numbers due to lack of food. Once it has set in, the climate anomaly usually lasts for a year and cannot be reversed.

Despite its inland location on a plateau in the Andes, Bogotá also feels the effects of the El Niño and La Niña phenomena. In recent years, normal seasonal rainfall has increased, and El Niño has exacerbated this trend, causing the city to adjust existing and implement new plans over the past two decades. In 2000, the *Plan de Ordenamiento Territorial* was approved, which identified ecologically relevant areas of the urban region. Dividing the area into urban, rural, and suburban expansion areas, it designates particular sites to be kept free of development for disaster prevention and defines areas with important ecosystems that should be preserved or restored. The plan also identifies land use for parks and public green spaces to provide adequate recreational opportunities for the population. All future urban development should observe sustainable principles, and the city has set out a series of ecological criteria in the *Estructura Ecológica Principal*, a supplementary document that details the primary elements of the city's ecological structure. These include parks and nature reserves.

Bogotá has numerous parks of varying sizes, the largest of which, the Parque Metropolitano Simón Bolívar, is one of the largest urban parks in the world, covering an area of 400 hectares. Besides this, there are several other large parks as well as a many smaller neighborhood parks. The *Estructura Ecológica* describes parks as being valuable for protecting the natural environment as well as for our interactions with it.

One of the most important nature reserves in the wider Bogotá area is the Parque Nacional Natural Sumapaz, established in 1977. Being the largest contiguous conservation area in South America, it consists predominantly of the typical treeless steppe vegetation of the Andean highlands, the *páramo*. The park lies above the tree line and has a humid climate. Temperatures range from 8 °C during the day to -3 °C at night with minimal seasonal variations. However, rapid weather changes occur, with 1,000 to 2,000 millimeters of annual precipitation, 75 percent relative humidity and frequent fog. Covered by a thick layer of black humus, the park creates conditions in which plants grow slowly but steadily and can grow to be very old. It has a rich variety of flora, which are optimally adapted to the conditions, as are the fauna: for example, the park provides a protected habitat for the rare Colombian mountain tapir.

The ecosystem of the *páramo* is able to store water for long periods of time and can feed springs even in times of drought. It is therefore vitally important for the water supply in the surrounding region. Due to a wider appreciation of the *páramo*'s unique characteristics, these landscapes are increasingly being designated as conservation areas that need protection from agriculture expansion, livestock farming, as well as raw materials extraction, all of which have been leading to ever-growing conflicts.

Since 2013, the protection of ecologically valuable areas has been extended to also encompass measures to cope with climate change. Included are better protection of areas of special importance for water management and biodiversity against other interests, as well as better recognition of the socioeconomic relevance of natural resources and environmental networks for the population. These revisions and additions to the *Estructura Ecológica* form the basis of a strategy for adapting to climate change.

Another important legal foundation is the Land Use Plan of 2020, which defines Bogotá as a compact, densely built-up city that in turn provides the basis for approving the declaration and protection of ecologically important compensation areas. However, Bogotá is already so densely built-up that each resident has only 4 square meters of public space.

EFFECTS OF CLIMATE CHANGE

By now, Bogotá has been exposed to climatic risks in the form of flooding and landslides for more than 100 years, and the frequency of such incidences is increasing. In the 30 years between 1985 and 2015, 165 floods and 158 landslides were recorded, making up 34 and 32 percent of all climate-related events reported in the city, respectively. Studies conducted by the Institute of Hydrology, Meteorology and Environmental Research (IDEAM) in Bogotá indicate that rainfall intensities correlate with the pattern of the La Niña and El Niño phenomena. With increasing precipitation comes an increased risk and frequency of landslides, putting especially illegal settlements on the slopes of the urban fringe at risk. As precipitation levels change, there is a real possibility that there will be a transition from a semi-humid to a semi-arid climate by the mid-21st century and to a more arid climate by the end of the century.

Changing temperatures offer further evidence of an expected climatic shift, and here too IDEAM sees a link to La Niña and El Niño. Mean temperatures, as measured by normal values for the 1971–2000 period, are forecast to continue to rise for the remainder of the 21st century, increasing gradually from 1 °C in the first decades to 4 °C in the final decades of the century. Estimated mean values for the period 2011–2070 vary from 10 °C at higher altitudes to 16 °C at lower altitudes, and for the period 2071–2100 from 12 °C to 18 °C. With the rise in temperature, the concern is that new diseases and the pathogens that transmit them could take hold. Other consequences could include food supply shortages for the population and greater pressure on the important ecosystems in the surrounding area that supply the city with water. Because levels of air pollution are already high and problematic, there is concern that this could lead to a further increase in respiratory diseases.

Since 2016, adaptation to climate change has focused on the preservation, restoration, and sustainable management of ecosystems, on reducing the ecological footprint, and in particular on safeguarding areas that serve as a water supply. For each of these, targets have been set for 2030. To mitigate the urban heat island effect, the level of urban vegetation must be increased, new urban developments must minimize surface runoff, and greenhouse gas emissions must be reduced by effecting a change in urban mobility and transportation.

The Disaster Risk Management and Climate Change Plan, *Plan Distrital de Gestión del Riesgo de Desastres y del Cambio Climático para Bogotá D.C., 2018–2030*, was drawn up to prepare the *Distrito Capital* (Capital District) for the impacts and risks of climate change and to develop corresponding resilient structures by 2030. To that effect, the main climate change goals include promoting low-carbon urban development, protecting ecosystems and water resources, and ensuring the well-being of rural communities and cities.

The priorities outlined in the plan are both comprehensive and general. They range from improving early warning systems for changes in climate and air quality parameters, to ensuring food security, protecting biodiversity, and improving public health. Ultimately, the most important goal is to reduce CO_2 emissions, which will be achieved primarily through more sustainable mobility and sustainable construction methods, as well as the creation of more green spaces in the city. By 2050, the *Distrito Capital de Bogotá* aims to plant 22,000 trees and increase the use of rainwater, and to protect a further 322 hectares of strategic ecosystems by 2030. Two thousand families living in the areas most vulnerable to climate change will also be resettled by 2030. Another plan is to implement 20 urban projects that mitigate the risks of climate change.

The plan emphasizes the importance of acting at a regional level: yet, to be effective, experience has shown that local municipalities must help in reducing the degree of risk at a local level and in finding opportunities for change that are replicable. In that regard, the recommendations for action in the *Plan Distrital* remain rather vague.

PARQUE 93 AND THE DEMOS P 93 MASTER PLAN

Parque 93 is a new city park in Bogotá and was designed by the office Grupo Verde with Martha Fajardo, Noboru Kawashima, and Ying-Fang Chen. The product of a ten-year design process, including a public participation phase from 2012 to 2014, the park is a 1.5-hectare oasis within a densely built-up area. Previously an undesigned open space, the site has been managed and maintained since 1994 by a local community-run organization, the *Asociación Amigos del Parque 93*.

The park has a large playground, a central open green area for games and exercising, and numerous mature trees that provide shade and give the park structure. With a wide range of different and variable seating, as well as a small library, a stage, and ample lawns, the park is well-frequented, and not just on weekends. Parque 93 is obviously well-kept and maintained, and functionally, ecologically, and aesthetically fulfills its purpose admirably.

Following the success of the park, Grupo Verde was commissioned to develop a master plan for the surroundings of the park in 2018. Entitled DEMOS P 93 (*Distrito Especial de Mejoramiento y Organización Sectorial*), its guiding principle is "The Healthy and Walkable City." In that sense, it identifies and documents opportunities for improving the green infrastructure and quality of public spaces to better serve the needs of the residents. Altogether, the master plan covers a 42-hectare area, with Parque 93 roughly in the middle, and proposes a mix of reuse, new development, and restoration. The upgrading of the public space is achieved through various small- and medium-scale changes as well as through experimental and low-lost natural interventions that can be undertaken on a step-by-step principle and rely on community involvement. What's more, temporary spaces will be created that afford local residents a more direct experience of nature through the use of urban greenery. The first phase is due to be

2
Design for Parque 93 by the office Grupo Verde.

3–7
The park provides multiple and variable places to sit and enjoy the park. Chairs can be moved into the sun or the shade. The large lawn is ideal for larger events such as yoga classes or civic meetings. A small lending library opens regularly for reading in the park. Due to its lighting design, the park is especially atmospheric at night.

PARQUE 93 AND THE DEMOS P 93 MASTER PLAN

put into practice in 2021 and will be implemented by the *Asociación Amigos del Parque 93*, local residents, and the district administration.

Judging by the visualizations and plans, DEMOS P 93 uses the park as the starting point for extending the green infrastructure into the urban surroundings. While the design emphasizes the social aspect of the urban spaces, many of the planned measures such as tree planting, providing shade in street spaces, along with light-colored surfacing, help mitigate the negative impacts of climate change. The urban design project is therefore a model for exemplary climate-resilient design in cities.

8, 9
Phase 1 of the DEMOS planning area around Parque 93 extends the park along the streets and improves the green infrastructure and street space. The detail shows the design of the street along the north edge of Parque 93 with new amenity areas and vegetation.

BOGOTÁ

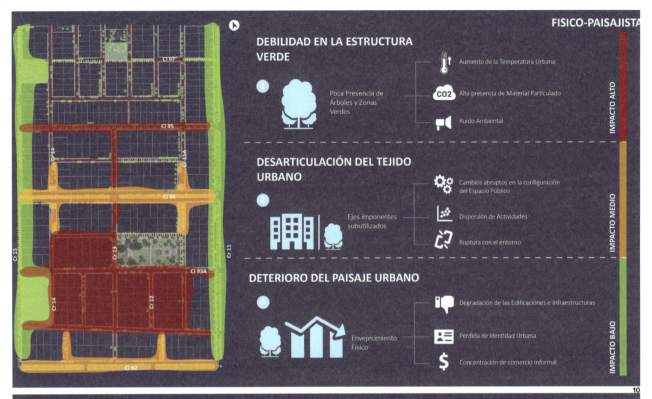

10
An analysis of the green infrastructure showing the problem areas. Red are high impact issues, such as too few trees and a lack of green spaces in a district. Orange are medium impact aspects such as barriers in urban permeability and fragmentation of the urban realm. Green are low-impact aspects such as deficiencies in the design of the streetscape.

11
An analysis of the socio-cultural situation reveals that changes of use from residential to commercial is one of the most serious problems (red), congestion is a further important problem area (orange) and inadequate public outdoor spaces (green) a lesser but also important aspect.

PARQUE 93 AND THE DEMOS P 93 MASTER PLAN

HUMEDAL SANTA BARBARA

In Bogotá, private corporations must allocate 15 percent of the land they build on for public use. Thus, in 2014, the owners of the Santa Barbara business center in the Usaquén district launched an open architecture competition in Colombia to redesign the public space and elevator access area at the base of six 25-year-old office towers. The competition for the 8,500 square meter site was won by the architecture office Obraestudio run by Juan Melo. A central aspect of their concept is the inclusion of typical local vegetation in the design of the plaza. As part of the competition entry, Obraestudio undertook climatic studies, considered the prevailing wind direction, and identified the climate for the planning area as corresponding to a wet savannah—from which it derives its name: *humedal* or wetland. This landscape, which can be found naturally in the areas around Bogotá, informed the design of the project, its vegetation, partially rugged appearance, colors, and overall ecosystem.

12
Wooden decking as a sustainable and CO_2-binding raw material.

13
Aerial view of the outdoor plaza area of the Santa Barbara business center with main plaza area at the back and various water features and plantings at the front.

14
The plaza with lush vegetation beds and an explanatory information panel.

15
View of the plaza areas between the office buildings.

HUMEDAL SANTA BARBARA

The publicly accessible area of the site is articulated as a transition between wet and dry surfaces that mediate between the elements of water and land. Distributed across the plaza are numerous elongated narrow water basins filled with plants and fed by collected rainwater. Both design and ecological considerations are well reflected in the choice of plants, which were sourced directly from natural locations in the wetlands around Bogotá—none were cultivated in garden centers or tree nurseries. Display panels provide details about the plants and their habitat for interested users of the plaza. The numerous pathways across the plaza and along the water features, along with the interspersed arrangement of benches (that conceal vents for the underground car park) and the interesting compositions of plants create a public space that is versatile and can be used and experienced in many different ways.

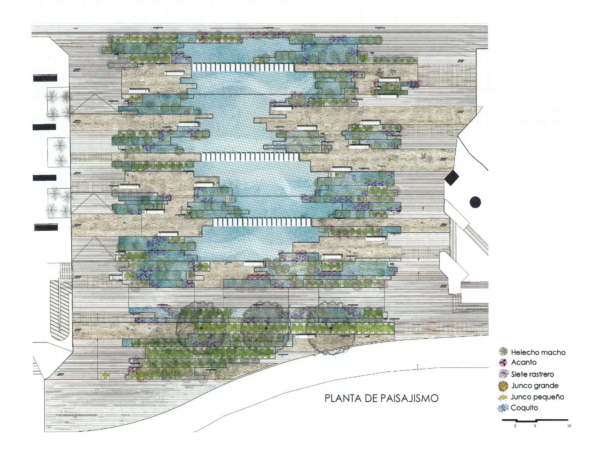

16
Plants around the water basins.

CORTE ARQUITECTÓNICO

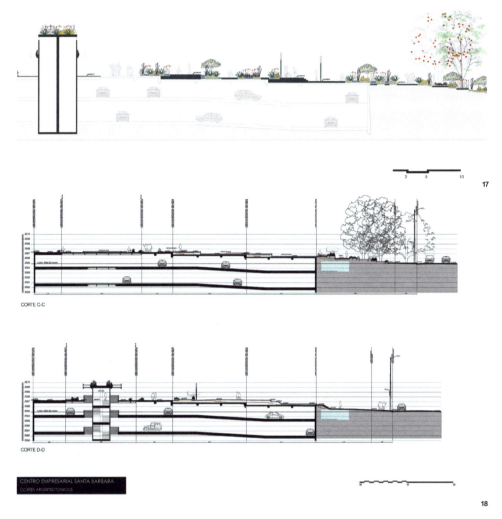

The COR-TEN steel-clad entrance to the buildings features a sculpture garden that lends this central area a sense of tranquility. All street furniture—benches, planters, and light fittings—were designed specifically for the project.

The plaza helps mitigate climate change by harvesting, desanding, and recirculating rainwater, on average some 110 cubic meters per day. That way, water evaporation through plant transpiration as well as the open water areas helps cool the public space. While rainwater is collected in a tank adjoining the underground car park, it travels from there through the pools and wetland beds. Located at the boundary of the site where it meets the street, the tank has several overflow points, should the volume of rainwater exceed the tank capacity and needs of the "wetland" on the plaza. An irrigation system ensures the native plant species in their wetland beds are kept moist. The underground car park is naturally ventilated, and the plaza is paved with natural stone and wooden decking.

17
Section through the plaza, with the height of the vegetation to indicate the scale.

18
Sections through the plaza showing several levels of underground parking, and the water tank that feeds and regulates supply to the water basins.

GREEN ROOFS AND FACADES

A conversation with Andrés Ibáñez Gutiérrez from the renowned Pontifical Xaveriana University in Bogotá provided interesting insights into new developments with respect to greening buildings and cities. One of the pioneers in this field, he uses the projects he manages in the city to give students the chance to learn about the impact of climate change, so that they can account for it in their own future design work. The main consequences of climate change that affect Bogotá are flooding due to insufficient drainage and sewer capacity to handle surface runoff, a marked urban heat island effect, especially in the historic downtown areas, and the long-standing problem of high levels of air pollution. While appropriately designed green roofs help retain rainwater, green facades have the potential to lower temperatures in the city and filter pollutants from the air. Although green roofs are not mandatory in Bogotá, there are now over 200,000 such roofs in the city, including greened roofings of underpasses. Most extensively greened roofs employ sedum species that are tolerant to the climatic conditions in Bogotá but are not native. Ibáñez sees potential for further research into suitable plant species, and especially native species, for planting on green roofs. While roofs cannot be seen from the street, green facades are all the more eye-catching. In Bogotá, these often take the form of complex structures attached to facades with integral irrigation systems and diverse plant species. They are, however, more complex to maintain.

19
Green roof on one of the buildings of the Xaveriana University campus.

20
Parque Bicentenario: Greening of the road tunnel with outdoor spaces at different levels.

21
A bench as a border for beds of perennials. The planted areas are fed by irrigation lines.

22
A green wall flanks the entrance to the road tunnel.

23
A series of gutters used as irrigated planting troughs for greening a wall.

24
Different kinds of plants green the facade of the Hotel B3.

GREEN ROOFS AND FACADES

LA CICLOVÍA

La Ciclovía—the temporary closure of city streets to allow only bicycle traffic—was "invented" in Bogotá in 1974. Initially, the civic organization *Pro-cicla* and the city's department for traffic and public transportation closed just two streets for use by cyclists only for a period of three hours. Then, 5,000 cyclists took part to take a stand against vehicle pollution and the lack of recreational facilities in the city. In 1976, the mayor eventually decided to declare strategically located streets for bicycle users and pedestrians only on Sundays and particular public holidays for a set period of the day. Since then, La Cicliovía has become a regular fixture.

Some two decades later, in 1995, La Ciclovía was expanded to encompass the idea of creating "the largest temporary park in the world." The idea was to improve quality of life for the city's inhabitants through cleaner air, less noise, more opportunities for physical activity and public health, as well as better equality and social integration. The city now has a dedicated department for regularly implementing the event, and numerous volunteers and police officers guarantee the smooth running of it. Also, publicity campaigns encourage residents to participate, whether by bike, on foot, or on roller blades. Over the years, more roads have been added, the time frame per day was extended, and the initiative now also takes place on all public holidays. Today, 121 kilometers of the streets in Bogotá are reserved for non-motorized traffic on Sundays and holidays from 7 a.m. until 2 p.m. The budget has increased more than tenfold since the initiative began, and some 1.5 million people regularly take part.

25
Public streets taken over by cyclists, skaters, and pedestrians during the Sunday Ciclovía.

The Ciclovía is no longer just about cycling: other sports, such as aerobics and dance, as well as accompanying activities also take place, and stalls sell food and other goods along neighboring streets. There are now multiple good reasons to spend time outside on and in the street without having to endure traffic noise and exhaust fumes.

While the social aspect is the primary motivation for most people, the initiative has helped the population see the benefit of roads without emissions. Bogotá's Ciclovía quickly became widely known and many other cities in Colombia and throughout South America have emulated the idea, allowing further urban populations to rejoice in the new-found freedoms of urban space. La Ciclovía automatically promotes public awareness of and engagement with the topics of nature and environmental protection. As such, it makes a positive contribution to the city's endeavors towards improving climate resiliency.

TOMINÉ REGIONAL PARK

In 1960, Bogotá's energy utility company elected to dam the valley of the Río Tominé to create a reservoir to supply water and electricity for the city. The village of Guatavita in the valley had to be sacrificed and was rebuilt from 1964 onwards on the banks of the new reservoir, the *Embalse de Tominé*. As it happens, Guatavita was of special significance to the region as the religious capital of the Muiscas, one of the most important Indigenous groups in Colombia. Their most sacred site is the Laguna de Guatavita, a small mountain lake located a few kilometers east of the much larger reservoir. The goldsmithing skills of the Muiscas are legendary, as well as the ritual of covering new kings with gold dust at their inauguration, and their subsequent cleansing in the waters of the lagoon. For this reason, the Muiscas have long been associated with the tales of El Dorado. After the construction of the dam and the flooding of the river valley, the landscape so closely linked with the culture and identity of the Indigenous tribe for millennia was lost. However, the new *Parque Regional de Tominé* picks up this historical thread and continues the history of the Muiscas and their close relationship to and respect for the landscape in its design.

The 4,900-hectare Tominé reservoir is located about 50 kilometers north of Bogotá and is now one of the most important water reservoirs in the entire region, playing a vital role in ensuring the quality of the city's drinking water. Not only does the lake supply fresh water to the capital, it also provides agricultural irrigation and is a source for energy production. In addition, it improves the water quality of its main tributary, the Río Tominé, by natural filtering, and acts as a buffer diverting excess water from the Río Bogotá—an important factor in flood control during the winter months.

However, the dam's construction caused significant environmental damage, altering the course of the river and affecting natural vegetation, which has been replaced by pine, acacia, and eucalyptus planting. What is more, this major transformation has severely impacted the native communities as well as the relationships between them, while the social ramifications have been significant.

Meanwhile, the project for the new *Parque Regional de Tominé* attempts to repair some of this environmental and social damage. Its goals include restoring characteristics of the landscape, improving the ecosystem and biodiversity, and increasing social and cultural support for the Indigenous people of the area. Set out in the Bogotá Development Plan 2016–2020, the project is an integral part of a longer-term vision for an "environmental cycle" between the city of Bogotá and surrounding regional parks. This envisages a network of interconnected public spaces that link up strategically important urban and rural ecosystems and thus expand the availability of open areas for recreation and long-term environmental education. In terms of environmental policy, the protection of the mountains to the east, the San Rafael reservoir, and the restoration of the Río Bogotá mark the first steps towards a sustainable development strategy. Special events for families, for environmental education and health, along with activities for seniors and for "good" natural, cultural, and sports-oriented tourism will appeal to a broad range of visitors.

To mitigate the effect of the projected rising temperatures and water shortages, additional rainwater retention reservoirs are being created for uses that do not require drinking-quality water, such as agricultural irrigation. Other major climate change-related goals include restoring forests and woodland, reducing erosion, restoring wetland areas, and reforesting with native vegetation. Over the next ten years, the park will become the largest regional park in Latin America to be developed sustainably. It will subsequently improve access to nature for

26
Laguna de Guatavita, a sacred site of the Indigenous Muisca people.

27
The new town of Guatavita on the banks of the Tominé reservoir and its surroundings. The original site of the town lies submerged beneath the reservoir.

28
The landscape around the Tominé reservoir.

TOMINÉ REGIONAL PARK

the residents of Bogotá and the neighboring communities—a major step forward given the comparative lack of public inner-city spaces relative to the population.

Compared with the affluent or rich cities in the northern hemisphere, the climate resiliency initiatives in Bogotá and other South American cities accord greater importance to the needs of society, and especially their poorer residents. Bogotá is undertaking projects at a large scale, and many of a socially progressive nature. They range from the restoration of a characteristic landscape to the climatic improvement of a neighborhood using its park as the point of origin for greening the district. Last but not least, smaller-scale interventions include greening buildings or creating parks on the cover of road underpasses. Even if only temporarily—as with the Ciclovía—the municipal government has invested considerable effort in increasing the number of green and open spaces available to citizens. The goal is to promote a climate-friendly urban way of life that is accessible to the residents and also replicable, thereby engaging the citizens in climate protection in a constructive way. This may motivate people to contribute personally, for example by switching from cars to bicycles for personal travel.

MEDELLÍN

Medellín's warm and sunny climate at an altitude of 1,500 meters above sea level has earned it the nickname "La ciudad de la eterna primavera"—The City of Eternal Spring. Colombia's second-largest city is the capital of the Antioquia region and has a population of 2.5 million, while the wider metropolitan region, which encompasses ten other municipalities in the Aburrá Valley to the northeast and south of Medellín has a population of nearly 4 million. It covers a total area of 1,152 square kilometers, a third of which is urban and two-thirds rural. The valley in which Medellín sits and through which the Río Medellín flows has a profile the shape of a cup with a wide base and steep sides. The planned, densely built urban areas lie predominantly in the flat base, which is about 10 kilometers long, while many informal settlements have sprung up on the edges as a result of migration from rural areas, a process that began in the 1960s. The main highway and railroad lines run north-south alongside the Río Medellín. The surrounding mountain ranges result in the development of different microclimates, and there are waterfalls and forests of high ecological value nearby. The Arví Regional Park, a 1,761-hectare area to the northeast of the city, can be reached quickly thanks to a cable car. It is not only a popular recreational destination but also the site of diverse educational programs for promoting environmental awareness.

Colombia's history has for decades been marred by armed conflict and even civil war, rooted in the extreme inequality of wealth and political power in the country. Peasant guerilla groups formed in the 1960s to fight the unjust distribution of land ownership and the military's support for the large landowners. Many farm workers are either Indigenous people or from the Afro-Colombian population. In the 1970s, several of the paramilitary groups entered the drug trade, most notably Pablo Escobar, who headed the Medellín Cartel until his death in 1993. During the heyday of Escobar's cartel in the 1970s and '80s, Medellín was one of the most dangerous cities in the world with an extremely high murder rate.

After a lengthy peace process that helped improve the political situation significantly, a peace treaty was signed in 2016 by the government and the FARC rebels (*Fuerzas Armadas Revolucionarias de Colombia*), by far the largest guerrilla group. The imbalances in land ownership, however, persist to this day, and drug trafficking has not ceased completely, operations shifting in some cases to neighboring countries such as Peru. The younger generation in Medellín is particularly conscious of the country's recent history. Some of them grew up abroad, their families only returning to their homeland after the situation had calmed. As far as drug trafficking and production are concerned, many are of the opinion that it will continue for as long as there are buyers around the world. Cause for hope, however, can be seen in the remarkable energy with which the new generation are standing up for their country and its transformation, and their commitment to guiding the country along the peaceful path that has begun.

Colombia is currently still the largest producer of cocaine in the world and the main supplier of heroin to the United States. As most of the drugs produced in Latin America are sold in the USA, the U.S. government has been pushing for decades for the destruction of drug plantations to limit supply. The U.S. Plan Colombia (2000–2015) employed military means along with the aerial spraying of plant poisons that not only destroyed coca crops, but often polluted entire swaths of land, poisoning them for the people living there, their crops and

1 (previous page)
The city of Medellín in the Aburrá Valley.

animals, as well as the rainforest. The long-term consequences for agriculture and the environment have been considerable.

According to the UN Refugee Agency, the civil war in Colombia, which has flared up repeatedly over the past 50 years, has caused the displacement of more than 8 million internal refugees, more than in any other country in the world. To add to that, Colombia also ranks second among those countries taking in refugees from abroad—currently about 1.8 million. The majority stem from neighboring Venezuela, where in recent years millions have fled the difficult political and economic conditions there. As more and more refugees flock to the cities, their populations swell still further. Medellín is one such example.

Developments that can alleviate the sometimes massive social upheavals that the city is exposed to therefore play a central role for the city's evolution as a whole and must always be considered when designing for climate change. Since the 1980s, the city has undertaken diverse and remarkable urban developments, and although the situation is significantly improved, the process is far from complete and the situation not yet stable.

In Medellín, these processes of adaptation involve not just political decision-makers but very often also the municipal utility company, the Empresas Públicas de Medellín (EPM). The EPM supplies the city and surrounding municipalities with water, gas, electricity, and telecommunications, and is also responsible for the city's sewer system and waste disposal. The EPM Group comprises 44 subsidiary companies with joint holdings in which EPM holds a majority stake. For EPM, sustainability and public participation are two important aspects, and the company's commitment to sustainable urban development and public green spaces is remarkable, often going beyond the company's actual remit.

The climate in Medellín is subtropical and, with a mean annual temperature of 15.8 °C, milder than in Bogotá. Temperature differences across the year are minimal: in the warmest month of August, the average temperature is 16.0 °C, and in the coolest month of November, 15.5 °C. With annual precipitation totaling almost 3,000 millimeters, the city receives significantly more rain than Bogotá. It rains every month of the year with average rainfall lowest in January, at 150 millimeters, and highest in April, at 350 millimeters. These conditions are favorable for vegetation, especially for many flowering plants, and Medellín is therefore also known as "the city of flowers."

EFFECTS OF CLIMATE CHANGE

The main challenges that climate change will bring are, firstly, that daytime temperatures will rise, and with it also the perceived temperature. The consequences range from reduced productivity to an increase in the decomposition of organic material. Second, dry periods will become more prevalent, causing groundwater levels to sink, which affects numerous ecosystems and in turn impacts agricultural production. Thirdly, an increase in the incidence of heavy rainfall events is predicted, increasing the risk and occurrence of landslides, which are of particular danger to those settlements on the steep valley slopes.

In the Climate Change Plan for the Aburrá Valley for the period from 2019 to 2030, the city and region outline the primary goals of reducing greenhouse gas emissions by 35 percent and adapting to climate change. Further strategies are outlined for education and science, urban planning, and business and politics. On a general level, the plan promotes improvements to energy efficiency and the prioritization of public transport. Nature conservation and land use considerations are to play a greater role. An information and early warning system will also be developed to anticipate potential disasters, for example for the settlements on the steep slopes where hydrometeorological conditions caused by El Niño can affect soil stability. Further goals include ensuring adequate food supplies and basic sanitation, and promoting public health and protection of the environment.

NEW TRANSPORT INFRASTRUCTURE

Alongside an environmentally conscious and sustainable urban development aimed at creating a better quality of life for the city's residents, a further important element is the development of a modern public transportation system. In Medellín this includes an elevated tramway that crosses the entire city from north to south, as well as tramways that connect the districts to the east and west of the city with the center. From the end points of these tramways, a system of cable cars, the metrocables, provides the last link for the residents of the informal settlements on the steep slopes. This combination of rapid transit systems connects the outlying districts to the city center, drastically shortening the journey to the residents' workplaces in the city. What once took two hours on foot and by minibus takes seven minutes by cable car. The combination of different

2
The new elevated tramway that crosses the city from north to south.

3
The new monorail connects the districts between the elevated tramway and cable cars.

4
A tramline along a busy street without a separate track bed.

5
The metrocable to the higher-lying districts offers panoramic views of the city.

6
The new, orange-colored escalators, barely visible between the dense agglomeration of houses in the Comuna 13 district, rising up a steep slope.

7
The striking design of the escalators.

8
The escalators are popular and well-maintained.

9, 10
The bike lane is on the street but separated from car traffic and the sidewalk.

NEW TRANSPORT INFRASTRUCTURE

modes of public transportation is part of a wider strategy to integrate mobility planning into urban development. Here a positive social effect is coupled with an ecological benefit. By reducing the need for outdated buses on steep and narrow streets, CO_2 emissions and fine particle dust was reduced along with greenhouse gases and other pollutants. In the case of CO_2, this amounts to nearly 20,000 tons per year. The city can now finance part of the operating costs for public transportation through emissions trading.

The various transit systems have been embraced by the population and are kept surprisingly clean. People are careful not to leave waste in cabins or harass fellow passengers. In one neighborhood built on a very steep slope in which the height distance from top to bottom is the equivalent of a 30-story skyscraper, the city has installed covered escalators to assist residents in overcoming the considerable height differences. In flatter parts of the city, bike lanes have been installed along many streets that clearly separate bike and road traffic to improve safety for cyclists.

GREEN CORRIDORS

For Medellín, expanding the green spaces and greening the urban realm is vital to improving its resilience to the negative effects of climate change. An ambitious green infrastructure program has been developed and already partially implemented. By linking up existing green spaces and creating new parks, the amount of public space per resident has increased by about 2.5 times. Green corridors—so-called *corredores verdes*—have been established along 18 roads and 12 waterways and some 9,000 trees and 350,000 shrubs have been planted since 2016. The success of this strategy can be seen in the reduction of local temperatures along key routes by on average 2 °C. The planting also helps improve air quality, provides shade for cyclists and pedestrians alike, and increases biodiversity. Complementing these green corridors are "green walls," vertical gardens that likewise serve to regulate the climate, improve air hygiene, and biodiversity. The green corridors project, which received support from the Kigali Cooling Efficiency Program and was undertaken in partnership with Sustainable Energy for All, was awarded the prestigious "Award for Cooling by Nature" in 2019 by the UK charity Ashden. The award text states, "Medellín shows how nature-based solutions can keep people and the planet cool."

11, 12 (opposite page)
Trees and lush greenery provide shade and cool temperatures for sidewalks and bike lanes. Evaporation from vegetation significantly lowers temperatures in the city.

GREEN CORRIDORS

PARQUE DEL RÍO

Parque del Rió is a project that promises to be transformational for the city and builds on and extends the Green Corridors strategy. The 20-kilometer-long park designed by the landscape architects Sebastián Monsalve Gómez and Juan David Hoyos has been under construction since 2014 and is currently only partially completed. Alongside creating significant new green infrastructure, the project aims to provide new routes for non-motorized traffic, to restore access to the riverbanks, and encourage biodiversity along the river.

13
Parque del Río: Road tunnel entrance with greenery above.

14
Large vegetation areas in the park are used to collect and hold rainwater.

Before the project most of the Río Medellín was channeled and additionally flanked by major traffic arteries, effectively dividing the city down the middle. The roadways in particular made it hard to reach the river. Stretches of these roadways have since been relocated into underground tunnels, making it possible to create new, high-quality public open spaces that provide access to the riverside, something that was not possible for 60 years. The river that once divided the city now serves as the structural axis for the park, and new bridges for cyclists and pedestrians connect the urban areas to the east and west of the river. Native species have been used as planting to restore the connection with the local landscape and promote public awareness of the native natural environment in an urban context. The park also features a pavilion for cultural activities run by the city's utility company.

So far two of the twelve planned sections have been completed and construction is expected to continue for up to 15 years. The intention and expectation is that new residential areas will emerge along the new green infrastructure, turning this environmental project into an important public amenity for improving the quality of life for many residents of the city. To address the impact of climate change, additional greening would help reduce the urban heat island effect and act as a natural buffer, collecting surface water runoff from heavy rainfall events before it enters the sewers.

15
The lounging areas in the park are popular. As the trees grow, they will provide more shade.

16
The linear park follows the course of the river. In 2018, its long paths were the site of an exhibition of works of art from the Prado in Madrid.

PARK LIBRARIES

Ecological resilience and social stabilization are two related aspects of urban development in Medellín. In addition to reforming urban mobility to prioritize less polluting public transportation and connect outlying low-income neighborhoods to the city center, the building of libraries in socially deprived areas is a further example of promoting resilience at multiple levels. Medellín's park libraries are built in green surroundings and form cool green oases in the city. Typically 1 to 2 hectares in size, they combine public space with educational, cultural, and social activities, and have a stabilizing effect on the respective neighborhoods. As a form of social acupuncture, they represent strategically placed, selected measures for transforming urban areas, inviting citizens to interact with their living environment and partake of urban life in new ways.

Located in the northeast of the city, Parque Biblioteca España was donated by Spain and opened in 2007. The building's striking composition of three rock-like volumes embedded on the side of a steep hill make it a local landmark. The buildings have, however, been closed for years pending essential renovation work. Another notable example is the Parque Biblioteca León de Greiff, named after Colombia's renowned 20th-century poet, who was a native of Medellín. Also situated on a steep slope in a neighborhood on the periphery of the city, its roof terrace and park are open to the public and provide impressive views over the city. Built in 2017 on the site of a former prison, it has created a new public space for people to learn, meet, and relax while also cooling the surroundings and improving the microclimate.

17, 18
The three distinctive buildings of the La Ladera Léon de Greiff library surround a small park that is illuminated at night.

100 NEW PARKS

Another urban development project aimed at improving the city's resilience to climate change is the creation of new parks and renovation of existing parks. A hundred sites throughout the city have been earmarked and some have already been completed.

An audit of the city by the municipal planning authority revealed several areas of the city without adequate lighting and other basic public infrastructure. A parallel study of EPM's own facilities revealed a similar pattern: the dark areas coincided with the locations of 144 water tanks that had been constructed on the outskirts of the city. However, as Medellín expanded, the informal settlements dotting the slopes of the Aburrá Valley enclosed the sites with the tanks. Unlit spaces in the middle of neighborhoods lacking adequate public infrastructure invite crime. As the operator of the water tanks, EPM turned to urban planning and architecture to address the problem, creating high-quality public spaces in the respective neighborhoods. Known as Unidades de Vida Articulada (UVAs), or places of social interaction, they are designed for people to meet, gather, and hold events, with areas for children to play and for families to escape the confines of their own four walls. Asphalt, brick, and concrete are replaced by trees, flowers, and other plants.

Thirty-two of the 144 existing water tank sites have since been selected for redevelopment as UVAs, and 14 of these are in areas with little other public space. The grounds around the water tanks have been made publicly accessible and redesigned with the help of public participation processes. Areas that were previously fenced off have been reconnected to their urban context as meetings spaces for the surrounding district. As many of the water tanks were located on elevated sites on the steep slopes, these public spaces are often more like urban balconies or terraces than conventional parks. The primary components of the UVAs are water and energy, and as such, they are frequently the starting point for local plans to provide lighting in the informal neighborhoods. Consequently, a hallmark of the UVAs is that they make urban utility networks accessible to the community, and this includes opening infrastructure facilities to other, sometimes unconventional uses. UVAs are therefore excellent examples of a shift in thinking toward a more socially resilient city that strives for better social equity. Three of the 100 parks are described below, each of which is different in its appearance and theme, illustrating the spectrum of possibilities.

PARQUE DE LA IMAGINACIÓN

The Park of the Imagination is located in District 8, Villa Hermosa, and some 27,000 people live in its immediate vicinity. Created in 2015, it encompasses 8,600 square meters of outdoor space and 2,200 square meters of buildings. The outdoor areas feature extensive play areas and sports facilities for people of all ages, as well as a lookout point with a view over the city. The theme of "water" is transported by an outdoor water feature and an open-air theater space within the circular perimeter of an open water tank. These two elements are defining for the identity of the park. The buildings house seminar rooms and computer rooms for public use, exhibition spaces for artistic, educational, and cultural activities, as well as music practice rooms. All facilities and services are free, and the facilities are open six days a week until the evening hours.

19–21
Stalls surround the water basin at the center of the Parque de la Imaginación, behind it a playground with sports equipment. The raw materiality of the architecture lends it a particular, atmospheric character.

PARQUE DE LOS DESEOS

Designed by the architecture office of Felipe Uribe de Bedout, the Park of Desires was completed in 2003. Rather uncharacteristically for the UVA, it is situated in the river plain in the north of the city, near the Botanical Gardens and the University of Antioquia. A large part of the 1.2-hectare site consists of a mostly sealed, sloping surface bordered by the Casa de la Música, completed in 2005, and the Planetarium. It serves as a space for events such as concerts or open-air cinema screenings, as well as workshops or guided tours. The House of Music has become an important meeting place for musicians and artists, with six rehearsal spaces for up to 250 people. On average, the rooms are used by more than 5,000 musicians every month for more than 12,000 rehearsal sessions.

22, 23
The main square of Parque de los Deseos, with the Planetarium and the House of Music in the background. With fountains, shaded seating areas, and a playground, it is an inviting space for all kinds of users.

The services provided by the Casa de le Música as well as the approximately 400 cultural events that take place each year are free. The park hosts 40 major events per year and has become an important venue in the city. Together with the planetarium, the park marked the beginning of the development of the northern part of the city. More facilities were built and now ten institutions, including the university, Botanical Gardens, a metro line, and the Ruta N, contribute to the social stability of the district and surrounding area.

During the day, the broad expanse of the Parque de los Deseos is used by schoolchildren who delight in playing in the double row of fountains, which is perfect for splashing and cooling down in hot weather. In the evenings, students from the nearby university make use of the plaza, and on weekends it is populated by families with children. The predominantly hard surfacing of the park gives it the character of an urban square. Interactive playground furniture helps explain scientific phenomena: there are acoustic shells that allow children to communicate over wider distances, a sundial, and a device that explains how solar eclipses occur.

Maintained by the EPM Foundation, the park was awarded Colombia's foremost design award, the "Lápiz de Acero Azul" in 2003, as well as an award for a public facility promoting interest in the sciences by Colciencias, a department of the Ministry of Science, Technology, and Innovation.

PARQUE DE LOS PIES DESCALZOS

The Barefoot Park is situated in the city center right in front of the main headquarters of the EPM public utilities company. The 3-hectare park invites its visitors to explore the different zones barefoot—running, playing, walking, or resting—and includes sand beds and play areas, a bamboo grove, and a paved area. Two shallow pools in the paved area allow visitors to dip their feet or wade through the water—a nod to wading through the cool, shallow streams of the countryside around Medellín—and additional sections with fountains provide plenty of opportunities for urban *joie de vivre.* The bamboo grove has a meditative quality, providing a calm space for mental and physical relaxation as a counterpoint to the sports and games.

Completed in 2000, the park was also initiated and funded by EPM and designed by Felipe Uribe de Bedout. The park is also home to the Water Museum whose interactive exhibits attract some 1,000 visitors a day, most of them schoolchildren. The museum exhibits explain the scientific, geographical, and ecological aspects of water in an accessible way and also details the work of the public utility, presenting different techniques for harvesting drinking water, treating wastewater, and generating energy. Further EPM activities, including electricity, gas, and telecommunications are presented in the museum. Like the park, the museum is financed and operated by EPM.

24–27
A pool of water in Parque de los Pies Descalzos. The bamboo grove is a tranquil, shaded space ideal for meditating or reading.

100 NEW PARKS

MORAVIA

Many of the people who came to the city in search of work or to flee the civil war settled in the outlying informal settlements and built homes for themselves with the materials they could find. The Moravia neighborhood is one such settlement that arose gradually in an area next to the Río Medellín between two major traffic arteries in the north of the city, not far from the bus station. In the 1970s, the area was used as a rubble tip for excavated material from new building projects elsewhere in the city. In 1977, in an attempt to prevent people settling there, the city turned the site into a municipal landfill, which quickly grew to a height of 30 meters and covered an area of 7 hectares. But it did not stop people settling; far from it, the landfill attracted more and more people in search of food and clothing or things they could turn into money by recycling or selling. Hundreds if not thousands of families lived permanently on the mountain of garbage in utterly unsatisfactory living conditions.

28, 29
Moravia, a former landfill site that has since been sealed and landscaped, is now crisscrossed by paths. Information panels detail the transformation it has undergone.

Fotografías comparativas del Morro de Moravia 1984-2014
Autor: Alcaldía de Medellín

En el año de 1984 cuando se cerró el botadero, la montaña de basura ya alcanzaba los 35 metros de altura en su cima, a sus alrededores sobre los desechos , cientos de familias poblaban el lugar. En el año 2014, 30 años después se ha dado una transformación ambiental, paisajística y urbanística en este sector de la ciudad.

Hoy con el proyecto "Moravia florece para la vida" se continua con la rehabilitación de este lugar por medio de procesos ambientales, que aportan al mejoramiento de la calidad de vida de los habitantes del barrio Moravia.

Alcaldía de Medellín

30
An information panel showing the landfill site in 1984 and after greening in 2014.

By 1983, the situation had spiraled beyond control with an estimated 15,000 people living on and around the landfill site. Moravia had become the most densely populated neighborhood in Medellín, and the contaminated environment and overcrowded living conditions presented a serious health risk for the residents. After several outbreaks of fire, the dump was closed in 1984. The neighborhood was declared a special intervention area in 1990, and in 2005 a public disaster zone. The impacts of the landfill site for the local climate include heat build-up due to lack of shade, toxic gas emissions, probably also including climate-damaging methane, and the risk of landslides in heavy rain due to the unstable soil conditions.

In 2004, two decades after the landfill was closed, a plan for the neighborhood was ratified that provided a basis for a series of critical improvements, including the construction of a network of sewers, business development measures to promote jobs and economic growth in the neighborhood, and the setting up of a network of social organizations. The people who lived on the landfill were relocated to newly built housing, some in other parts of the city. In 2009, ground cover was applied to the landfill to minimize toxic gas emissions, and some 50,000 trees and shrubs were planted on the hill. Within a short space of time, the former landfill became the largest garden in the city. Plant species were selected that, together with appropriate bacteria, can break down toxic residues into its harmless constituents. Modernization initiatives in the neighborhood included walkways and bridges over the flood canals, new health centers and free public bicycles.

Moravia remains one of Medellin's most densely populated neighborhoods with a population that now exceeds 40,000. But the 30,000 square meters of green space on the hill of the former landfill as well as the formation of cooperatives that have had a positive impact on social cohesion, and a more equitable distribution of housing and job opportunities, have led to Moravia becoming a landmark example of urban transformation. The example also demonstrates how an urban community can emerge in the second generation of immigrants that is a social advancement over their parents' generation. The redevelopment and infrastructure measures, coupled with the establishment of social facilities have created conditions in which residents can identify positively with their district—and in turn their city—and can make use of opportunities for education and play their part in economic and political life. The parallel aspects of improved social cohesion, adequate access to green and public spaces, and mitigation of the negative effects of climate change have brought major improvements for the common good of the residents of Moravia and will hopefully pave the way for its future development.

GREEN ARCHITECTURE

The increasing awareness in Medellín's urban society of the need to protect the environment and adapt to climate change can be seen in new architecture projects that pioneer ecological qualities and resilience. Aside from incorporate greening measures, these projects relate to the public space around them, establishing a beneficial interaction between architecture and its green surroundings. It is precisely this symbiosis that is so important for building climate resilience in cities but is all too often inadequately addressed. The three projects discussed here present exemplary approaches.

CIVIC CENTER OF THE DEPARTMENT OF ANTIOQUIA

The Civic Center of Antioquia, also called Edificio Plaza de la Libertad, was completed in 2010 and impressively demonstrates the interplay between a building's architecture and its outdoor spaces and how it can respond sensitively to a site's cultural and natural conditions. Designed by the architecture offices OPUS and Toroposada Arquitectos, the building responds visibly and tangibly to the environmental and climatic conditions of the tropics. It draws on traditional elements of regional architecture, such as terraces, bridges, and balconies, reinterpreting them in a contemporary form for its ultra-modern design. At the same time, the site is a model for the incorporation of vegetation into the urban spaces of the city, creating spaces of luxuriant natural richness along with corresponding opportunities for people to experience it up close. The striking design of the facade recalls the forests of the surrounding natural landscape.

The site of the building is designed to be a permeable public space connecting to the surrounding urban environment. Its green spaces are planted with native species, helping to reduce the urban heat island effect, and providing a habitat for native fauna and a place for staff and visitors alike to relax and enjoy the greenery. The use of vertical shading elements on the facades reduces the need for air-conditioning and for indoor lighting.

31
The grounds of the Civic Center are planted with native species.

32 (opposite page)
A water basin in the outdoor areas of the Civic Center.

MEDELLÍN

EPM BUILDING

The EPM building is the headquarters of Medellín's public utilities company. In the early 1990s in the spirit of progressive, socially inclusive urban planning, the decision was made to situate it in one of the poorer neighborhoods of the city as a catalyst for promoting urban development. Combining six individual towers into a single building, the EPM headquarters is an intelligent, LEED-certified building that stands next to Barefoot Park. In addition to a rooftop garden, it includes green walls, green roofs, and a green facade facing the park. Sixty percent of the plants used are native species. In 2017, the roof was fitted with a photovoltaic system with 1044 panels, which went into operation in 2021 and is expected to generate enough electricity to cover 5.5 percent of the building's electricity needs. Its environmentally friendly design and intelligent systems have made the EPM building a symbol of progressive and innovative architecture in Medellín for almost 30 years.

33, 34 (opposite page)
A partially greened wall at the entrance to the EPM building in which the municipal utility company has its headquarters.

RUTA N

Ruta N is a business and innovation center designed by the architecture office Estudio Transversal in 2011 that stands out not just through its striking architecture but also its lush green surroundings. Located opposite the University of Antioquia not far from the Parque de los Deseos, the complex is part of the regeneration of the northern part of the city. A central aspect of the architecture is the courtyard, which is enclosed on three sides and planted with a variety of tropical plants. The native species, selected with the help of the city's Botanical Gardens, require little irrigation and no pesticides. The names of the species are shown on information panels with QR codes for those interested in finding out more online. The outdoor areas around the building link up with the green space of the university campus opposite as well as with the green facade of the building complex.

35, 36–37 (next page)
The Ruta N building, with its distinctive street corner, has a courtyard and lush garden of tropical plants that opens onto the street. Together with the greened walls of the building facing the courtyard, it cools the building and provides fresh air.

MEDELLÍN

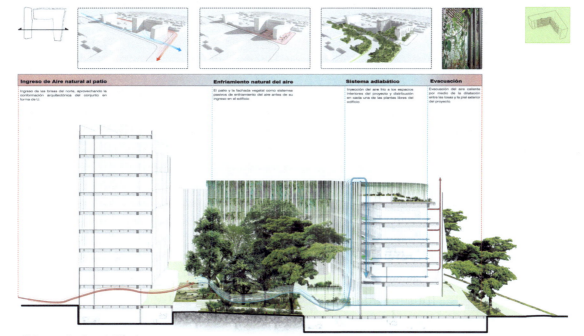

38
The Ruta N passive cooling system: Air is cooled by the plants in the garden and on the facade and drawn into the building's interior.

39
The Ruta N facade passively controls direct light incidence: Folds in the facade act as an innovative means of solar shading, providing the interior with indirect natural light.

GREEN ARCHITECTURE

The Ruta N building has a number of features that heighten its sustainability: all interior lighting is fully automated using light sensors to minimize energy consumption. The indoor temperature regulation employs adiabatic cooling rather than mechanical systems: cool air is drawn into the building and warm air expelled via the terraces. The lush vegetation of the greened courtyard provides a vital basis, and the structure of the facade ensures good air circulation: all office spaces can be ventilated between the wall and ceiling. Rainwater is harvested, filtered, and used for toilet flushing and irrigation of the gardens. The building's users can charge their mobile devices free of charge in the public spaces using solar power, and park their bicycles in one of the many bicycle racks. The project demonstrates that when green infrastructure is appropriately integrated into the overall concept, it can benefit the building considerably. Ruta N was the first building in Colombia to receive LEED Gold certification.

After decades marred by endemic political violence, widespread drug crime, and uncertain social and living conditions, Medellín has gradually transformed into a city abounding in new perspectives for the new millennium. The residents increasingly identify with the city, and the improving political situation and decline in violence has made it possible to devote more attention to environmental protection and adapting to climate change. Funding made available for such measures in Medellín always also has a social component. The city has undertaken to improve the city's climate resilience through expanding green infrastructure, greening buildings and the city along important streets as well as the public park along the Río Medellín. At the same time, it has expanded its public transport system, connecting lower-income neighborhoods to the city center, and constructing new educational facilities. Formerly fenced-off infrastructure has been made available for public use to create numerous new parks that also serve to provide relevant social facilities. Although the ongoing peace process is still not conclusively resolved and the challenges of climate change are only gradually beginning to become clear, the steps the city has achieved so far over the past decades are both remarkable and inspiring, far beyond the boundaries of Medellín.

RIO DE JANNEIRO

With 6.7 million inhabitants, Rio de Janeiro is the second-largest city in Brazil, situated in the state of the same name, in the southeast of the country. One of its nicknames is *Cidade Maravilhosa*—Beautiful City—which is easy to understand given its picturesque location between the Atlantic Ocean and a large bay, the *Baía de Guanabara*, and its wooded mountainous backdrop and expansive white beaches. The city itself lies an average of 31 meters above sea level. Currently the metropolitan region has 13.3 million inhabitants, a number that is expected to rise to 14.8 million by 2035.

On January 1, 1502, the Portuguese explorer André Gonçalves came across a settlement on the banks of Guanabara Bay, which he initially took to be a river. This assumption together with the month of discovery—Rio for river and Janeiro for January—gave the city its name: River in January, Rio de Janeiro. At the time some 3,000 Native American Indians lived in the village and the white Europeans who settled there referred to them in their language as Cariocas, which is now the common term for the inhabitants of Rio de Janeiro. Copacabana—the name of the city's most famous beach—is another example of a term that has persisted over the ages, and means "clear water." The official founding of the Portuguese city—initially as São Sebastião do Rio de Janeiro—took place on March 1, 1565.

Today, Rio de Janeiro is considered one of the most beautiful urban centers in the world and is correspondingly a tourist magnet. Despite no longer being the actual capital of Brazil since 1960, it is still considered the cultural capital of Brazil and is the second most important economic center in the country. It hosts numerous cultural exhibitions and international conferences: in 1992 and again in 2012, the UN Conference on Environment and Development convened there, and it is no coincidence that South America's first Olympic Games were held in Rio in 2016. At the same time, Rio de Janeiro faces major urban development challenges, including implementing infrastructure and social improvements in the many populous *favelas*, as well as tackling the high crime rate in the city overall. Other tasks that lie ahead include ensuring adequate sanitation facilities such as clean drinking water and a properly functioning sewage system in many neighborhoods—both of which are further compounded by the effects of climate change.

The UN Conference on Environment and Development held in Rio de Janeiro in June 1992, often also known as the Earth Summit or Rio Conference, was remarkable because, for the first time, environmental and development topics were considered together in front of a global audience. Since then, the goals of the conference have been closely associated with this city. Representatives from 178 countries and many non-governmental organizations debated urgent environmental issues and development goals for the 21st century and adopted the concept of sustainable development as an international guiding principle. In addition, economic efficiency, social equity, and the safeguarding of the natural basis of life were declared of equal importance and as essential for survival. The conference resulted in the Rio Declaration, Agenda 21, and internationally binding conventions on climate protection, biodiversity conservation, and combating desertification. Together with the Statement of Forest Principles, these have formed the basis for global cooperation on environmental and development policy.

1 (previous page)
The city of Rio de Janeiro lies in a scenic setting of water, rocky outcrops, and wooded hills, among them the landmark of Sugarloaf Mountain.

Among the political pioneers of development and climate policy initiatives in Brazil is the longtime mayor of Rio de Janeiro, Eduardo Paes, who chaired the global C40 cities network from 2014 to 2016 and under whom Rio's *Resilience Strategy* was adopted. The latter explicitly refers to the goals of the Rockefeller Foundation's 100 Resilient Cities organization, as do various programs of the C40 cities and other organizations.

Paes's first term in office also coincided with the 2016 Olympics, which was accompanied by a number of major infrastructure projects, among them the extension of the subway and the introduction of a rapid bus system in neighborhoods farther from the city center. As described later in this chapter, he was also instrumental in promoting the large Porto Maravilha urban redevelopment project.

Rio de Janeiro was one of the first cities to quantify its greenhouse gas emissions by sector in 2000. In this context, the sectors most responsible for greenhouse gas emissions were transportation (37 percent), waste (16 percent), and industry (12 percent). The mayor subsequently introduced goals to reduce greenhouse gas emissions to 20 percent below 2005 levels by 2020.

As a member of the Carbon Neutral Cities Alliance, Rio de Janeiro has also committed to becoming carbon neutral by 2050. An important project in this context is the recycling of organic waste. Brazil is among the top ten producers of food waste in the world. Up to 30 percent of fruit and vegetable harvests are sent to landfill and some 40,000 tons of food are disposed of every day, 5,000 tons in Rio alone. A pilot project that began in 2018 employs biomethanation, a process that produces electricity, biofuels, and compost while also reducing the emission of climate-damaging methane gas from landfills. While ideally the goal—as with any waste—should be to reduce the production of organic waste in the first place, the City anticipates that this process will help appreciably reduce greenhouse gas emissions. Other positive initiatives include the extension of the public transportation network to better serve residential and work districts with poor mobility infrastructure. Even though the aforementioned subway extension to the west of the city and the connecting rapid bus system has helped significantly, the extensive infrastructure project was not completed until after the 2016 Olympics. Bike Rio, a modern bike rental system for public use was also founded in 2018. Beyond that, the network of footpaths has been extended, and a reforestation program was started to replant deforested hillsides to secure them against further erosion and potentially catastrophic landslides. Since 1989, more than 12 million trees have been planted in Rio's urban area.

At an altitude of just a few meters above sea level, Rio de Janeiro's climate is tropically humid, with a mean annual temperature of 23.6 °C. While February is the warmest month, with temperatures reaching 27 °C, in July, the coldest month, they drop to only 20 °C due to warm ocean currents from the Atlantic. As a result of weak seasonal variation, the temperature amplitude between summer and winter is only 6.8 °C. Neither frost nor snowfall has occurred since weather records began. Total annual precipitation is 1,250 millimeters, with the least precipitation in August (45 millimeters) and the most in January (170 millimeters). Due to the warm temperature of the Atlantic Ocean, the relative humidity is often very high at 75 to 90 percent from October to January. This can give rise to localized short showers and thunderstorms that can deposit large amounts of rainfall locally.

EFFECTS OF CLIMATE CHANGE

Brazilian cities have long viewed climate change as a risk that will somehow be averted and have given comparatively little thought to adaptation measures. Yet this changed in 2016 when Rio de Janeiro became one of the first cities in the country to adopt a climate change adaptation strategy, the *Estratégia de Adaptação às Mudanças Climáticas da Cidade do Rio de Janeiro*. Alongside monitoring changes to climate parameters, the scenario also considers other emerging trends such as the aging of society, and the decreasing rate of population growth, as well as increasing land consumption as the city expands. This strategy will serve as the basis for a future climate change adaptation plan.

The Climate Change Adaptation Strategy looks in detail at the potential threats to specific areas of the city. Existing climate records make it possible to identify ongoing trends, for example that hot days are becoming more frequent, that mean annual temperatures are rising by 0.05 °C per year, that heat waves are lasting longer, and cold days are becoming less frequent. It also shows that the occurrence and intensity of rainfall is increasing, especially at higher elevations.

The predictions for the future climate in Rio de Janeiro were made by the National Institute for Space Research, using climate model calculations. For one thing, they forecast that the current trend of rising temperatures is expected to continue within a range of 1.16 to 2.42 °C, and for another, that both minimum and maximum temperatures will increase by 2040. This will be least pronounced in the districts closest to the coast, and higher in the more inland areas, so that the temperature gradient—already noticeable today—will continue to rise depending on proximity to the sea or to forested areas. The number of days with maximum temperatures above 25 °C and minimum temperatures above 20 °C will also increase.

A declining trend is forecast for annual precipitation, which could sink to between 700 and 800 millimeters, especially in those parts of the city where current precipitation is already lower, and also in the generally rainier summer months of December through February. Compared with the current mean annual precipitation of 1,250 millimeters, this forecast represents a marked decrease. In some areas, such as forested or mountainous regions, this is likely to be less severe, so that these regions have potential for harvesting rainfall. Periods without rain are forecast to last longer than before, up to 16.5 days, and simulations suggest that the frequency of extreme rainfall events with considerable precipitation is expected to decrease. At the same time, the strategy notes that simulations based on regional climate models alone are still highly uncertain. The results could potentially be more reliable if intense but not extreme rainfall events are taken into account. To improve the predictive reliability of the results, the models could also factor in urban heat island effects, the degree of surface sealing and infiltration of the soil, as well as energy fluxes in the city.

But forecasts based on climate model data are only one source of information on the effects of climate change in Rio de Janeiro. Literature reviews and expert interviews offer further insight. For example, these sources indicate rising sea levels and the formation of higher waves as potential hazards from the sea, as well as landslides, heat waves and flooding, the emergence of heat islands, and longer periods of drought.

For a city with such a long coastline, ocean waves are especially relevant because they determine the design of the shoreline and the promenades, and in turn influence the lifestyle of the Cariocas. Needless to say, an expected rise in sea levels also causes an increase in waves. Damage resulting from storm surges has been reported from as far back as the 19th century, and scientists' records indicate an increase in the frequency of strong waves since 1980. Clearly, the city is estimated to be very vulnerable to the effects of rising sea levels. It would affect developments near the shore as well as the lagoon, where higher levels of saltwater intrusion could affect its ecological balance.

The occurrence of prolonged droughts and potential disruptions to the water supply were not evaluated in the climate strategy, because the vulnerability analysis only examined vegetation cover in the mountains and water catchment areas.

An additional major risk in parts of Rio is landslides and mud and debris flows following heavy rainfall events. Those most affected are the inhabitants of the *favelas*, the slum settlements built on slopes, where serious incidents in the past have actually caused fatalities. Moreover, mudslides reaching the lowlands have led to silting up of the drainage systems. In recent years the frequency of such events has increased, and since 2011 those residential areas most at risk from landslides have been equipped with an early warning system to alert the affected population in advance. A study on the probability of landslides in combination with rainfall levels showed that the most critical period is in summer between December and March. However, the modeling scenarios cannot yet adequately predict the frequency of heavy rainfall events; in addition, they do not take sufficient account of the city's topography so that proper preventive protection cannot yet be guaranteed.

Heat waves and the heat island effect are further problems that model calculations are as yet unable to predict with sufficient accuracy. Nonetheless, observations and measurements indicate an increase in the occurrence of hot spells. Sea winds play an important role in cooling the city, especially when architecture and vegetation along coastal stretches do not block air flow and allow the wind to be channeled up into the built-up urban areas behind. From this perspective, ventilation is also an area that needs to be studied in more detail.

Due to its geographic location, the city is prone to flooding. While Rio de Janeiro extends across mangroves and marshes, it lacks both stormwater retention facilities and flood protection measures. Building along the coast has also not adequately considered the dynamics of the sea. Computer modeling of the terrain and gradients can be used to determine susceptibility to flooding, however, this does not consider accompanying precipitation or floodwater run-off. Nevertheless, it can serve as a planning tool to limit building developments and urban densification in critical locations.

The scientists and climate experts who authored the Climate Adaptation Strategy are themselves quite critical of the lack of data and the difficulties this presents for the city and planning agencies to respond adequately to climate change. In the absence of systematically collected environmental data, it is hard to determine whether a particular event can be attributed to global climate change. The greatest risk, according to the authors, is a lack of knowledge about the coastal environment of the city, and it is this that presents the main obstacle to planning appropriate responses to climate change.

Emilio Lèbre La Rovere, a professor at Rio de Janeiro State University and director of Centro Clima, also points to the rapid growth of Brazil's cities. In 1940, Brazil had 40 million inhabitants, 10 million of whom lived in cities; by 1990, this figure had risen to 100 million, two-thirds of whom lived in cities. Infrastructure could not be developed quickly enough, and growth did not follow an overall strategy. In Rio de Janeiro, lack of space has caused construction to rise up the steep mountain slopes, but without suitable geotechnical stabilization of the soil the risk of landslides increases. The most serious landslide yet occurred in 1966 and is still remembered by many, especially those living in the *favelas*. Disasters of this kind are an example of the catastrophes that can occur when the consequences of climate change coincide with social problems.

PORTO MARAVILHA

Brazil's largest urban redevelopment project, the transformation of Rio de Janeiro's port area began in 2010 and is scheduled to be completed over a 15-year period. An area of 500 hectares that includes an elevated highway, warehouses, a publicly inaccessible shoreline, the city's oldest *favela*, and the former arrival point during the slave trade is undergoing comprehensive renewal and will be transformed into a completely new urban district.

As in many large port cities, the waterfront was freed up for redevelopment due to a shift in freight shipping to large container ships. Due to greater automation of goods handling, less manpower is required but more container storage areas and greater water depths for container ships. As the existing port area was unable to provide such facilities—a situation familiar from other cities—a new location was found outside Rio. Subsequently, the old port facilities and warehouses were no longer needed, accompanying housing and office spaces also stood empty, and historic buildings were threatened with decay. The redevelopment has however made it possible to redesign much of the port area and introduce new uses while taking into account its great cultural significance.

Several major events, including the hosting of the 2014 World Cup, the city's 450th anniversary in 2015, and the hosting of the 2016 Summer Olympics, which Rio was awarded in 2009, provided added impetus to implement the project and complete significant parts by 2016.

There is clearly great potential in such an extensive urban development zone for creating new public space in the vacated areas. Of relevance are not only new outdoor recreational areas and new architecture with educational and cultural facilities, but also making a connection to the history of the place and what it means for the people living there. For example, work on the redevelopment of Porto Maravilha brought to light evidence of Brazil's history of the slave trade that was either forgotten or was no longer visible. These have been reinstated, giving back the people a piece of their history and dignity. Here, resilient urban development also means reconnecting with diverse histories and promoting cohesion and understanding between the different groups in Rio's multicultural urban society. Alongside implementing technical innovations, the redevelopment therefore carefully and respectfully maintains the social and cultural connections of the people with their homeland.

ORGANIZATION

Adjoining Guanabara Bay, the Porto Maravilha project area is implemented as a consortial urban development in public-private partnership. Public land is designated as construction areas that private developers can then build on to a greater extent that the building regulations would normally allow. In return, developers must invest the added value this generates in infrastructure and educational and cultural facilities.

The aim is to improve urban infrastructure, reduce traffic and environmental pollution, to make available some 5 million square meters for construction, create new parks and squares, plant trees along 40 kilometers of roads and clean up mangrove areas. Furthermore, the redevelopment is also expected to create 20,000 jobs, not least by attracting technology and other innovative companies. New housing is intended to improve the situation for the local population and attract new residents, and the latest and existing cultural activities should improve the appeal of the rejuvenated quarter for tourists, while also referring to its historical and cultural heritage.

INFRASTRUCTURE

Considerable progress has been made to date, and the character of the former port has changed dramatically, especially along the waterfront. The first major project was the demolition of the elevated highway, the so-called *Perimetral*. Built in 1950 as a 5.5-kilometer-long elevated roadway above the water's edge, it was an important link but separated the port area and ferry dock of the nearby city of Niterói from the old town. Between 2012 and 2015, the road was demolished with traffic redirected along a new route with tunnels, including a 3-kilometer stretch that is the longest road tunnel in Brazil. For one thing, the ground-level road beneath the former Perimetral was replaced by a 3.5-kilometer-long promenade for pedestrians and cyclists, but also a new tramway line with a total length of 28 kilometers links the area to a nearby metro line and the city center. When completed the new area will have 70 kilometers of roadway, 650,000 square meters of sidewalk and 17 kilometers of bike lanes. The planting of 15,000 trees should increase the percentage of greenery in this zone from 2.46 percent today to 10.96 percent. Less visible, but no less important, is the renewal of 700 kilometers of sewers and drains in preparation for rising sea levels, as well as the connection of the area to the modern fiber-optic network.

2
The former elevated highway of the Perimetral in a photo from 2010 bisects the urban realm as a dominant and noise-emitting structure.

3
The open spaces beneath the Perimetral were used by the local population but, despite their central location, were not the focus of public life in Rio due to the noise of the highway.

MAUÁ SQUARE WITH NEW MUSEUMS

Bordering the central square of the port area, Praça Mauá, are now two new museums, the Museu de Arte do Rio, or MAR, which opened in 2013, and the Museum of the Future, Museu do Amanhã (literally: Museum of Tomorrow) which followed in December 2015. The MAR consists of a historic building from the early 20th century, the Palace of King John VI, to which—by means of an undulating roof structure—an elegant new modern building has been connected by the Brazilian architecture office Bernardes Jacobsen Arquitectura. Although an art museum, the MAR is not aimed just at the art world and tourists but is also explicitly for the neighborhood. In fact, schools are regularly involved in projects, and exhibitions often relate to the history of the city and of the surrounding district. The Museu do Amanhã, by contrast, is a completely new building constructed on an old pier. Designed by the architect Santiago Calatrava, it is a striking and expressive building that is immediately recognizable from far and wide. Using both artistic and scientific means the museum addresses some of the most pressing problems facing humanity: climate change and overpopulation. In this regard, the architect describes the building's sustainable approach as making the most of the natural resources of the site: the water of Guanabara Bay is used as cooling for the air-conditioning, while solar energy is harvested using photovoltaic panels incorporated into the wing-like elements of the roof. The wings move so that they can adapt optimally to the angle of the sun to maximize energy yields. These earned it the Best Innovative Green Building MIPIM Award in 2017.

To the west of Praça Mauá, next to the cruise ship terminals and various event halls, is a long public space for pedestrians, cyclists, and the tramway. Old warehouse walls are covered in large murals painted by the Brazilian artist Eduardo Kobra, including the work "Ethnicities," which with an area of nearly 3,000 square meters—17 meters high and 150 meters long—is the largest piece

4
The new urban space gained by demolishing the Perimetral with some of the newly planted urban trees.

PORTO MARAVILHA

5
The art museum, Museu de Arte de Rio, MAR, comprises an old and a new building joined by a roof canopy.

6
The modern building for the Museum of the Future, Museu do Amanhã.

7
Bench next to the Museum of the Future with solar shading in the shape of a palm tree.

8
The front end of the Museum of the Future resembles ...

9
... the prow of a cruise ship moored next to it.

RIO DE JANEIRO

of street art created by a single artist in the world. It depicts portraits of five faces representing the continents participating in the Olympic Games. With the arrival of the Olympic torch, the mural was inaugurated on August 4, 2016. A few minutes away on foot from Praça Mauá is the AquaRio seawater aquarium, which also opened in 2016. Housed in a converted historic building, it is the largest aquarium of its kind in South America.

In the open space between the buildings, especially between Praça Mauá and the aquarium, the tramway lines are embedded in a lawn. The ground is therefore unsealed and can absorb rainwater and also release it back into the atmosphere at ground level as evaporation, cooling the otherwise predominantly sealed urban area. The cooling effect here is less pronounced than from trees, which have a larger surface area and provide shade, which helps prevent the ground from heating up. Trees were also planted, however as very young plants that have not been tended well since. At present, they have next to no climatic benefit, and it does not look like they will develop greatly into large trees that can provide shade and regulate rainwater. From a climate-conscious urban planning perspective, it is disappointing to see that a newly redeveloped site with award-winning architecture and top-class engineering has given so little consideration to sustainable planting.

10 Detail of the mural "Ethnicities" by the artist Eduardo Kobra showing Mursi, a native African from Ethiopia.

11 Another detail of the mural "Ethnicities" showing a Huli man from Papua New Guinea with his typical red and yellow face painting.

12 The AquaRio marine aquarium, the largest aquarium of its kind in South America.

172

13
The greened track bed for the new tramway. Larger, more mature trees stand alongside the buildings.

14, 15
These trees will need to grow significantly before they can provide adequate shade to those sitting on the benches on sunny days.

RIO DE JANEIRO

THE CULTURAL SIGNIFICANCE OF THE PORT AREA

Further west of the Aquarium, also within walking distance, are several renovated warehouses that reopened in 2006. Known as the *Cidade do Samba*, they house the samba schools and their extensive collections of props and costumes. Samba schools are cultural associations with up to 5,000 members who prepare for participation in the carnival. In the purpose-built *Sambódromo*, the annual parade of the schools is a vital part of the carnival in Rio de Janeiro. This tradition is closely linked to the history of the Afro-Brazilian population, whose roots are in turn closely interwoven with the urban area of Porto Maravilha, where vast numbers of slaves arrived in the country: Porto Maravilha was in effect a center of the slave trade, and for 350 years slavery was a key motor of the Brazilian economy. About 40 percent of the approximately 10 million Africans sold as slaves ended up in Brazil, significantly more than in North America.

The story of many slaves in Brazil began with their arrival at Valongo wharf in the port of Rio de Janeiro. Now slightly inland from the current water's edge, the old dock, the *Cais do Valongo*, was only rediscovered in 2011 during construction of the Porto Maravilha project. It was built in 1811 as a dock for ships carrying African slaves destined for the plantations in the interior or other parts of Brazil, or for work as servants in the households of Rio de Janeiro, then the country's capital. Over a period of just 40 years, it is estimated that approximately 900,000 slaves passed through the port into the country—about a quarter of all the African slaves shipped to South America. This site was therefore the largest slave port in the world.

Slavery was only officially abolished in Brazil in 1888. While the former slaves were then free on paper, they did not have access to education, property, or reasonable opportunities for equal participation in society. Appealing to the responsibility of today's society to remember the victims of slavery, the Cais do Valongo is now a public memorial commemorating the crimes against humanity committed as part of the slave trade. Added in 2017 to the UNESCO World Heritage List, the archaeological site is now managed by the National Historic and Artistic Heritage Institute. It also honors the contribution of the Afro-Brazilian population to the cultural, economic, and social development of Brazil and the Americas.

16
The Cais do Valongo, now a World Heritage site, was from 1811 onwards the arrival point for an estimated 900,000 captives from Africa over a period of 40 years.

17
The Instituto de Pesquisa e Memória Pretos Novos (IPN).

PORTO MARAVILHA

Not far from Valongo Wharf is the Cemetery of the New Blacks, *Cemitério dos Pretos Novos*, which was discovered in the late 1990s, also by chance, on a private property. Tens of thousands of Africans who died before or shortly after arrival in Brazil between 1770 and 1830 were buried here. At present, this area is the site of a memorial as well as the Institute for Research and Remembrance which examines and highlights traces of the slave trade, providing regular tours along with information on Afro-Brazilian culture.

Also near Valongo Wharf is the Valongo Hanging Garden. Created in 1906 as part of a revitalization program for the port area by the garden architect Luís Rei on the slope of Morro da Conceição, it was designed as a romantic garden and continuation of a retaining wall. The small garden is located 7 meters above street level and measures 1,530 square meters. Originally intended for public recreation, it has flower beds, lush planting, a water tank with irrigation system, and four marble statues of Greek gods. Situated not far from the former slave market, the garden was intended as a pleasant and uplifting distraction from the gloomy past of the neighborhood. After a long period of neglect, the garden was restored as part of the Porto Maravilha redevelopment and is now also part of the cultural heritage of the quarter.

In fact, many of the residents near the port are descendants of the slaves of the past. After they were liberated in 1888, many former slaves moved from the northeast of Brazil to larger cities such as Rio de Janeiro or São Paulo in search of work. One such area where they settled was the hill Morro da Providência, where the city's first *favela* arose, and many more were to follow.

18
View of the Morro da Providência ("Providence Hill") *favela*.

19, 20 (opposite page)
Part of the Valongo Hanging Garden and a building on its steep slope.

The development of the Porto Maravilha area is exemplary in its awareness of the sensitive history of the site. Less focus was given, however, to mitigating the effects of climate change. Opportunities to plan for climate resiliency are greatest when an urban area is comprehensively renewed or replanned, but unfortunately this chance was not fully exploited. Given that the population of the downtown area is declining, it is important for the city to make these neighborhoods attractive as places to live. Greater climate resiliency, with public urban spaces and generous green infrastructure could support this goal. While the current renewal is at least a major improvement, there is certainly potential for further related efforts in the future, although these will take time.

CORREDOR VERDE RECREIO

In recent decades, urbanization has focused in particular on the coastal region west of where the city of Rio Janeiro was founded more than 450 years ago, greatly altering the original landscape. Most notably, the natural water cycles and water balance have been heavily affected by the draining of wetlands and the channeling or underground routing of most of the 267 rivers and streams passing through it. While the city still has significant national, state, and local conservation areas, most of these zones are disconnected from one another, and many are also threatened by the continuing expansion of the city and the demand for land for building. As so often, the paradox is that ongoing construction and the accompanying destruction of the natural ecology contribute significantly to the natural threats to which the city is exposed. The greatest threat comes from water, whether from heavy rains, storm surges, or flooding and ensuing erosion. To counteract this, the city has designated eleven areas as important existent ecosystems that in the long term should be connected under the name "Carioca Mosaic." The Carioca Mosaic was developed in 2015 by the Ministry of the Environment to preserve and restore the ecosystem of the Atlantic Rainforest. Including an ecologically sensitive lagoon system, the first green corridor to be safeguarded is also located in the western part of the city. One segment of this is the greenway in the Recreio district, which connects several natural parks and lies in a lowland area with valuable ecosystems, lagoons, and canals.

The Recreio district in the west of the city has grown rapidly in recent decades, partly through the creation of "gated communities," enclosed, secure housing complexes for the middle and upper classes, and partly through the construction of new informal settlements in the lowlands. Both have led to the destruction of sensitive ecosystems. The Corredor Verde project started in 2012 with the aim of redressing this damage and creating new habitats for flora and fauna. Financed by compensation programs for the construction measures of the Olympic Games, the green corridor comprises over 320 hectares of protected areas and 60 hectares of public outdoor spaces. The water bodies in the project area are home to locally endangered species such as caymans, capybaras, and beach butterflies.

MASTERPLAN

21

22

23

24

21
Development plan for the Corredor Verde in Recreio showing the proposed changes.

22
Concept for the Corredor Verde showing the protected zones, transitional areas, and green residential areas, as well as bodies of water, squares, greened streets, and their interconnection to promote ecological biodiversity.

23
Sketches of specific aspects of the green corridor: Protected areas, biodiversity, street greening, hybrid-use street spaces, green residential areas, and the Sandra Alvim Walkway.

24
Sectional view showing proposed greening and accompanying improvements to the amenity value of the existing situation.

CORREDOR VERDE RECREIO

While the project aims to improve and preserve biodiversity, it also improves the resiliency of this western fringe of the city to the expected impacts of climate change. A significant aspect here is to reconnect the previously fragmented nature landscapes while creating greened streets as buffer zones and green islands as ecological stepping stones. Developed areas are also to be greened, both by planting native woody species and promoting green roofs and facades. New bike lanes and sidewalks and better public transportation options aim to encourage the use of "clean" mobility. Involving local residents in the project planning and investing in raising environmental awareness are also key components of the project. Initial results and goals of the planning process, which began in 2012, were presented to the residents in various public events. After all, the long-term success of the project can only be guaranteed, if the people either involved or affected become more aware of the importance of biodiversity and ecosystems for their own quality of life and well-being.

The Chico Mendes Municipal Natural Park is part of the green corridor and has been protected since 1989. Located in a level area that comprises mostly a lagoon and Atlantic rainforest, this ecosystem is based on sandy, mostly salty soils. Together with strong sunlight and wind they provide a habitat for special plant formations with bromeliads, cacti, and other water-storing plants. The typical fauna consists mostly of birds and reptiles and few mammals. Throughout the year plants provide flowers and fruits for the animals.

25
The body of water in the Chico
Mendes Municipal Natural Park,
a core part of the Corredor Verde.

26–28
The Casa Firjan is home of the Industry Federation of the State of Rio de Janeiro. Firjan assists companies in sustainable development and improves competitiveness by providing technological solutions, promoting innovation, and assisting with professional training. Examples of their sustainable and forward-looking facilities include a Fab Lab, trend labs, support for project development and training, exhibitions, and cultural activities. Firjan embraces the spirit of Rio de Janeiro's role as a hub of global sustainable development. The building features a green roof, a greened enclosure for the building's cooling plant, and a solar energy plant.

CORREDOR VERDE RECREIO

Eight years after starting the project, the measures have not yet been fully implemented. So far, the protection of conservation areas has been enhanced, invasive plant species removed, and native species planted. Endangered animals have been given more space and protection by fencing off core areas, and they can also be better monitored as a result. A large *favela* adjoining one of the canals poses a bigger challenge as the lack of sewage treatment and eutrophication of the waters has a negative impact on aquatic life. The caymans, for example, are predominantly male, because the decay of organic material means that the water temperature is too high for the female eggs to mature. The capybaras, in turn, pose a risk for humans because they carry ticks that can transmit Lyme disease. Overall, however, the project has had positive results. Its nature-oriented approach is appropriate for enhancing outdoor spaces and connecting biotopes, in turn supporting the ecosystem. At the same level, green infrastructure helps improve biodiversity, and conservation areas have been stabilized and can act as a buffer to climate change.

As it happens, Rio de Janeiro is the site where the concept of sustainable development was recognized as an international guiding principle three decades ago and where important networks for environmental preparedness originated. Now the city has itself made significant local efforts to leverage major development projects for the sustainable transformation of urban areas and the improvement of infrastructure. These include reducing greenhouse gas emissions by extracting methane gas from landfill sites, building a comprehensive rapid bus system to reduce private car traffic, and saving energy for public city lighting. The climate goals the city set for itself in 2012 were met two years later.

However, the biggest challenge that Rio faces, along with most other cities, is that only about 1 percent of the city is being newly or redeveloped at any one time. Since the remaining 99 percent already exists, the effort required to transform it to meet future needs is that much greater. Options for adapting neighborhoods to new climatic challenges are more limited, and the costs also considerably higher. That notwithstanding, pre-existing historical and cultural conditions must also be considered.

A further aspect that is often not properly understood from a European perspective is that for many nations climate change is not always the most pressing issue. Like many other countries in the southern hemisphere, Brazil faces huge social and economic challenges, high levels of poverty, strong population growth, an influx of people from rural areas to the city, and massive destruction of the natural environment. Many of the country's cities have therefore experienced a haphazard sprawl. As a consequence, the provision of sewage treatment and stormwater management has not kept pace with actual development, and infrastructure is therefore often lacking where it is needed. The combination of long-standing social problems and the growing consequences of climate change has compounded the challenges that cities face. Nevertheless, Rio de Janeiro was one of the first municipalities to elaborate an adaptation strategy and is on its way to developing a corresponding adaptation plan with concrete measures. Rio is also going to great lengths to mobilize material resources, motivate social energy, and develop ingenious planning solutions to address the many challenges it faces, including climate change.

MANAUS

MANAUS AND THE AMAZON BASIN

With an estimated 2.2 million inhabitants, Manaus is the seventh-largest city in Brazil and the capital of Amazonas, the largest state in the country in terms of area. Given that 60 percent of the population of Amazonas live here, Manaus is also known as the "Metropolis of the Amazon." Situated just 3 degrees south of the equator, the city is so intimately connected with the rainforest and its main rivers that it cannot be considered independently of its wider surroundings and sensitive ecosystem, which is of global climatic importance. The climate is tropical, with a mean annual temperature of 27.4 °C and an annual rainfall of 2,145 millimeters. While temperatures remain mostly uniform throughout the year, rainfall varies from an average of 56 millimeters in August to 295 millimeters in the rainiest month, March.

Officially designated a city on October 24, 1848, Manaus only acquired its current name on September 4, 1856, when it was named after the Manaós tribe of Indians, meaning "Mother of God." In 1866, the Brazilian Emperor Pedro II issued a decree permitting merchant ships of all nations to navigate the Amazon. Soon after, Manaus became a destination for international trade routes, which quickly brought the city rapid prosperity. Regular services were even introduced for long-distance shipping and from 1877 ships traveled regularly from Manaus to Liverpool, and from 1881 to New York. Today, ships are still an important means of reaching destinations along the Amazon, although these journeys are neither especially comfortable nor romantic: a trip from Manaus to Belém on the Atlantic coast, for example, takes between three and five days and the lowest price category entails sleeping in your own hammock, usually very close to your neighbor. Instead, air travel has taken over as the primary mode of transportation in and out of Manaus, as there are only a few sufficiently well-developed long-distance road connections to the city.

1 (previous page)
The city of Manaus on the Rio Negro.

2
Boats used to transport people and goods up and down the larger rivers.

Beginning in 1870, the production of rubber and ensuing international trade heralded a boom period for the city. As the center of rubber trade, Manaus attracted jobseekers from all over Brazil as well as from other parts of the world, who were needed to create access routes in the rainforest and to extract rubber from the rubber tree (*Hevea brasiliensis*). For a while, the percentage of foreigners in the population rose to over 5 percent. By the end of the 19th century, Manaus had established a reputation as a particularly open city for its day, banning slavery in 1884, four years before the Lei Áurea, the "Golden Law" abolishing slavery throughout Brazil. Thanks to the economic boom, Manaus was the only city in Brazil with electric lighting on its wide streets in the 1890s, with a proper water supply and system of sewers and, starting in 1899, Brazil's first electric tramway. By then, the city had also become known as the "Paris of the Tropics." Several prestigious municipal buildings were erected at this time, including the Palace of Justice and, most notably, the Opera House, which today still radiates the grandeur of the city's glory days. The market hall, which opened in 1882 and is located directly on the Rio Negro, likewise displays an extravagant Art Nouveau style and is still in use today, offering a wide variety of regional products, fruit and vegetables, spices and herbs of all kinds, as well as meat and fish. Designed by Gustave Eiffel and modeled on the market halls in Paris (*Les Halles Centrales*), it is built of structural elements shipped from France and is considered one of the most important examples of steel architecture of the late 19th century.

From 1910, the price of rubber, which had secured the city's prosperity for decades, fell due to the emergence of new production methods in Asia. In the decades that followed, Manaus could not maintain its former economic importance and wealth, and it was not until 1957, when the city was declared a free trade zone—in order to promote regional development—that the economic relevance of Manaus saw a renewed upturn as companies could import their raw materials almost duty-free. From this time on, new housing was also created for the people moving to the city, and the *Cidade Nova* (New City) was founded. Due to industrial growth as well as a high birth rate of over 4.7 children per woman, the population rose rapidly from 300,000 to 800,000 between 1970 and 1985, and to over 2.2 million by 2020. Today, the *Cidade Nova* is the largest district of the city.

Manaus is situated at the confluence of the Rio Negro and Rio Solimões, which then flow on eastward as the Amazon River through the Amazon Basin named after it. It then reaches the Atlantic Ocean north of the city of Belém. Traveling by boat from Manaus to the *Encontro das Águas* where the Rio Negro and Rio Solimões meet is an awe-inspiring experience because, due to their different temperatures, densities, flow velocities, and sediment loads, the colors of the dark blackwater river (Rio Negro) and the brownish whitewater river (Rio Solimões) mix only gradually over a distance of 10 kilometers. This impressive natural phenomenon has been declared a site of Brazilian Natural Heritage by the National Historic and Artistic Heritage Institute (IPHAN).

3, 4
The Teatro Amazonas, built during the rubber boom in 1896.

5
The Adolpho Lisboa market hall.

6
The Largo de São Sebastião. The Monument to the Opening of the Ports to Friendly Nations (Monumento à Abertura dos Portos às Nações Amigas), stands in the middle of the patterned San Sebastián Square. Built in 1899 to commemorate the opening of the ports of the Amazon River to foreign trade in 1866, it was constructed entirely of materials imported from Europe.

7
The Palácio Rio Negro, built in 1903 by the German "rubber baron" Karl Waldemar Scholz, is now a museum.

MANAUS

8, 9
The confluence of the Rio Solimões (brown-colored water) and the Rio Negro (dark-colored water). They mix gradually over a distance of 10 km.

MANAUS AND THE AMAZON BASIN

CLIMATE CHANGE IN MANAUS

As is mandatory for all Brazilian cities, Manaus sets out stipulations for the development of the city in an urban planning document, which was last updated in 2014, however, the city has no specific climate adaptation plan. In a research project into whether Manaus' planning practices are adequately addressing the impending crisis of climate change, the authors had to turn to the city's Environmental Code from 2011 as the last legislative document to include climate-relevant measures. The document broadly divides measures into the focal areas "disaster prevention," "health," "mobility," "sanitation," and "waste," and further categorizes them according to their climate change focus: "climate plan," "adaptation," "cooperation," and "mitigation." As a result, measures for adapting to climate change are incorporated into other urban development activities in Manaus. Having said that, statements expressly related to mitigating the negative consequences of climate change are not made. Of particular relevance, however, is that a connection is consistently drawn between the climate of the city and the climate of the surrounding rainforest. One study even points out that nitrogen oxides emitted by vehicular traffic and industry in Manaus affect the climate of the rainforest by impairing rain formation. In this respect, the development of an emissions register, systematic climate measurements, and projections of the expected effects of climate change on the city would represent important first steps towards building resilience to climate change on the one hand, and protecting the ecosystems of the Amazon Basin on the other.

AMAZONIA

The name Amazonia or Amazon Basin refers to both the river system and the Amazon rainforest that is so vital for the world's climate. While the entire area covers about 7.5 million square kilometers, some 5.5 million square kilometers thereof are tropical rainforest. About 60 percent of this area lies in Brazil, with other parts in neighboring Peru, Colombia, Venezuela, Ecuador, Bolivia, Guyana, Suriname, and French Guiana. In Brazil, the Amazon Basin covers, in addition to the state of Amazonas, part or all of the states of Acre, Amapá, Maranhão, Mato Grosso, Pará, Rondônia, Roraima, and Tocantins. In total, it accounts for almost two-thirds of Brazil's land area.

Of the roughly 30 million people populating the Amazon Basin, 17 million live in Brazil. More than 2.7 million belong to Indigenous peoples, and in Brazil alone 220 different Indigenous peoples live in the Amazon Basin. Their settlement territories and protected natural areas account for about 45 percent of the total area. There are 180 different indigenous languages, and most Indigenous people also speak Portuguese. Outside the cities, the people live mainly from fishing, hunting, and the fruits of the vegetation, occasionally also from subsistence farming. The waters of the Amazon Basin account for one-fifth of all freshwater reserves on earth, and the Amazon River is the main river of this drainage basin, which is the largest in the world in terms of area. It also contains the largest volume of water in the world outside the oceans. Depending on precipitation, the water levels of the rivers can rise or fall by several meters. Even in the dry season,

the Amazon River is 10 to 20 kilometers wide, and during the rainy season, an additional 20 to 60 kilometers of riparian rainforest is flooded. Any development must therefore adapt to the widely varying water levels, and in zones prone to flooding, building is only possible on river embankments. The river is typically 30 to 40 meters deep, in some places up to 100 meters. About 30 percent of the known animal species of Amazonia live in and near the Amazon. Among the approximately 2,000 known freshwater fish species are piranhas, electric eels, and the river dolphin—revered as a sacred animal by the Indigenous people—which has a pink coloration on the underside of its body. The banks are also home to numerous water birds such as herons, storks, ibis, and spoonbills, all finding their food in the water.

Not only is the Amazon the world's largest contiguous landscape area but also its largest contiguous rainforest. It is estimated that about 10 percent of the planet's known animal and plant species live in the Amazon rainforest, and the degree of biodiversity is greater than anywhere else in the world. So far, tens of thousands of plant species have been identified and described, including countless medicinal plants, more than 2.5 million types of insects, 1,300 bird species, 430 kinds of mammals, and more than 3,000 fish species, as well as amphibians and reptiles—and new species are still being discovered. Since the flora grow in different interrelated layers, the ecosystem of the rainforest contains a particularly large biomass: the tallest trees are 60 to 80 meters high, below them grow the trees that can manage with less sunlight, while almost no sunlight reaches the ground. Hence, larger animals mostly stay in the high treetops in the light. Given this large biomass, it is surprising that the soil is not very fertile. The humus layer is only a few millimeters thick because nutrients are immediately utilized by animals and then absorbed and stored by plants. As a result, the soil of the Amazon rainforest is among the poorest and most infertile in the world. When cleared, it is only suitable for agricultural use for a limited period, before the soil gets depleted after just a few years. If the soil is then left to its own devices, however, the rainforest will not regrow back to its original state.

10
The vegetation is able to adapt to fluctuating water levels, as seen here in a tributary of the Rio Negro at high water.

188

11
The water level can vary by more than 12 m.

12
Buildings are constructed on firm ground above the flood line.

13
The banks and houses built on them are at risk of erosion from high water and heavy rains.

14
Many houses are built on stilts for safety, as water levels vary greatly over the year.

MANAUS

CLIMATE CHANGE IN THE AMAZON BASIN

Although the full influence of the Amazon rainforest and its importance to the world's climate is not yet fully known, there seems to be no doubt that, due to its size, abundance of water, and location near the equator, its significance for its wider surrounding environment and probably for the climate of the entire world must be immense. Due to the strong solar radiation throughout the year and the abundance of water, the rainforest produces enormous amounts of evaporation, which in turn has an evaporative cooling effect and creates clouds. The effect of the enormous cooling capacity extends a long way. As such, the Amazon Basin is also known as the "air conditioner of the earth." The clouds release rainfall mainly south of the Amazon, in the distant metropolitan areas of São Paulo and Rio de Janeiro, and in the agricultural areas of Brazil, Paraguay, and Argentina. Sometimes, this airborne water transportation is referred to as "flying rivers." Without the rainforest and its abundance of water, South America would bear similarity to Africa at the same latitude, with extensive deserts, semi-deserts, savannahs, and steppes.

In addition to directly affecting the weather and climate, the rainforest, like all forests, is an excellent carbon sink. During the day, the trees convert carbon dioxide (CO_2) into oxygen and sugars; when darkness falls at night—which is the same length as the day near the equator—the process is reversed, with slightly more CO_2 being sequestered than released overall. By and large, the Amazon River absorbs 5 percent of anthropogenic CO_2 emissions; the only part of the world to store significantly more is the ocean.

15
Giant water lilies *Victoria amazonica* *(regia)* grow naturally in wet clearings.

While the Indigenous peoples' use of the rainforest can be considered sustainable for the most part, modern Brazil has destroyed large parts of the rainforest through deforestation, fires, and slash-and-burn agriculture. To date, about 20 percent of the rainforest has already been cleared, primarily on the southern and eastern fringes. The following statistic illustrates the scale of the problem: 89 percent of the Amazon's greenhouse gas emissions are attributed to changes in land use, and only 3 percent to agricultural use. Even though emission levels declined for a while, they have started rising again since 2014.

The impact of rainforest destruction on Indigenous peoples, biodiversity, and the Amazon hydrological cycle is immense. Not only does clearing change the climatic function of the areas concerned, which are then typically used for agriculture or construction, it also changes a carbon sink into a carbon source. The additional CO_2 production emanating from the areas cleared in Brazil amounts to 1 to 2 gigatons of CO_2 per year. Given that global greenhouse gas emissions total 50 gigatons, this amount is very significant. The destruction of the rainforest has already led to a warming of 0.8 to 0.9 °C in the deforested region, and the dry or low-rainfall period has grown longer. If deforestation continues, a tipping point will be reached, irreversibly altering the entire regional climate. In all likelihood, the impact on carbon storage, biodiversity, and local, if not global, climate would be severe, and experts fear a decrease in precipitation and the drying up of the Amazon region. The effects would be felt far away, for example in São Paulo with its population of more than 20 million inhabitants. During the dry and hot summer of 2014 the lack of rainfall in São Paulo was attributed to deforestation of the Amazon rainforest and other forests near the city. Since then, the Paulistas, the inhabitants of São Paulo, have started to build water tanks and cisterns in order to be more independent in the event of future reductions of the urban water supply.

Studies have shown that after global warming of about 4 °C, the tipping point would be reached for the central, southern, and eastern Amazon, causing the forest to start to turn into savannahs. The scientists Thomas E. Lovejoy and Carlos Nobre estimate that the tipping point for the Amazon is 20 to 25 percent deforestation due to the negative synergies of clearing, climate change, and slash-and-burn agriculture. It is hard to determine exactly when this point will be reached, and we may only know once it has passed. Many indicators suggest that the tipping point is not far off. Exceptionally serious droughts occurred in 2005, 2010 and 2015/16, and these may be the first clear signs of climate change. And the opposite is also occurring more frequently than in the past: in 2009, 2012, 2014 and 2015, there were severe floods with water levels exceeding 29 meters. Since records of annual water levels started to be kept in 1902, such high levels have only occurred in 1909, 1922, and three times in the 1970s. The spate of extreme events over the past 20 years may indicate that the rainforest system is changing. In view of this, scientists and climate activists are pushing for the deforested area to remain below 20 percent of the total rainforest to avoid risking reaching or even exceeding the tipping point. At the 2015 climate conference in Paris, Brazil committed to reforesting 12 million hectares of forest by 2030, with much of this reforestation taking place in the southern and eastern Amazon, where the extent of clearance has been greatest to date, in order to preserve the wider-scale hydrological cycle and other positive effects of the rainforest.

A major influence on rainfall and the said hydrological cycles in the rainforest is the relationship of the two seas surrounding the continent, the equatorial Pacific in the west and the tropical Atlantic in the east. Here too, climate change is bringing more frequent unusual fluctuations—such as the effects of El Niño and La Niña, which have clearly impacted on the Amazon rainforest. For example, a whole series of droughts have been attributed to either warming in the eastern Pacific due to the El Niño phenomenon or warming in the tropical Atlantic. And the effects of climate change on trans-regional flow patterns may very well have an influence, too.

THE BOTANICAL GARDENS

The Adolpho Ducke Botanical Gardens in Manaus, also called the Museum of Amazonia (MUSA), are named after the Italian-born botanist and ethnologist, who died in 1959, and is essentially a showcase of the rainforest ecosystem. One of the most respected experts on the flora of Amazonia, Ducke had studied the tree system of the Amazon rainforest, documenting 900 species and 50 genera. The Botanical Garden is part of a 100-square-kilometer protected reserve of the rainforest, which also marks the boundary between the developed area of the city and the rainforest. Managed by the National Institute of Amazonian Research (INPA), the Botanical Garden is a 500-meter-wide and 5-kilometer-long strip on the edge of the forest reserve. Essentially a "living museum,"

16
Giant water lilies *Victoria amazonica (regia)* in the MUSA Botanical Garden.

the theme of the garden is the typical primary rainforest, its plants, animals, and Indigenous peoples. Displays and exhibits describe the habitats and systems of the rainforest in the museum building and in the natural environment of the Garden. Special attractions include a lake in which the impressive giant water lilies *Victoria amazonica (regia)* grow, a maze of paths through the different ecosystems of the forest including explanations of trees and flora, and a 42-meter-high observation tower with three viewing platforms at different heights for observing the different layers of the forest. From the very top, one has an impressive view of the expanse of the rainforest, where the trees grow to about 40 meters high.

An additional archaeological and ethnographic collection also details numerous aspects of the lives of the rainforest's various Indigenous peoples. Apart from that, a corresponding archaeological and ethnological research center attached to the museum is dedicated to preserving the archaeological heritage of the Amazon and researching the way of life and cultural knowledge of Indigenous ethnic groups. Under the motto "Living Together," the museum works to preserve the cultural, biological, and social diversity of the Amazon Basin and to promote interaction between Indigenous communities and modern Brazil.

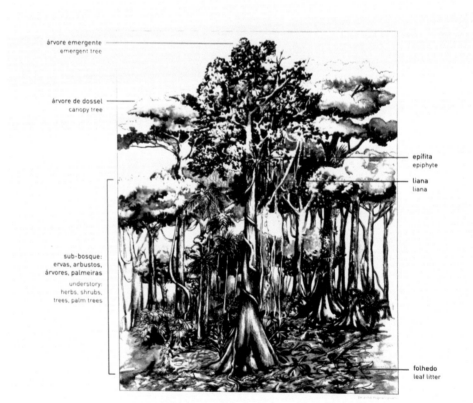

17
A display panel in the MUSA Botanical Garden, explaining the layers of plant growth in the rainforest.

18–22
Views from the observation tower in the MUSA Botanical Garden. The tower begins at the base of the trees and extends high above the treetops, making it possible to view successive levels of the rainforest and the forest from above.

193

THE BOTANICAL GARDENS

THE INPA AND THE ATTO RESEARCH PROJECT

The National Institute of Amazonian Research (INPA) was founded in 1952 and is renowned around the world for its research on the natural environment and socioeconomic living conditions of the Amazon. Initially, it focused on studying the flora and fauna of the region, whereas today the focus lies primarily on the sustainable use of natural resources and the interrelationships between climate and environment, with specific research fields encompassing ecological dynamics, society, environment and health, technology and innovation, and biodiversity. Using models and large-scale experiments, researchers undertake predictive modeling of the future climate of the rainforest, including the area of the city of Manaus. Its urban climate modeling aims in particular to identify ways to reduce the urban heat island effect resulting from climate change.

The research institute itself lies in an interesting section of the forest with rich regional flora. Plants are labeled with their botanical name and potential pharmaceutical uses, and its waters are home to animals such as otters, turtles, and manatees, the largest animals living in fresh water.

About 150 kilometers direct northeast of Manaus in a still largely undisturbed part of the rainforest lies the Brazilian-German research station Amazon Tall Tower Observatory (ATTO). Founded in 2009 by INPA, the University of Amazonia (UEA), and the German Max Planck Institutes for Chemistry and Biogeochemistry, this collaborative project has been scientifically studying the Amazon rainforest and its interaction with the climate. Alongside research facilities at ground level and lab containers, the centerpiece for data collection is a 325-meter-high tower and two 80-meter-high research masts. These are used to study meteorological and atmospheric processes, fluxes in trace gases and aerosols, matter life cycles in plants, and a variety of other ecosystem aspects at different heights within and above the treetops of the rainforest. The tallest tower has been in place since 2015, and INPA estimates it will take 10 to 20 years to obtain sufficient useful data. Their findings will be used to improve climate models and understand the importance of the Amazon Basin for the Earth's climate system.

23 (opposite page)
View into the crowns of the trees from the observation tower in the MUSA Botanical Garden.

CONSEQUENCES OF THE DESTRUCTION OF LARGE PARTS OF THE RAINFOREST

Unique in both its characteristics and its dimensions, the rainforest completely surrounds the city of Manaus. As such, it plays an absolutely fundamental role for the city's climate and how it will change in future. To date, Manaus has undertaken little to prepare for climate change. The free trade zone has fueled rapid urban growth, and the city has focused accordingly on providing housing and public infrastructure. However, its position in the middle of the rainforest makes it all the more important for Manaus to develop a sustainable approach to climate change adaptation, both to maintain good living conditions and to ensure continued preservation of the tropical rainforest.

The destruction of the Amazon rainforest has been ongoing for decades despite open knowledge of the enormous negative consequences this has and despite ever more urgent warnings by scientists, environmental activists, and citizens' initiatives. Deforestation, often through slash-and-burn, mostly affects the eastern and southern edges of Amazonia, for example in the Brazilian states of Para and Mato Grosso. Here one can already see the feared and predicted formation of dry savannahs. Key players responsible for deforestation are stakeholders in agriculture, agriculture-related industries, and mining, as well as their organizations or parties at a political level who ensure their interests are upheld. These groups largely dispute the negative consequences of deforestation for the climate, or simply place their own, shortsighted business goals above the long-term common good.

24
The extent of areas used for mining minerals in the rainforest only really becomes apparent from the air.

In 2019, the Brazilian state of Para alone saw a 30 percent increase in logging in just one year. Critics attribute this to the change in federal government on January 1, 2019, when the newly elected right-wing conservative President Jair Bolsonaro took office. And indeed, the new government has since shown greater interest in more intensive economic exploitation of land in rainforest areas, especially the mining of mineral resources, as well as a much lower inclination to protect it. Existing mechanisms are being undermined by decisions such as the transfer of responsibility for defining Indigenous territories and the Brazilian Forestry Agency to the Ministry of Agriculture, the affiliation of the National Water Agency with the Ministry of Regional Development, the closure of the Climate Change Council, and the downsizing of the Environment Council. In essence, climate change has largely disappeared from the federal government's policy agenda and is either downplayed or seen as inevitable. Instead, permits are being granted for large-scale agriculture and mining projects, hydropower plants and the like in rainforests and Indigenous protected areas. Revisions made to land use plans now favor agricultural interests.

In addition, most of the agricultural land is not even used to grow food for the regional population. Instead, the majority is used to cultivate soybeans for the globalized agricultural economy or for cattle breeding. The cattle, likewise, are not bred for local consumption but predominantly for export, either as live animals or as beef. Soy is exported primarily as livestock feed for fattening animals around the world. After the land has been cleared for large-scale agricultural use, new roads are being built, and with farming come pesticides and veterinary medicines. In fact, since 2019, 239 new chemicals have been approved for agricultural use in Brazil and, according to Greenpeace, 43 percent of these are highly toxic with correspondingly harmful effects for human and animal health.

25, 26

The majority of climate experts agree that preserving the Amazon rainforest is of major importance for the climate of Brazil, and for South America as a whole, and probably also plays a significant role in balancing the global climate. Even though much still needs to be done to fully understand its systems and interactions, it is clear that this unique landscape needs protecting as effectively, quickly, and comprehensively as possible. In this context, the work of modern science is often given more credit and accorded greater value than the knowledge of the Indigenous people who live in the region. Given that they have lived in the rainforest for several thousands of years and have learned to use their natural environment sustainably over a very long time, their traditional experiential knowledge should be regarded as a valuable resource and preserved accordingly. In fact, Indigenous cultures generally possess a wealth of knowledge about the animals and plants in their habitat, which can enrich modern scientific understanding, for example, when using plants and roots as remedies. More than anything, though, modern Western society can perhaps learn most from the basic attitude of Indigenous peoples toward the rainforest, which is one of mindfulness rather than a desire for domination and exploitation.

A further important factor in protecting the rainforest is politics, and in the case of the Amazon rainforest, that also means international politics. Brazil must be able to count in the long term on the international support it already receives, especially from the global North. This ranges from Brazil's inclusion in international institutions and support for local NGOs, to import bans on products that damage the rainforest and, just as importantly targeted publicity campaigns.

Finally, to return to Manaus: Amazonia's largest city will benefit in the long run from rainforest protection. In the near future, however, work is needed to ensure that the well over 2 million citizens who live in Manaus are better protected against the effects of climate change, and that the city becomes more resilient to the impacts of probable extreme weather events such as floods and droughts. While essential, studying and mitigating the effects on the urban climate does however not constitute adapting to climate change. Green infrastructure needs to be expanded, retention areas for stormwater need to be created, drought-tolerant vegetation must be selected, and existing parks need to be retrofitted to make them more resilient to climate change so that severe weather events such as heavy rainfalls do not cause significant damage.

25, 26
The 53,421 m² Parque Senador Jefferson Péres near the Palácio Rio Negro arose as part of the restoration and uncovering of previously filled-in streams *(igarapés)*. This allows rainwater to flow away without causing lasting damage to the park, even during heavy rainfall.

MANAUS

BRASÍ
LIA

Brazil's capital is a new city planned on the drawing board in 1956 and officially established just four years later in 1960. Initially only the major infrastructure was completed, and other government and municipal buildings were built in the following years. Although the idea of a new capital city centrally located in the interior of the country had been enshrined in the first republican constitution in 1891, it did not come to fruition until 1956 when the then President Juscelino Kubitschek made it reality. The site of the new city was strategically chosen to stimulate development in the interior of Brazil. As early as 1950, an area of 5,800 square kilometers was selected in the central highlands on the border between the states of Goiás and Minas Gerais. This is now the Federal District, *Distrito Federal do Brasil*, and corresponds exactly to the municipality of Brasília, which today comprises 31 administrative regions. Since 1997, the core area of Brasília, which is called Plano Piloto and encompasses the area of the initial design by the urban planner Lúcio Costa, has been an independent administrative region. The Federal District is largely responsible for administrating both the levels of the city and the state, and there are joint legislative and executive branches of government with the governor simultaneously performing the function of the mayor. Some state functions are also performed by the federal government. Originally designed for 500,000 inhabitants, it now has a population of 3 million and an estimated 4.4 million in the wider metropolitan region. Today the third-largest city in the country, Brasília's population continues to grow, though Brasília is not one of Brazil's fastest-growing cities.

The city's name derives from the name of the country, which in turn derives from the national tree Pau Brasil (*Caesalpina echinata*) and its amber-colored wood ("brasil" is the Portuguese word for "amber"). Mainly found in Atlantic coastal forests, the tree has great civilizational and cultural significance because of the color and resilience of its wood. In the past, dye was extracted from the wood, which today is mostly used to fabricate the bows of musical instruments. The bark and the natural dye continue to be used in medicine. Accordingly, research is being conducted into whether the tree extracts have medicinal properties suitable for the treatment of cancer.

The anthem of the capital heralds the city as the "City of Hope," and indeed, moving the federal government to a newly planned city untainted by historical burdens was a symbol of great hope for the future of the country and its political system. In addition, modern urban planning promised to provide better living and working conditions. It represented an opportunity to overcome the cramped living conditions, limited public outdoor and green space, and poor ventilation typically seen in cities that have evolved over longer time periods.

A cross in the center with four diverging arrows, starting in the middle and pointing in all directions, symbolizes the radiation of politics, i.e. the National Congress, into the country. At the same time, the motto "Venturis Ventis" (coming winds) also refers to the theme of expectations for the future.

2

1 (previous page)
Model of the city of Brasília in the administrative region of Plano Piloto. The National Congress is in the foreground in the middle of the central axis running vertically, flanked by the ministries. Crossing it is the arc of the axis with the residential quarters, the *supercuadras*.

2
The coat of arms of the city of Brasília.

An urban planning ideas competition was held to determine the master plan for the new capital along with designs for the individual buildings, the results of which were presented in 1957. Of particular importance was that the competition be held among Brazilian urban planners and architects. Amidst the background of that time, the intention was to develop Brazil's own formal language and autonomy that expressed both modernity as well as efficiency. Following the competition, Lúcio Costa was selected as the urban planner and Oscar Niemeyer as principal architect of the new city of Brasília, while major green spaces and gardens were designed by Roberto Burle Marx. From the arrangement of buildings, streets, and open spaces to the formal characteristics of the architecture and gardens—this team set about the comprehensive planning of the city, starting out from optimal circumstances that otherwise would not have been possible in cities already well developed.

The urban design is strongly influenced by the principles of Modernism and the Athens Charter, written in 1933 during the IV International Congress of Modern Architecture (*Congrès Internationaux d'Architecture Moderne*, CIAM) and published in Paris in 1943 by Le Corbusier, under whose direction it had been developed. The Charter was a response to the problems facing many cities since the turn of the 20th century: rising population density and insufficient open space in central areas of cities, air pollution caused by trade and industry, uneven availability of housing, and ever greater distances to surrounding nature caused by urban sprawl. The model of the functional city designed according to the principles of modern town planning, as set out by Le Corbusier and others in the Athens Charter, was intended to prevent the well-known problems of the 19th-century city from ever occurring in the new Brazilian capital. In this ideal arrangement, administrative, business, consumer, and cultural facilities were to be established in the city center, while residential, industrial and commercial areas were to be located around the center but separate from one another. The various sectors were connected to each other by roads, but with green space between them, whereas satellite towns in the periphery would serve solely as housing. Many cities and districts around the world were planned or developed along the lines of the Athens Charter with the express intention of improving housing conditions and creating more green space in the cities. At the same time, however, the separation of urban functions disrupted the traditional fabric of cities and, more seriously, led to an increase in private vehicular traffic and public transportation use. As a result, congestion, air pollution, and other impacts grew and are now well-known as symptoms of functional urban planning in many cities.

The initial idea from which the layout of Brasília sprung was a cross drawn by Lúcio Costa that probably denotes an existing intersection of two roads in the open landscape where the new city was to be built. At the intersection of these two main axes Costa positioned the bus station. Placed along the east-west axis—the so-called Monumental Axis—were the government buildings, the ministries, the National Congress with the Senate and the House of Representatives, the Presidential Palace, and the Supreme Court, and in the opposite direction, the TV Tower. At over 300 meters wide, the axis has two-way traffic with several lanes of traffic in each direction and wide lawns in between, with additional water features near the TV Tower and at the National Congress.

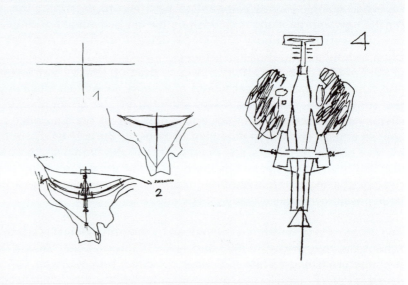

The north-south axis—the residential axis—is not quite as wide as the Monumental Axis and curves slightly with the topography. Likewise flanked by broad lawns planted with groups of trees and shrubs, it is lined by a succession of so-called *supercuadras* or superblocks, neighborhoods for up to 5,000 residents each. The uniformly designed residential buildings are often raised off the ground to allow public space to pass beneath and to create partially shaded areas. Each *supercuadra* is 300 × 300 meters, and four such blocks form a neighborhood unit with amenities for everyday needs, restaurants, and public spaces, all reached via a primary access road from the main traffic axis. Once one is accustomed to the principle, orientation is easy since all the neighborhoods are laid out similarly.

3
Initial sketches of the plan for the city by Lúcio Costa.

4
The Monumental Axis of Brasília from the National Congress in the background to the Rodoviário bus station that is located at the intersection of the two main axes. Between the two roads lies a broad expanse of green. The artificial Lago Paranoá can be seen in the very background.

BRASÍLIA

5–9
A residential *supercuadra* with open shaded green areas, large trees, and places to sit outdoors. The partially elevated buildings provide shade, allow air to circulate, and connect the outdoor areas around the buildings.

BRASÍLIA

The *supercuadras* are connected to each other by the main expressway with its extensive green space. From within a neighborhood unit, the city appears relatively compact, with greenery close by and short distances to shops and other facilities. Overall, however, the city is very sprawling and almost impossible to experience without a car—partly due to the long distances involved, and partly due to a lack of pedestrian and cycle paths. By and large, the expanses of green space are kept in good condition, with lawns mowed and hedges trimmed, and they serve as a pleasant backdrop for motorists, conveying the impression of a well-kept city in the countryside.

Many of the major public buildings and government facilities are striking Modernist structures built of concrete in sculptural forms. Some have accompanying water features that increase local air humidity and create a more pleasant microclimate for spending time outdoors. For example, in 1991, a large pool of water was added in front of the east face of the Congresso Nacional, the parliament building with the downward-arcing domed roof for the Senate and the upward-arcing bowl-shaped roof for the Chamber of Deputies in the center of the Monumental Axis. The ministries line up in identical-looking blocks of equal size on either side of the Monumental Axis to the west. Only the Ministry of Justice and the Ministry of Foreign Affairs have their own distinct architecture and lie between the National Congress and the other ministries, indicating the special importance of these two institutions for the country's political system. These two buildings are also surrounded by water, and the arcade of the Ministry of Justice, the Palácio da Justiça, even features a sequence of waterfalls. By comparison, the Ministry of Foreign Affairs, the Palácio Itamaraty, is surrounded on three sides by a water basin, with an open garden area separating it from the rear street space as well as a semi-open roof garden. Both gardens were designed by Roberto Burle Marx.

As the first contemporary architectural monument of its kind, the entire administrative district, the *Plano Piloto*, was accorded World Heritage status by the UNESCO in 1987. The monumentality of the public buildings, the quality of the residential areas, the picturesque character of the open spaces, and the character of housing with its community building qualities for diverse social groups are to be protected.

Since it was founded, Brasília has grown considerably and many of the new neighborhoods bear little relation to Lúcio Costa's plan, arising either as informal settlements or as independent satellite towns. Political upheavals such as the military dictatorship between 1964 and 1985, as well as economic crises and new urban planning philosophies have prevented the consistent extension of the city in the Modernist style. The ambitious vision could only be realized at the beginning. Meanwhile, the monofunctional zoning of the districts, its huge dimensions, and the subsequent dependency on vehicular transportation are now seen as weaknesses of the city's planning. Even Lúcio Costa and Oscar Niemeyer are said to have later critically questioned some aspects of the "experiment."

Brasília is located on Brazil's central plateau in the mid-west of the country, 1,000 to 1,200 meters above sea level in the highland steppe known as the Cerrado. With pronounced rainy and dry seasons and an annual precipitation of 1,500 to 1,700 millimeters, the Cerrado has a semi-humid tropical climate. It constitutes

10 (opposite page)
A so-called *cobogó*, seen here at the bottom right of the picture, serves as an air-permeable screen for residential buildings.

11, 12
The Parliament building, or Congresso Nacional, seen from the south: the smaller, convex dome houses the Senate Chamber and the larger, concave bowl the Chamber of Deputies. The view from the north shows the two 28-story office towers—one for each chamber—with the water basin in front, which was added in 1991.

BRASÍLIA

13
The Ministry of Justice, Palácio da Justiça, with its great arcades, the water basin, and concrete waterfalls in front of the facade.

14
The waterfalls emerging from the front of the facade of the Ministry of Justice.

15, 16
The building of the Ministry of Foreign Affairs with its large arcades is surrounded by a water basin with plants. The planting beds are located on beds created in the water.

17
The semi-open roof garden of the Ministry of Foreign Affairs, a much-vaunted example of Roberto Burle Marx's garden design.

18
The garden inside the building transitions directly into the adjacent outdoor space.

BRASÍLIA

the second-largest biome in South America and is the most species-rich savannah in the world with more than 10,000 plant and 200 mammal species, as well as a large number of birds, fish, reptiles, and amphibians. This species composition is adapted to the intermittently dry climate and nutrient-poor soils. Likewise adapted to living in the highland steppe are the Cerrado's more than 80 Indigenous peoples who have existed in a sustainable manner for many generations.

Due to land use demands of mechanized agriculture and related industries, the Cerrado's ecosystem is under massive threat. More and more of the originally forested savannah landscape is being cleared for monoculture farming such as soy, corn, and cotton, for planting monocultural forests for pulp and charcoal production, or for creating new pastureland. A further factor that contributes greatly to the destruction is the building of dams. Every year, some 30,000 of the originally almost 2 million square kilometers of land are lost, and today only about 55 percent of the Cerrado has its original primary vegetation.

The climate in Brasília is tropical, with an annual mean temperature of 20.6 °C, varying over the year between 13 °C and 28 °C, although the diurnal temperature fluctuation can be greater than seasonal temperature differences over the year. Annual precipitation totals 1,500 millimeters, with a dry season from May to August, and a rainy season with usually short and heavy rains from October to April.

Another key aspect of Brasília's climate is the frequently low relative humidity of less than 30 percent. In the rainy season, it averages 70 percent, but in the dry season, which can last up to five months, it can be much lower with higher temperatures. With this in mind, a large artificial lake, Lago Paranoá, was created when the city was built in order to increase humidity levels. Stretching from south to north around the east edge of the main city, it is fed by the river of the

19
The landscape of the Caatinga near Brasília.

same name and its tributaries. The lake has three islands, a total surface area of 48 square kilometers, and an average depth of 12 meters, extending to 38 meters at its deepest point.

EFFECTS OF CLIMATE CHANGE

The document "Climate Change in the Federal District and the Integrated Development Region," published by the Distrito Federal government in 2016, contains climate data for Brasília from 1960 to 2010 along with projections for future trends of the climate parameters temperature and precipitation until 2100. Besides a broad overview of the risks posed by climate change, the document also refers to reports by the UN's Intergovernmental Panel on Climate Change (IPCC), which describes global warming for the period 1901 to 2012 for the different regions of the world. On the continents temperatures have increased by up to 2.5 °C, much more than the oceans, where temperatures have gone up by 0.8 °C. Temperature increases for Brazil over the same period correspond in amplitude to the continents—2.5 °C in most urbanized regions—but are much less in the densely forested Amazon region, at between 0.6 and 0.8 °C. For this reason, the Amazon Basin is one of the regions with the lowest rates of global warming in the world.

For Brasília, the numbers of days per year with low relative humidity (30 percent or less) has increased over the last 50 years from an average of 24 to 50 days per year. The temperature amplitude between daily maximum and minimum temperatures has decreased by almost 2 °C. Less pronounced were changes in precipitation levels. Brasília has, however, seen an increase in extreme rain events and storms, some of which are strong enough to uproot trees and cause damage to buildings. At the same time, for example in 2014 and 2015, there were also extreme droughts with high temperatures and exceptionally low relative humidity levels, at times as little as 10 percent. Such levels are not just stressful in bioclimatic terms, but also significantly increase the risk of fire. In 2016, there were more than 17,000 outbreaks of fire in the Cerrado savannah, the highest level in five years, and more than 17,000 hectares of savannah and agricultural land were destroyed. In view of this, a state of emergency was declared for agriculture in the Federal District in June 2016, and corn harvests alone were estimated to be 70 percent lower than expected. Finally, in November 2016, water was rationed due to the drought in Brasília.

In 2009, the Brazilian government introduced a National Plan on Climate Change and also established a Panel on Climate Change (PBMC), to which 360 scientists and researchers belong. Its task is to study how Brazil can respond to global warming and its consequences in a proactive and responsible manner. In 2015, the PBMC produced a *First National Report on Climate Change* (*Primeiro Relatório de Avaliação Nacional sobre Mudanças Climáticas—RAN1*), on which the Federal District's document on climate change is based. *RAN1* details trends for mean temperature and precipitation levels over successive 30-year periods in this century for the six Brazilian regions of Amazonia, Atlantic, Pantanal, Caatinga, Cerrado, and Pampas. Based on model calculations, these predictions detail changes in levels relative to the reference period 1961–1990, given an increase in CO_2 levels in the atmosphere. For northeast Brazil, the results indicate an increase in temperature and a significant reduction in precipitation. By the end of the 21st century, temperatures may rise between 2 °C and 6 °C in this region, mainly during spring. For the Brasília region, precipitation is forecast to decrease over the course of the 21st century, especially during the wet season, as there is already little rainfall in the dry season, although the scale of reduction is still rather vague. The analysis suggests a trend towards longer dry seasons, with precipitation occurring increasingly in concentrated heavy rainfall events.

By 2040 the Cerrado is expected to experience a 1 °C increase in temperature and a decrease in precipitation of between 10 and 20 percent. In the years up to 2070, thus the predictions, temperatures will rise by 3 to 3.5 °C and precipitation decrease by 20 to 35 percent. Finally, by the end of the century, the temperature increase will reach values between 5 °C and 5.5 °C, while precipitation will decrease between 35 and 45 percent.

Compared with the goals set out in the 2015 Paris Climate Agreement, in which a maximum temperature increase of no more than 2 °C was agreed, such levels of warming with a simultaneous reduction in rainfall represents a dramatic scenario. With rising temperatures, the photosynthetic capacities of the plants of the Cerrado are expected to decrease, in turn resulting in a decline in biomass. Also, if water availability decreases drastically, as the model calculations suggest, extreme and prolonged droughts will follow, increasing the risk of fire still further. In such cases the Cerrado adds to the carbon burden on the atmosphere due to lack of water.

The *Report on Climate Change* is aimed at decision-makers and raises the important question of how Brasília, a city with more than a million inhabitants, can become more climate-resilient and, given its location in a sensitive natural area, how it can limit the effects of climate change to which it is exposed. In the preface of the document, André Lima, then Minister of the Environment and President of the Environment Council, already points to non-climatic factors that contribute to the magnitude of the impact. This includes the water shortage, which is rooted in excessive consumption and in weaknesses in the water collection and distribution system. Also, due to increasing land use and sealing in the Cerrado, the water absorption capacity of the soils is greatly affected, so that the Minister calls for better conservation of water to protect headwaters and replenish groundwater. In addition, new methods of water conservation and harvesting must be exploited. He specifically warns that the ecosystem infrastructure needs to be preserved and restored, and asks how much green infrastructure will be needed to mitigate the negative impacts of climate change.

Because the predictions are based on model calculations with a grid cell resolution of 20 × 20 kilometers, the document calls for the findings to be scaled up to regional standards and for the results to be reevaluated accordingly. This would provide decision-makers in politics and administration with a more precise basis for their actions. Following up on the conclusions of the measurements and forecasts through the introduction of laws and regulations to bring about changes in land use and reduce the consequences of climate change is an important task for the future.

ECOVILA ALDEIA DO ALTIPLANO

Naturally, every city needs a functioning infrastructure to supply its inhabitants with food. In the best-case scenario, this food comes from the surrounding area and reaches consumers soon after harvesting or processing thanks to short transport routes that in turn limit emissions. An exemplary initiative in this context is the Aldeia ecovillage, founded by Fabiana Peneireiro in 2015 near Brasília, just 20 kilometers from the National Congress. Run on a solidarity-based principle, the farm operates as an agroforestry venture. Peneireiro's objective is to grow healthy food in harmony with the goals of conserving and developing the landscape. Due to its proximity to the city, it is closely linked to its consumers, who are mainly people who want to know where and how their food is produced, and who have chosen to patronize this sensitive but also strenuous way of farming: Peneireiro's agroforestry approach combines the cultivation of woody plants, i.e., trees, shrubs, or perennials, with arable crops of herbaceous vegetable or fodder plants. The so-called "New Forest Code" of 2012, which in principle aims to protect the country's forests against economic interests, though controversial in many detailed provisions, permits agroforestry as a means of restoring ecosystems as long as it maintains or improves the basic ecological functions of the area in question. All interventions must benefit people and other living things. Hence, agroforestry has been legally recognized and given a role in food production.

Fabiana Peneireiro has written several scientific publications, including a technical guide on how to reconcile ecosystem conservation with food production in the semi-arid landscape of the Cerrado and Caatinga areas of northeast Brazil. Now part of Brazil's new Forest Code, this guidance is being applied by agricultural education institutions throughout the country. At home in Aldeia, Peneireiro not only dedicates herself to the sustainable production of agricultural products, but also takes the time to explain her concept of solidarity-based and sustainable agroforestry in a clear and detailed manner to guests, professional colleagues, and other interested parties. Her goal is to create a balance between economy and ecology based on a knowledge of plant successions and the characteristics of local ecosystems. By constantly alternating the variants of edible crops that are relevant to the local ecosystem, one not only expands the resources for further plant growth but can also use them to restore a plant community after damage. In agroforestry, certain species are given the opportunity to develop over a longer period of time, while others have a shorter lifespan, perish, and form humus for subsequent species, with their root systems remaining in the soil. These different life cycles correspond to the natural dynamics of the habitat and its requirements for light, moisture, temperature, nutrients, and other growth factors. As plants grow to different heights, this can be taken into account through mixed planting: some plants need ample sunlight and grow taller while others thrive better in the shade. The combination of different plants optimizes the use of space as well as the use of resources such as water, light, nutrients, and soil organisms. Although agroforestry is labor-intensive, it is also very productive—and can exist in harmony with the natural environment.

An important part of the social and economic dimension of solidarity agriculture is having a reliable consumer base. Committing themselves to buying the products over a certain period and paying a fixed, pre-calculated price, the patrons

20

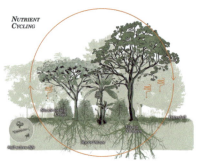

21
22

2 to 3 years

7 to 10 years

23

20
The natural environment of Ecovila Aldeia do Altiplano.

21
The water and nutrient cycle. Mixed crop cultivation and carefully timed planting reduce the economic risks of dependence on a single crop season, and the incidence of pest infestation or disease.

22
Coordinated tree planting makes optimal use of the resources of water, sunlight, and nutrients.

23
Intensive cultivation adapted to the Cerrado and the development of plants as part of the agroforestry venture.

BRASÍLIA

24
Fabiana Peneireiro shows off the fruits of her labors.

25, 26
Fruit and vegetables ready for pickup by the consumers on Saturdays. The produce varies depending on the season and yield.

27
Mixed crop cultivation in Fabiana Peneireiro's agroforestry concept.

28
Rainwater is collected.

ECOVILA ALDEIA DO ALTIPLANO

pick up their freshly harvested food every Saturday. While they get to know the community and the place of production, they themselves also have the opportunity to work, plant, and harvest. Needless to say, the produce varies with the season and ranges from bananas, papayas, lemons, squash, cassava, lettuce, arugula, kale, almonds, string beans, tomatoes, and cilantro. While the producer does not bear the entire risk, consumers receive regular, healthy, and fresh local produce, and the region is sustainably managed and developed. For this system to succeed in the long term to the benefit of everyone, prices for food must be fair. The primary motivation of the various participants is not to pay less for food, or to earn more by farming. Their main interest is in helping each other, solving problems together, sharing their knowledge, and making things happen that are beneficial to the community and the landscape.

THE UNIVERSITY OF BRASÍLIA

Only two years after the city was founded, the University of the Federal District was opened. Its founding director was the ethnologist and writer Darcy Ribeiro, after whom the main building is now named. Ribeiro, who died in 1997, is considered one of Brazil's most important scholars of the 20th century. Called the Central Institute of Sciences (ICC), the university's main building was designed, like most of the important buildings in the administrative district, by Oscar Niemeyer. Its long construction time from 1963 to 1971 is a factor of the building's size: it is an unusually long building, extending for almost 700 meters, and comprises two long parallel volumes that start straight, curve in the middle and end straight again, rather like the main axis of the city plan. The logo of the university reflects the building's shape.

The two building volumes are made of precast concrete elements that were assembled on site, an innovative construction method at that time. Spaced 3 meters apart, concrete fins project up to 30 meters into the air, connecting the different parts of the buildings. A main access corridor for pedestrians runs along the inner edge of these long volumes at ground level flanked by a long strip of garden, while car access and deliveries are located below ground. The gardens were designed by the garden architects Miguel Alves Pereira, Nelson Saraiva dos Santos, and Paulo de Melo Zimbres, and the building shields them from dry winds and helps improve the humidity in the central area through plant transpiration.

Considering that the building's design reflects Niemeyer's interpretation of Modernism, it is a child of its time both architecturally and as a reflection of the political-educational attitudes of the 1960s. Then, the anthropologist Darcy Ribeiro and educator Anísio Teixeira had envisaged an educational concept that would be free, state-organized, secular, and tailored to the needs of a country developing into a modern industrial nation. The university, both building and institution, was to be structured in such a flexible way that it could respond to and accommodate new perspectives. A further important aspect was financial autonomy that should enable the university to develop freely and independently. To this day, the university's founding document, the Magna Charta from 1962,

remains valid. At the outset, practically the entire institution was located in the main building, which incorporated several faculties, but over the decades the university has grown considerably, and many more buildings have since been added in the spacious university grounds.

Another structure that is notable for its striking architecture is the Rectory. It comprises two cuboid volumes set slightly apart, between which is a space covered by a deep, open concrete grid ceiling, and traversed by a series of access ramps. The open courtyard is planted with diverse vegetation and has a water basin. Further water basins are placed in front of the two building sections facing the prevailing wind so that air blowing towards the structure carries moisture from the pools, adding to the evapotranspiration cooling effect of the vegetation. In early 2019, however, the water basins had no water in them, and retrofitted air-conditioning units were clearly visible, suggesting that the natural cooling mechanism is no longer sufficient to cool the building. It is not clear whether this should be attributed to rising maximum daily temperatures caused by climate change, or whether the pools were defective, or whether the users' climate comfort expectations had risen. Given that the pools were dry during the rainy reason, it is unlikely that their climatic cooling effect will be utilized or be deemed sufficient during the dry season. Precisely in the dry period, the grass in the city and the campus dries out and the trees have no foliage, so do not transpire. Consequently, plant transpiration cannot contribute to natural cooling and humidity levels in the dry months.

29
Model of the University of Brasília. The main building is particularly striking due to its size and long, curved shape.

THE UNIVERSITY OF BRASÍLIA

216

30
Shaded and greened connecting walkway between the two parts of the main building.

31
A broad green strip extends the length of the building between the two elongated wings of the main building.

BRASÍLIA

Maintaining partnerships with universities around the world, the University of Brasília is considered one of the best in the country. In fact, out of its roughly 43,000 students, 1,000 study architecture. Of particular interest in the context of climate change adaptation is the university's environmental institute Laboratório de Controle Ambiental (LACAM), headed by Professor Cláudia Naves David Amorim. As part of the Faculty of Architecture and Urban Development, it conducts research into sustainable architecture, the architectural bioclimate, natural and artificial lighting, thermal behavior, acoustics and energy efficiency of buildings, and the economical use of water in buildings. Also, LACAM is part of a Brazilian network that certifies the energy efficiency of buildings, which is mandatory in Brazil for public buildings.

32
The Rectory has recently had air-conditioning installed.

33
The water basins that were originally in front of the elevated Rectory allowed the breeze to carry moisture and cool air into the courtyard and the building. Sadly, without water they no longer serve their purpose.

BRASÍLIA

34, 35
The partly open and partly covered inner courtyard of the Rectory promotes airflow. Openings to the rooms and the vegetation in the courtyard are likewise carefully positioned. However, without water in the basin, there is no evaporation and no associated cooling.

THE UNIVERSITY OF BRASÍLIA

As a completely new city, the center of Brasília was designed according to the urban planning principles of the classical Modernist period with the aim of creating an ideal urban environment. Such ideals are frequently born out of a desire to remedy preceding negative experiences, like poor housing and living environments, long distances between the place of work and place of residence, and so on. In this respect, Brasília remains a compelling example of the uncompromising implementation of the modern ideas of the time.

This comprehensive urban plan also included the design of spacious public buildings surrounded by extensive green areas. The openness of these modern functional structures makes it possible to cool them largely without artificial air-conditioning. In addition, the strategic use of plants and water surfaces improves the humidity of the local microclimate in a region often prone to very dry humidity levels. By raising the *supercuadras*, the residential blocks off the ground, shaded outdoor areas have also been created in local living environments. This works for as long as the plants and water basins are maintained, but as soon as this is neglected and air-conditioning is used in its place, a negative spiral is set in motion. Energy consumption increases, thereby indirectly amplifying the effects of climate change, and as temperatures gradually rise, the energy required for cooling with air conditioners grows in turn. It is therefore now more important than ever to seek out less energy-intensive methods for maintaining tolerable temperature and humidity levels for people inside buildings and in outdoor areas.

Climate change presents Brasília with a considerable challenge. Despite the Minister of the Environment's call for more green infrastructure and measures to reduce water consumption, there is as yet little evidence of action in response to the findings of research and projections on climate change. The regional climate is characterized by highly pronounced dry seasons and at the same time Brasília is increasingly finding itself faced with water shortages while demand steadily increases, because the city is now much larger than it once was and is still growing. Other important issues that Brasília needs to address—as climate change continues—include stormwater management and new transportation concepts to cut down on private vehicle use, as people currently still rely heavily on their cars due to a lack of suitable alternatives.

MONTE VIDEO

Montevideo is the capital of the Oriental Republic of Uruguay, as the country—the second-smallest in South America—is officially known. Located in the country's extreme south, the city extends for 30 kilometers along the Río de la Plata, and its 1.4 million people make up about 40 percent of the population of the entire country. The name Uruguay comes from the vocabulary of the Guaraní, one of South America's Indigenous peoples, and means "river where the bird lives" or "river of painted birds." In fact, the rivers running through Uruguay strongly define and ensure the character of this country's green and very fertile interior. The largest of them is the Río Uruguay, which constitutes the country's western border with Argentina and, together with the Río Paraná, feeds the Río de la Plata, a 290-kilometer-long and up to 220-kilometer-wide estuary delta opening onto the Atlantic. By the time it reaches Montevideo the delta is already so wide that the opposite shore is no longer visible and the point at which it meets the open sea is practically indistinguishable.

Founded in the 1720s, Montevideo began to expand, from 1861 onwards, beyond the walled boundary of the densely built old town. The new quarters are more spacious, and the streets are lined by trees, often on both sides, that have since grown to a considerable height and provide ample shade. Culturally, Montevideo is known for its extremely long carnival season and its reputation, next to Buenos Aires, as the origin of the tango.

1 (previous page)
The promenade along the Río de la Plata is 18 km long and over great distances without trees. It is a popular place to stroll on summer evenings.

2
Seen from above, one can see that the trees that shade the street have grown taller than many of the buildings.

3
Large cassia trees provide sufficient shade for the street space.

4
A street thrown into pleasant shade by tall plane trees.

Since the 1950s, the country has been nicknamed the "Switzerland of South America." Uruguay is considered the safest, most politically and socially stable country in South America. Thanks to a broad middle class, prosperity is quite evenly distributed, and education and literacy rates are rather good. In its 100-year-old democracy, referendums rank highly and—unlike in Switzerland—women have been able to vote since 1937.

Agriculture is the country's most important economic sector, and over 80 percent of the agricultural land is used for cattle farming. Reportedly, Uruguay has four times more cattle than inhabitants. Most of the livestock is bred for meat production, with only a small proportion producing milk. Meat is produced for consumption within the country as well as for export, mainly to China and Europe. Also, a diverse range of agricultural crops, including cereals such as soy, rice, sesame, and corn, are cultivated for both food and animal feed. Other crops include tea, tobacco, cotton, grapes, fruit, and vegetables. Surprisingly, holly (*Ilex paraguariensis*) is not cultivated in Uruguay despite that fact that its leaves are used to prepare mate tea, which is drunk widely in public all over Montevideo.

The country's many green pastures are not the only clear indicator of the favorable agricultural conditions due to ample rainfall and warm temperatures. There is rarely ground frost in winter. Furthermore, the typical trade winds are also beneficial throughout the year, transporting moisture from the sea in summer and cooler, drier air from the interior in winter.

Montevideo, like the rest of the country, lies in the humid subtropical climate zone with warm temperatures and regular rainfall. The annual mean daily temperature is 21.5 °C, rising to a maximum mean of 28.5 °C in summer (November to April). For four months of the year daytime temperatures exceed 25 °C and sink to a mean minimum of 12.2 °C. Montevideo has an average of 7.7 hours of sunshine daily, slightly more in the summer months. The annual average relative humidity is 73.8 percent, rising only slightly in summer when it can reach 82 percent. At temperatures exceeding 25 °C, conditions can get quite muggy, with a relative humidity of more than 75 percent. In winter, the air is not too dry, rarely falling beneath the lower comfort limit of 35 percent at 25 °C. Rain falls throughout the year on an average of 5.9 days per month, slightly more in summer than in winter, but without distinct rainy and dry seasons. As is typical for its climate zone, Uruguay is experiencing increasingly frequent violent storms, especially in spring and fall.

Characteristic of the humid subtropical climatic region are semi-evergreen humid forests, laurel forests, swamp lands and upland prairies. In the humid forests, trees grow very densely and can reach heights of up to 50 meters. Like the rainforests, they form several layers though lack the same degree of biodiversity. Some animal species are native only to this habitat, including flamingos and certain alligators.

5, 6
Parks such as Parque Rodó provide a variety of green spaces and water features for sitting outside in the sun and also in the shade.

MONTEVIDEO

7 (opposite page)
Plane trees in the downtown Plaza de la Constitución provide welcome shade on warm, sunny days.

8, 9
In the old town, there are few trees due to the narrow streets. To remedy this, sections of the streetscape have been converted into parklets as places to sit. Bollards separate them from the roadway, and they are greened with planters arranged between the backs of the benches, thus separating the sections.

MONTEVIDEO

EFFECTS OF CLIMATE CHANGE

Although the country is responsible for only 0.15 percent of global greenhouse gas emissions, it is just as affected by climate change as other countries that produce higher levels of emissions. In 2017, the country committed to reducing emissions of the greenhouse gases CO_2, CH_4 and N_2O to the levels set out in the Paris Climate Agreement.

In Uruguay, more than 93 percent of the population live in cities and 70 percent in coastal areas. Since extreme climate events are more frequent and severe in urban areas, they potentially affect almost all the country's inhabitants, albeit to differing degrees. The Ministry of Environment's 2021 *National Adaptation Plan to Climate Change in Cities and Infrastructures* identifies droughts, floods, heat waves, hail, tornado storms, storm surges, and rising sea levels as impacts attributable to climate change. Already today, flooding is undeniably becoming more pronounced, along with the extent of the damage this causes to homes and roads. In 2015, for example, 20,000 people were temporarily required to leave their homes due to flooding. Other expected consequences of climate change include the emergence of new vector-borne diseases, transmitted through particular mosquito types, and a reduction in species biodiversity.

10
The shoreline and the ground floor zone of the buildings near the waterfront are at risk of flooding.

So far, Uruguay has seen a rise in sea level of almost 20 centimeters. Since 2000, there have been three or four severe storm surges, depending on estimates, with water levels of 3 meters or more above normal. Indeed, longer-term forecasts predict the possibility of a 1-meter rise in sea level and storm surges with waves up to four meters high. If these forecasts come to pass, the result would be massive flooding of the shores and promenades as well as adjacent urban areas of Montevideo. Likewise anticipated are increases in annual precipitation and especially heavy rainfall events.

In 2010, the government set up an interdisciplinary working group on climate change to elaborate how the city can adapt to mitigate the negative effects of climate change in the country, and in Montevideo in particular. Published in 2014, the city's first climate change plan, the *Montevideo Program on Climate Change*, is a response to the changes observed in the period from 2010 to 2014 and concentrates on reducing greenhouse gas emissions.

According to the climate change plan, areas with most CO_2 emissions correspond to those with the greatest concentration of informal settlements. The residents of these areas will also potentially be most affected by the negative impact of climate change because they have fewer of their own social and economic resources, including food and recreational opportunities, with which to counter the negative effects, damage and destruction. What's more, people are directly exposed to the natural risk of storms and rising sea levels due to a long stretch of coastline in that zone.

A climate action plan for the Montevideo metropolitan region with the neighboring towns of Canelones and San José had already been adopted at the sub-national level in 2012. Developed in cooperation with the United Nations Environment Programme (UNEP), the *Climate Action Plan* focused on reducing greenhouse gas emissions, emphasizing particularly the importance of involving local actors and residents, who, as those most familiar with local climatic conditions, were invited to participate in the actions. Basically, this approach sees climate change not solely as an environmental problem, but as a complex process of sustainable development. As such, it proposed coordinated action at environmental, economic, and social levels, and considers both positive and negative synergies with sustainability goals.

In May 2014, a newly created task force embarked on a participatory planning process to implement the measures set out in the resolutions of the *Climate Action Plan*. So far, more than 30 workshops have been organized with over 700 participants, ranging from key local stakeholders such as civic organizations to municipal experts and managers from local administration. Based on the results of the workshops, climate profiles were then developed as a "link" between greenhouse gas emissions and the results of the participatory processes. These were then supplemented with calculations from climate models and scenarios. In a subsequent step, possible options for reducing emissions and implementing corresponding adaptation measures were identified, discussed, and prioritized according to their cost-benefit ratio. Finally, all the studies, analyses and trade-offs were translated into a plan that sets out strategies for the region along with corresponding projects and tasks for the various stakeholders.

Four years later, in September 2018, the City of Montevideo published a *Resilience Strategy*, which has four key pillars: the first is urban development and transportation, the second, social equality and diversity, the third, a social and solidarity economy, and the fourth, environmental management. This last pillar encompasses using new technologies to prevent ecological impact from waste disposal, improving rural areas, strengthening civic commitment to environmental protection, and reducing risks by improving resilience. Certainly, Montevideo's public urban space is the obvious place in which to develop social and environmental resilience to climate change. For this purpose, a set of guidelines details the use of plants, biodiversity conservation, green infrastructure, and water-permeable pavements, along with better ways of using and overseeing public open spaces. Likewise, sustainable stormwater management is to be developed, based on experience already gained in pilot projects. This will include rain gardens, watercourse restoration, renewal of green spaces, permeable paving, green roofs, green city squares, and the creation of floodplain and retention areas. An initial selection of measures will be implemented in the urban areas most at risk of flooding. Furthermore, Montevideo is joining the Edible Cities Solutions Network, initially in an observing capacity to gain knowledge and ideas for the use of urban open spaces for food production.

Also in 2018, a three-year project began to develop the aforementioned *National Adaptation Plan to Cimate Change for Cities and Infrastructure*, which was completed in 2021. Its primary goals for the first three years after adoption are to build capacity for improving the resilience of cities and infrastructure facilities, and to implement concrete development strategies for cities and regions. By analyzing future climate scenarios and their potential impacts for four selected urban areas, the plan aims to develop forecasts for the country as a whole. These projections are to be incorporated into urban and regional planning tools as indicators of resilience and climate change adaptation.

With a *National Climate Change Policy* that sets out a framework for the next three decades up to 2050, Uruguay is among those countries adopting a long-term approach to planning and preparation. The climate change policy includes both ways of reducing the impacts of global warming by decreasing greenhouse gas emissions as well as plans for adapting to environmental changes. These address three distinct planning areas: cities and infrastructure, coastal areas, and agriculture. For each of the three areas, the policy identifies expected risks, corresponding mitigation and improvement measures, and establishes an appropriate investment plan.

This approach of implementing strategies and measures based on adaptation plans that specifically consider social impacts is noteworthy, not least because economic and social sustainability goals and climate change measures are incorporated into regular planning processes. Both Uruguay and its westerly neighbor, Argentina, claim to be the only two countries to have defined their Nationally Determined Contributions (NDCs) to climate change by 2025 to a higher level of detail than that outlined in the United Nations Framework Convention on Climate Change. The approach focuses primarily on urban areas, as this is where most of the population lives and where urbanization is expected to continue.

Among the intended instruments, risk assessment based on risk maps is of particular relevance for elaborating adaptation strategies to mitigate the effects of climate change. In this regard, climate change risks influence land use planning: flood risk maps, for example, provide an essential basis for deciding which spaces not to develop, and which residential areas are most exposed to the risk of flooding. By keeping these areas free or potentially resettling residents, the dangers posed by flooding can be minimized. Similarly, other risks can be addressed that may not yet be clearly identified, for example the exposure of coastal areas to storm surges, again for the period up to 2050. Universities and specialist partners are developing corresponding risk maps.

Still, other climate risks, such as droughts, extreme precipitation and humidity, unusually strong winds, as well as the change in frequency and intensity of such extreme events, have as yet received little attention. Heat waves, for instance, which have become more frequent and can last for more than three to four days, pose a health risk in urban areas, especially to the elderly and children. The resulting excessive use of air conditioners is likewise problematic due to their high energy consumption. In this context, it is particularly important to develop guidelines for upgrading public space and using vegetation in urban areas to reduce heat build-up.

In Montevideo, as in Uruguay as a whole, data on climate change risks mostly relate to their impact on society and the economy. Accordingly, priority is given to measures pertaining to changes in land use and the reduction of greenhouse gas emissions. Measures aimed at influencing specific climate parameters, such as reducing urban heat island effects, avoiding the consequences of prolonged droughts, and ensuring adequate ventilation of affected areas currently play a lesser role. In its prioritization of direct actions to protect the population and economic basis, Montevideo's approach therefore differs starkly from that of most other cities.

THE NATIONAL RESETTLEMENT PLAN

The most serious risk posed by climate change in Uruguay is flooding. In the last decade alone, more than 67,000 people in 60 cities across the country have had to be evacuated due to flooding. In 2010, a *National Resettlement Plan* was introduced that aims to mitigate or eliminate these risks in the long term by providing assistance and financial support to people living in flood risk areas. Because an estimated 60 percent of the population are potentially affected, the plan focuses particularly on those living along rivers or in contaminated areas who lack the funds and resources to relocate to a safer area on their own. The plan aims to also provide a safe, long-term solution for these residents. To this end, the government is making new land available: under the program, relocated families should be involved in the construction of a new house that will then become their own property. Alongside improving flood protection, the resettlement program also aims to halt or even reverse social division and urban sprawl in the country.

While the Ministry of Housing and Spatial Planning provides the funding and technical assistance, the regional municipalities make land available for resettlement and provide the requisite technical infrastructure such as water and electricity, as well as electrical and sanitary installations. The resettlement process also includes a wide range of accompanying social support programs to help people get settled in their new surroundings, find work and schools, and to contribute and have a say in the new neighborhood. The new settlement regions are designated in urban areas with access to public transportation and educational facilities. By involving families in the process, the intention is that neighborhoods will develop as sustainably as possible. The vacated land is then converted into public outdoor areas, such as parks, where flooding does not have such major consequences. This should prevent new informal resettlement of this land.

Since 2010, 55 resettlement agreements have been signed, 34 of which have been completed and another 21 were in progress at the end of 2019. More than 2,100 households have relocated over this period, clearly demonstrating the success of the program. Most of the affected areas were along the Río Uruguay and other rivers where flooding caused significant damage in 2009 and 2010. Montevideo, for example, has accommodated 894 inhabitants in a new settlement.

INSTITUTE OF DESIGN, UNIVERSITY OF URUGUAY

Among the institutions doing important work on climate change adaptation is the Institute of Design at the Faculty of Architecture, Design and Urbanism of the Universidad de la República de Uruguay. Founded in 1959, it has focused primarily on teaching and research in the context of landscape architecture. With the increasing interdisciplinarity of landscape architecture, the Institute began in 1999 to explore new theoretical and methodological approaches. In the context of climate change, it initiated a research program for landscape design and public spaces that encompasses both theoretical and applied planning approaches and spans both large-scale landscape planning and small-scale design. The aim of the project is to elaborate generally applicable statements on the functions of outdoor spaces. These can then be applied to specific planning scenarios and their respective uses to positively influence the quality of life of the population through their sustainable design. One example is the elaboration of a general methodology for analyzing, evaluating, and developing guidelines for the planning and management of public urban parks in Montevideo. Publishing its results at regular intervals, the Institute has now produced an impressive body of high-quality work—such as the outstanding project for an approximately 25-kilometer-long section of the promenade in Montevideo, to which some 20 researchers contributed. Included in the formulated guidelines and recommendations for the future development of the promenade are built structures, vegetation, lighting, and street furniture. The planners also bore in mind the activities of its users, as well as the need to protect historical monuments, and microclimatic conditions. What's more, specific measures for conserving and enhancing the natural and urban environment were then developed from an analysis and evaluation of these recommendations and corresponding planning proposals. Some of the projects have since received international acclaim, for example *Montevideo a cielo abierto: El espacio público* (Montevideo Open Air: Public Space) was commended by the jury of the XIV Pan-American Architecture Biennial in Quito, Ecuador, and *La frontera del agua: El paisaje costero de Uruguay* (The Water Frontier: The Coastal Landscape of Uruguay), which won first prize at the first Latin American Biennial and the third Mexican Biennial of Landscape Architecture.

Montevideo certainly is an interesting city for landscape architects and urban planners, not least because its parks and urban spaces are actively used and well frequented. Whether sitting or strolling along a section of the 18-kilometer-long promenade in the evening or spending time in one of the city's many parks, the mate tea-loving Montevideans have a pleasantly relaxed pace of life that lacks the hectic rush of many other cities. That the city and the small country have long been aware of climate change is undeniably beneficial for the population. Alongside developing strategies for reducing greenhouse gas emissions and implementing precautionary measures to mitigate the effects of extreme weather events, the city's strategies have a strong social focus: they are aimed not just at improving the resilience of nature, the urban realm, and infrastructure but also at creating healthy and sustainable living conditions for the residents. While resettlement programs are certainly a last resort for preventing disasters resulting from extreme weather events, the Uruguayan resettlement plan goes a step further than just preventing health risks or loss of life or livelihoods through flooding or contamination: it also enables them to improve their living conditions and overall social situation. By combining climate resiliency with social improvements, the decision-makers in politics and the administration have demonstrated remarkable farsighted awareness of the upcoming challenges presented by climate change and the need to find sustainable solutions. The strong research focus of the university is an additional asset, providing government agencies with the scientific and experimental backing for their adaptation plans and the concrete implementation strategies that follow from them.

LANDSCAPE ARCHITECTURE AND THE RESILIENCE OF CITIES IN TIMES OF CLIMATE CHANGE

Around the world, reports of heat waves with sustained extreme temperatures, of extensive forest fires and burning steppes, and of tidal waves and flooding with fatalities and injuries, seem to be increasing, and with them news of unprecedented damage to buildings, roads, and railroad lines. Such extreme weather situations are the result of the warming of the atmosphere, the oceans, and land masses, which, according to the 2021 Assessment Report of the Intergovernmental Panel on Climate Change (IPCC), can clearly be attributed to human actions. To avoid even greater consequential damage, considerable efforts are necessary to mitigate the effects of extreme weather events as well as to reduce greenhouse gas emissions.

As part of the 2015 Paris Climate Summit, numerous countries committed to strive to limit global warming to between 1.5 and a maximum of 2 °C, but for the most part the measures needed to achieve this have been vague. For years, the IPCC has been warning that global efforts and actions to meet the 1.5 °C target are still insufficient, and in its most recent Sixth Report, it stresses that global warming will exceed 2 °C during the 21st century unless greenhouse gas emissions are drastically reduced in the coming decades. While the possibility of limiting global warming and concomitant unpredictable climate change still exists, the Report states clearly that the regional impacts of climate change—intense heat, higher ocean waves, heavy precipitation, droughts, and tropical cyclones—are expected to intensify in the near future.

The accounts of the cities in the Americas featured in this book show that climate change is already becoming an important factor in their future development in order to protect their inhabitants and urban infrastructure. In fact, many cities have developed and are adopting climate change adaptation plans and strategies, both to contribute to reducing greenhouse gas emissions and to improve their resilience to projected extreme weather events. That these will occur is inevitable, but the timing, magnitude, and ensuing damage they will cause is hard to predict. Cities must therefore ready themselves for such uncertain eventualities and develop appropriate adaptation plans, translating them into concrete measures that must then be put into action. These plans must also be coordinated with other, existing development plans. Therefore, a key requirement is that future urban planning must consider urban green space sufficiently across the entire metropolitan area of a city and employ it as functional green infrastructure to mitigate climate change. Dealing with rainwater must also be actively incorporated into planning processes in a more differentiated way: water from heavy rain is a potential cause of damage but at the same time water is vital for vegetation and helps cool local microclimates. Finally, urban development plans need to exploit the possibilities offered by landscape architecture to a much greater degree. The projects presented in this book illustrate the broad variety of approaches and possibilities.

Landscape architecture as an interdisciplinary profession that strives to create and develop sustainable and climate-responsive open spaces and cities has an increasingly important and also partially new role to play in the context of climate change. In short, landscape architects can contribute significantly to climate-adapted and resilient urban development through the appropriate design of open spaces, the choice of climate-tolerant vegetation, use of water features, and relevant material choices. Construction methods that are more resilient and better able to adapt, green infrastructure that complements and augments gray infrastructure and architecture, planning processes that involve the inhabitants and, where necessary, assist in ensuring food security, and traffic planning and the distribution and expansion of urban green in the urban realm, are all tasks that landscape architecture can address and influence.

The projects in North and South America detailed in this book present diverse individual and pioneering ways of adapting cities with foresight and appropriately deployed green infrastructure to improve their urban resilience while adapting to the currently foreseeable consequences of climate change. Cities and their various stakeholders—governments and planning departments, clients and investors, landscape architects and researchers—must urgently reappraise and reimagine the role of landscape architecture in urban projects, designs, and strategies. The projects, developments, and research discussed in the previous chapters pave the way towards more climate-responsive urban development. As the climate changes, cities need not just more, but also more effective and better connected and coordinated landscape design. Without this, we will see a widespread rise in the use of air-conditioning along with an accompanying leap in energy consumption, we will see buildings raised on stilts to survive rising sea levels, and the artificial humidification of outdoor environments to ensure that they remain healthy, comfortable, and indeed livable at all.

1
Business premises on Plaza Independencia in downtown Montevideo—nearly every room has an air-conditioning unit, which is energy-intensive to operate, resulting in high CO_2 emissions.

2
Houses raised on stilts to survive rising sea levels and high waves—will this be the new face of city waterfronts in the future?

3
An outdoor water mist cooling system in a square in Buenos Aires—compared with the natural evapotranspiration of plants and trees, this is both costly and energy-intensive.

LANDSCAPE ARCHITECTURE AND THE RESILIENCE OF CITIES

MORE LANDSCAPE ARCHITECTURE

While levels of CO_2 emissions must be reduced in the respective emitting sectors, ideally tending towards zero, previously emitted greenhouse gases will remain in the atmosphere for a long time to come. Carbon sinks are one of the most effective ways of rapidly reducing their concentration, and the most well-researched of these sinks, aside from the oceans, are forms of vegetation such as forests, peat marshes, and grassland, which produce water and oxygen from CO_2 via photosynthesis, and sequester carbon. While densely built-up cities typically lack the space for sufficiently large areas of forest, vegetation still plays a very important role beyond its function as a greenhouse gas sink. In most cities, there is good potential to create more public green spaces, and this can also be achieved relatively easily, with few side effects, and without excessive cost.

Climate change has raised the profile of urban green space significantly: it has the potential to mitigate urban heat island effects, and to retain and infiltrate rainwater. In hot weather, green space cools the local microclimate through evapotranspiration and by providing shade, and in times of heavy rains, it acts as a means of retaining and cleansing water, in turn replenishing groundwater levels. All in all, cities need to better recognize the role that urban green can play and to promote and incorporate it into their climate change adaptation plans and strategies.

Vegetation also serves multiple important functions in adapting cities to respond better to climate change, as many examples have shown. Surprisingly, only a few of the climate change adaptation plans described in this book specifically identify the benefits of green infrastructure or advocate functional green planning. Similarly, comparatively few cities—notable exceptions are Toronto, Vancouver, and Medellín—highlight the importance of public green space and explicitly specify larger planting boxes with appropriate substrate for STREET TREES

4
A model example of the necessary marking of a public green space in Montevideo that also tasks local residents with the maintenance of the space.

or detail the appropriate maintenance of trees according to their species and age. The climatic benefit of trees only acquires its full potential with age. Where street trees are planted in too constricted conditions, are not adequately watered, or are poorly maintained, their life expectancy is shortened dramatically. Replacing a mature tree with a new, usually smaller specimen significantly reduces the climatic effect of planting at that location, and this is only recovered once the young tree has grown sufficiently large, assuming it is properly and regularly maintained over its lifetime. This principle applies to the replacement of any tree, whether due to age or construction works for new buildings, traffic planning, or other gray infrastructure. As such, not just the number of street trees needs to increase significantly, but also their longevity so that future generations can truly benefit from their climatic effect. The changing climate also subjects existing trees to new stresses: new pests and diseases, humidity levels, and water availability can challenge the vitality of the existing stock of trees and the respective public authorities must be provided with sufficient, ongoing financial resources to adequately respond to changing demands through planning, new planting, and maintenance. Toronto's *Complete Streets*, Vancouver's Stanley Park, or the *Rain Gardens* in New York City and Montevideo are all good examples of appropriate responses. To maximize the evapotranspiration capacity of the trees, they require a constant supply of water during the growing season. Water retention trenches in the planting areas beneath the root zones can help bridge dry spells by collecting stormwater runoff, which can supply vegetation with water for longer than conventional tree boxes.

GREEN INFRASTRUCTURE fulfills multiple functions at once and should be networked as far as possible throughout the city. Interconnecting green infrastructure in dense urban areas improves their climatic benefit by maximizing the transfer of the cooling and humidity-producing effect across a larger contiguous area. Excellent examples of green infrastructure that both collect water and provide controlled drainage include Hunter's Point South Park in New York City, the Campus Martius Plaza in Detroit, Buffalo Bayou Park in Houston, Parque 93 in Bogotá, the Green Corridor and Parque del Río in Medellín, to some extent the Porto Maravilha area and the Corredor Verde Recreio in Rio de Janeiro, the large green spaces in the center and residential areas of Brazilian cities, and the inner-city parks in Montevideo.

Another productive form of urban green is URBAN GARDENING, which can range in size from individual beds, such as those in front of City Hall in Vancouver, to larger facilities for farming produce for markets in Detroit or community farms in Toronto. Cities often designate specific areas for this kind of public green space, and this has a dual benefit: gardened areas reduce the amount of green space the city has to maintain, and at the same time these areas are usually managed very intensively. Many garden colonies plant heirloom varieties, counteracting the decline of species and cultivating biodiversity. Urban gardening also benefits the community, as it promotes the exchange and knowledge of plants and cultures and raises awareness of the climate and its changes. Produce is grown close to home, shortening transport distances and reducing CO_2 emissions resulting from deliveries. On a larger scale, they can also help cover some of the nutritional needs of populations whose supply of healthy foods cannot be guaranteed all the time. Home-grown food is more likely to be consumed, and any leftovers used for composting, in turn raising awareness of food handling and reducing food waste, both of which contribute significantly to climate change. Finally, urban gardening is an ideal interim use for derelict land, which can be found in all cities.

MORE EFFECTIVE LANDSCAPE ARCHITECTURE

Landscape architects are called upon to develop and leverage the possibilities that their profession offers for mitigating climate change. In contrast to constructing buildings or traffic infrastructure, landscape architecture is characterized by flexibility, and this is a particular asset in times of climate change. Green spaces can change and adapt, even though the full climatic benefit of plants, and especially trees, only becomes apparent as they grow and mature. Against this background, projects must be conceived for longer planning horizons of one or two human generations; it is no longer sufficient to simply plant site-appropriate vegetation or design single- or multipurpose open spaces. Similarly, green spaces must be designed to withstand the impact of more frequent heavy rains or more extensive dry spells and drought without incurring lasting damage. Construction methods may need to be more robust than in the past, and at the same time surfaces may need to be more water permeable and made of different materials. Hence, designers planning today must take into account the expected impacts of climate change for the coming decades, preferably even a century, in their designs and constructions. A CERTIFICATION SCHEME needs to be devised that, like the LEED rating system for buildings, certifies the sustainable qualities of a green space, its accordance with UN criteria, usability, and material properties, and especially their resilience to climate change.

Hunter's Point South Park and Governors Island in New York City are two examples of parks that have been appropriately designed and built. Both respond proactively to the impacts of climate change. Their topography takes account of predicted rises in sea level and incidences of saltwater flooding by placing key areas of the parks and their vegetation above the flood line. They are designed to accommodate an influx of floodwater and to manage the runoff of water without incurring damage but also without limiting the range of uses they can accommodate. In fact, the opposite is the case and both parks have quickly become magnets for visitors of all kinds.

Houston's Buffalo Bayou Park was also stress-tested for its resilience by Hurricane Harvey without sustaining major lasting damage. Owing to its topography the upper reaches of the park were not affected for as long as the lower-lying areas by the rapidly flowing waters that filled the park. To take these conditions into account, the constructions were designed for durability and quick reinstatement or cleaning after a weather event. Typical strategies included reversing the mistakes of the past where rivers were straightened or buried in covered canals. Instead, the river has been given room to flow and meander more slowly. What's more, a park built along a river is in many ways an optimal situation, providing a nearby amenity for adjoining residential neighborhoods, improving local biodiversity, reducing traffic flows, and linking neighborhoods and districts either side of the river via pedestrian bridges and cycle paths. As a natural stormwater collector, it must be designed to withstand higher water levels and greater water masses, and in turn protect the surrounding urban areas from flooding.

In the context of climate change, CLIMATE, WATER, and VENTILATION, as well as air hygiene, are becoming ever more important factors for urban development. The retention and utilization of water, the evaporative capacity of vegetation, and the provision of open bodies of water are particularly relevant. Urban green spaces must, however, also be able to accommodate large masses of water caused by sudden and heavy rain events without requiring extensive reinstatement afterwards, especially when such events become more frequent. Until recently, the method has been to discharge such excess water as quickly as possible into the drains, or to allow it to percolate into the soil in bioswales and be stored in underground tanks. Many such retention tanks are made of plastic and how these survive or disintegrate over time in the soil is not yet known. The risk is that they could contribute to microplastics in the soil and water, which is not a good, long-term prospect for maintaining good soil resources. Water that is drained away can no longer be utilized either, although it does replenish groundwater. Given that cities are also subject to hot spells and periods of drought, it makes sense to intelligently collect and reuse any rainwater that accumulates. Rainwater cisterns are a common solution, particular for smaller properties and houses, although the water must be oxygenated to ensure it remains of good quality.

In many warmer climates, it is already common practice to recycle rainwater and graywater. When water is scarce, it avoids depleting surface water or groundwater reserves. An excellent example of this is the Olympic Village district in Vancouver, where the multistory housing blocks are designed to harvest rainwater. The roofs extend even beyond the buildings' footprints to maximize the surface area for collecting rainwater, which is then collected and stored in large cisterns next to the underground car park, rather than in the surrounding soil. It feeds the flower beds and water basins and is oxygenated as it circulates, ensuring a near constant supply of good-quality water.

At a more general level, we must also raise awareness of the environment and the interplay of such ecological factors, especially in the context of today's modern urban lifestyles. Thus, the impact and effects of climate change should be COMMON KNOWLEDGE, as only then can the population understand what constitutes a "green city" and contribute to making cities more resilient. Landscape architects and planners, but also clients must be the driving force in a broad understanding of the need to change our urban way of life as well as the necessity of new kinds of open spaces. Along these lines, academic institutions and research initiatives such as the CALP research group at the University of British Columbia are pioneering new methods and have developed citizen-centered media such as the Future Delta video game and Citizen's Coolkit for climate-smart action at a neighborhood level. Universities play indeed an important role here in developing pan-disciplinary approaches to tackling climate change, both in terms of conducting research findings and in disseminating the knowledge gained to society. Citizens of all ages need to become aware of the impacts of their own actions. This can also happen directly on site, such as in the rain gardens of the Levy Park and Midtown Park in Houston or the water features of the Parque de los Deseos in Medellín, which communicate the relevance of water to children as they play.

BETTER CONNECTED LANDSCAPE ARCHITECTURE

Green infrastructure can be even more effective in mitigating the effects of climate change when implemented in combination with buildings and gray infrastructure. It not only helps reduce their negative impacts, for example by counteracting heat build-up from facades, but also enhances their largely static systems by introducing a measure of adaptability, creating design options that are overall more flexible and interconnected.

In most cases, supply and disposal utilities for BUILDINGS bypass the surrounding open space. However, interconnecting buildings with the green spaces around them offers new opportunities for living and working in the context of climate change. In the case of Vancouver's Olympic Village, for example, rainwater is also used—once the rainwater cisterns are full—to supply graywater to the building, in this case for flushing toilets. In drier seasons, the same quantity of water is then drawn from the city's water supply to irrigate the vegetation in the grounds. This approach to supplementing the varying incidence of rainfall over the year can on balance—at least mathematically—lead to cost and energy savings (by reducing water entering the sewers for treatment) and ensure that green spaces are adequately maintained year-round. Although the advantages of using graywater in buildings have long been known, they are unfortunately not yet common practice even in new buildings, despite being easy to incorporate. The design of buildings can likewise respond to climatic conditions, as seen in the Supercuadras in Brasília, which provide well-ventilated, shaded outdoor spaces in the transitional areas between the housing blocks and open spaces. These spaces augment the larger public green spaces, providing an ideal local recreational and leisure amenity for residents of all ages. Another example is the modern Ruta N office building in Medellín, which actively utilizes the cooling capacity of adjoining green areas for ventilating and cooling its indoor spaces. By combining green infrastructure with the structural design of buildings, it is possible to reduce energy demand for cooling in summer and heating in winter, and in turn CO_2 emissions by a relevant order of magnitude. Similarly, greening buildings with green roofs and facades, as well as the greening of road tunnels, are now well-proven construction technologies that have a measurable cooling effect and are well researched. Shallow gradient roof surfaces can also be used to retain rainwater runoff. When implemented together with an underground cistern, water can be pumped back onto the roof during dry periods so that a green roof can provide largely uninterrupted evaporation. When applied at a larger scale, this can have a demonstrable impact on the climatic conditions of a neighborhood through the cooling effect of the roof or facade surfaces. Individual isolated green roofs and facades also have an effect, but only for the building in question, and at best its direct neighbors or adjoining urban space.

TRAFFIC INFRASTRUCTURE such as streets, parking lots, sidewalks, and other paved areas occupy a large proportion of the surface area in cities, and generally contribute to heat build-up through their materials and construction methods. They are also predominantly monofunctional spaces, primarily for traffic, which in turn causes significant pollution, sometimes to the extent of being hazardous to health. However, roadways also offer particular potential for greening along their borders, and by dint of their interconnection, for climate-friendly alternative forms of mobility such as skating, rollerblading, or cycling. Roadside greenery, and especially trees, rain gardens, rainwater harvesting facilities in traffic islands, and similar climate-responsive spaces turn simple roadways into streetscapes that reduce the impacts of climate change while still serving as urban connectors, especially for zero-emission forms of mobility. By improving the quality of these spaces, they can become local places for people to meet in their neighborhoods or in the city. In fact, there are many examples of such opportunities for climate-friendly enrichment of streetscapes, as seen, for example, in Toronto's *Complete Streets* and *Green Streets* initiatives, in the reclaiming of Times Square in New York City for pedestrians, the Ciclovía in Bogotá and other cities, and the Parklets in Montevideo. Medellín has been particularly progressive with the creation and expansion of its rail-based public transit network and system of cable cars. These have reduced emissions and drastically reduced journey times for citizens using more climate-friendly and faster means of transportation. By connecting the outlying districts to the central urban areas, it has also improved the residents' identification with their city. As a result, roadways can be redesigned to accommodate more climate-friendly modes of transport, at the same time improving their qualities for local residents: better air quality, less noise pollution, a better quality of life, and in turn better communication and interaction with each other.

All of these examples illustrate the many imaginative ways in which landscape architects can help cities improve their resilience to climate change, and highlight why landscape architecture should be accorded a central role in addressing climate change in cities.

5, 6

7, 8

9

5, 6
Fairford Avenue in Toronto before and after its transformation into a *Complete Street*.

7, 8
Ryerson Avenue in Toronto before and after refitting with a bioretention system.

9
Water-permeable surfacing, suitable for allowing stormwater runoff to seep into the ground into an appropriately permeable base course.

BETTER CONNECTED LANDSCAPE ARCHITECTURE

REFERENCES/ SOURCES

RESILIENCE AS A FACTOR OF URBAN DEVELOPMENT

International Panel on Climate Change (IPCC)
https://www.ipcc.ch/

Koska, T. (2013): Schwarz auf weiß: Arbeit und Berichte des Weltklimarates (IPCC). Bundeszentrale für politische Bildung
https://www.bpb.de/gesellschaft/umwelt/klimawandel/38497/weltklimarat

Reckien, D. et al. (2018): Equity, Environmental Justice, and Urban Climate Change. In: C. Rosenzweig et al. (eds.), *Climate Change and Cities: Second Assessment Report of the Urban Climate Change Research Network*, 173–224. Cambridge: Cambridge University Press. doi.org/10.1017/9781316563878.013

Rechid, D., Jorzik, O. (2019): Schlüsselstellung der Städte beim Kampf gegen den Klimawandel. *Earth System Knowledge Platform*, January 31, 2019 [www.eskp.de], 6. doi.org/10.2312/eskp.041.

Seto, K. C., Dhakal, S. et al. (2014): Human Settlements, Infrastructure and Spatial Planning. In: Edenhofer, O. et al. (eds), *Climate Change 2014: Mitigation of Climate Change. Contribution of Working Group III to the Fifth Assessment Report of the IPCC*. Cambridge and New York: Cambridge University Press, 923–1000.

Agenda 2030 and the 17 Goals for Sustainable Devleopment, see
https://sdgs.un.org/goals

Weiland, U. (2018): Stadt im Klimawandel. Bundeszentrale für politische Bildung.
https://www.bpb.de/politik/innenpolitik/stadt-und-gesellschaft/216883/stadt-im-klimawandel

United Nations Environment Programme (2021): Adaptation Gap Report 2020. Nairobi.
https://www.unep.org/adaptation-gap-report-2020

TORONTO

CLIMATE CHANGE

For general information on Toronto, see:
https://www.toronto.ca/services-payments/water-environment/environmentally-friendly-city-initiatives/

Toronto: CanopyTO, Tree Canopy Study, 2018
https://www.toronto.ca/legdocs/mmis/2020/ie/bgrd/backgroundfile-141367.pdf

Toronto: Complete Streets Overview
https://www.toronto.ca/services-payments/streets-parking-transportation/enhancing-our-streets-and-public-realm/complete-streets/overview/

Toronto: Green Streets
https://www.toronto.ca/services-payments/streets-parking-transportation/enhancing-our-streets-and-public-realm/green-streets/

Toronto: Toronto Green Streets Technical Guidelines, 2017
https://www.toronto.ca/legdocs/mmis/2017/pw/bgrd/backgroundfile-107514.pdf

Toronto's First Resilience Strategy
https://www.toronto.ca/ext/digital_comm/pdfs/resilience-office/toronto-resilience-strategy.pdf

Toronto: TransformTO: Climate Action for a Healthy, Equitable & Prosperous Toronto Implementation Update 2017 and 2018
https://www.toronto.ca/wp-content/uploads/2020/02/92f8-TransformTO-Climate-Action-for-a-Healthy-Equitable-Prosperous-Toronto-Implementation-Update-2017-and-2018.pdf

URBAN GREENERY

Roman, L. A., Scatena, F. N. (2011): Street Tree Survival Rates: Meta-Analysis of Previous Studies and Application to a Field Survey in Philadelphia, PA, USA. *Urban Forestry & Urban Greening* 10(4): 269–274.

Hilbert, D. R., Roman, L. A. et al. (2019): Urban Tree Mortality: A Literature Review. *Arboriculture & Urban Forestry* 45(5): 167–200.

Kwon, C./DTAH (2014): Canopy Size and Climate Change. Growing Trees in City Sidewalks.
https://www.csla-aapc.ca/sites/csla-aapc.ca/files/CONGRESS2014/Clara%20Kwon%20-%20FINAL.pdf

Moll, G. (1989): The State of our Urban Forest. *American Forests* 95: 61–64.

Roman, L. (2006): Trends in Street Tree Survival, Philadelphia, PA. Master of Environmental Studies Capstone Projects. 4. University of Pennsylvania. *Scholarly Commons*, May 28, 2006.

URBAN AGRICULTURE

Nasr, J. (2012): Interview with Joe Nasr: Urbane Landwirtschaft wird für Architekten Routine werden, *Bauwelt* 39. 2012.
https://www.ryerson.ca/carrotcity/graphics/_publications/_bauwelt/BW_39_12_Nasr%20(1).pdf

Gorgolewski, M., Komisar, J., Nasr, J. (2011): *Carrot City: Creating Places for Urban Agriculture*. New York: Monacelli Press.

PROJECTS

Lobko, J. (2012): Toronto Brownfield Redux. Artscape Wychwood Barns and Evergreen Brick Works. In: *ICOMOS 17th General Assembly*, Paris, France. http://openarchive.icomos.org/id/eprint/1178/1/II-3-Article3_Lobko.pdf

Lobko, J., Torza, M. (2015): The West Don Lands Story: The Tale of how former industrial lands became the home of the Pan Am Games and a new neighbourhood. *Spacing* 36 (Summer 2015).

VANCOUVER

CLIMATE CHANGE

City of Vancouver: Climate Change Adaptation Strategy. 2018 Update and Action Plan, City of Vancouver, Sustainability Group
https://vancouver.ca/green-vancouver/climate-change-adaptation-strategy.aspx

City of Vancouver: Climate Change Adaptation Strategy 2020 Progress Update Council Meeting – October 20, 2020
https://council.vancouver.ca/20201020/documents/P1-Presentation.pdf

City of Vancouver: Greenest City 2020 Action Plan
https://vancouver.ca/files/cov/Greenest-city-action-plan.pdf

City of Vancouver: Greenest City 2020
Action Plan Part Two: 2015–2020
https://vancouver.ca/files/cov/
greenest-city-2020-action-
plan-2015-2020.pdf

City of Vancouver: Climate Emergency
Action Plan Summary 2020–2025
https://vancouver.ca/files/cov/
climate-emergency-action-plan-
summary-2020-2025.pdf

City of Vancouver (2021): Coastal
Adaptation Plan False Creek final
report
https://syc.vancouver.ca/projects/
false-creek-coastal-
adaptation-plan/final-report.pdf

City of Vancouver: Symbols of the City
of Vancouver
https://vancouver.ca/news-calendar/
city-symbols.aspx

Pacific Climate Impact Consortium:
Plan2Adapt
https://www.pacificclimate.org/
analysis-tools/plan2adapt

Zuehlke, B., Jaccard, M., Murphy,
R. (2017): Can Cities Really Make a
Difference? Case Study of Vancouver's
Renewable City Strategy.
http://rem-main.rem.sfu.ca/papers/
jaccard/ZuehlkeJaccardMurphy-
Vancouver_Renewables_Report-
March%202017

OLYMPIC VILLAGE

Durante Kreuk: Olympic Village
Vancouver
http://www.dkl.bc.ca/PROJECTS/
PROJECTS_001/PROJECT_001.html

Bayley, Roger (2010): *The Challenge
Series: Millennium Water: The
Southeast False Creek Olympic
Village – Vancouver, Canada.* Chapter
06: Water and Building Landscape.

City of Vancouver (2007): Southeast
False Creek. Official Development
Plan.
https://bylaws.vancouver.ca/odp/
odp-southeast-false-creek.pdf

City of Vancouver (2006): Vancouver
Southeast False Creek. Public Realm
Plan
https://vancouver.ca/docs/sefc/
public-realm.pdf

GREEN ROOFS

Zinco: Fetthenne und Dickmännchen.
Deutsches Architektenblatt, Ausgabe
Ost, 07/2018, 49.

CALP

CALP: Citizen's Coolkit in Climate
Change & Urban Forestry.
https://calp2016.sites.olt.ubc.ca/
files/2020/07/2019-Aug_Coolkit-In-
design-v26-jul8-2020-reducedsize.pdf

CALP, Sheppard, S., Cheng, Z.
(2016): Citizen's Coolkit on Climate
Change & Urban Forestry: A visual
"do-it-yourself" toolkit for engaging
neighbours on your block. Test version
3.0.
http://calp2016.sites.olt.ubc.ca/
files/2017/10/Coolkit-revision-
22.compressed.pdf

PCIC

Pacific Institute for Climate Solutions:
Annual Report 2017–2018. Special 10th
anniversary edition.
https://pics.uvic.ca/about/pics-
annual-reports-strategic-plan

NEW YORK CITY

CLIMATE CHANGE

Washburn, A. (2013): *The Nature of
Urban Design: A New York Perspective
on Resilience*. Washington, D.C.: Island
Press.

Rice, D. (2019): By 2080, Global
Warming will Make New York City
Feel Like Arkansas. *USA TODAY*,
February 12, 2019.
https://eu.usatoday.com/story/news/
nation/2019/02/12/global-warming-
climate-change-shift-climates-
south/2847860002/

Kasang, D. (2019): Küstenstädte – das
Beispiel New York. In: Lozán J. L. et al.
(eds.), *Warnsignal Klima: Die Städte*.
Hamburg: Verlag Wissenschaftliche
Auswertungen | GEO Magazin, 82–90.
doi.org/10.25592/uhhfdm.9358.
www.klima-warnsignale.uni-hamburg.
de

Rice, A. (2016): This is New York in
the Not-so-Distant Future. *New York
Magazine*, September 5, 2016.
https://nymag.com/intelli-
gencer/2016/09/new-york-future-
flooding-climate-change.html

Plitt, A. (2019): The Trends that Defined
New York City in the 2010s. *Curbed
New York*, December 26, 2019.
https://ny.curbed.
com/2019/12/26/21038024/
nyc-trends-development-real-estate-
parks-2010s

Connell, C. (2018): How NYC is
Preparing for Climate Change.
Time Out, October 3, 2018.
https://www.timeout.com/newyork/
things-to-do/how-NYC-is-preparing-
for-climate-change

RESILIENCE

NYC Parks: Design and Planning
for Food Resiliency: Guidelines for
NYC Parks, 2017
https://www.nycgovparks.org/
planning-and-building/planning/
resiliency-plans/flood-resiliency

Climate Resiliency Design Guidelines,
Version 3.0, 2019 and Version 4.0, 2020
https://www1.nyc.gov/assets/orr/
pdf/NYC_Climate_Resiliency_Design_
Guidelines_v4-0.pdf

Arup: New York City Green
Infrastructure
https://www.arup.com/projects/
new-york-city-green-infrastructure

City of New York: Waterfront Action
Agenda: Transforming New York City's
Waterfront 2011
https://www1.nyc.gov/assets/
planning/download/pdf/plans-
studies/vision-2020-cwp/waves-
agenda.pdf

GOVERNORS ISLAND

Flavelle, C. (2019): New York City Wants
to Put a Climate Change "Laboratory"
on Governors Island. *New York Times*,
October 6, 2019.
https://www.nytimes.com/2019/10/
06/climate/governors-island-climate-
change-new-york.html

West 8 Urban Design & Landscape
Architecture: Governors Island Park
and Public Space Master Plan
www.west8.com/projects/
governors_island/

West 8 Urban Design & Landscape
Architecture: Governors Island The
Hills
www.west8.com/projects/
governors_island_phase_2_the_hills/

West 8: Governors Island—The Hills.
*Landezine – Landscape Architecture
Platform*, July 18, 2016.
landezine.com/index.php/2016/07/
opens-tomorrow-governors-island-
phase-2-the-hills-by-west-8/

American Society of Landscape
Architects: Governors Island Park
and Public Space Master Plan
New York City
https://www.asla.rg/2012awards/
085.html

REFERENCES/SOURCES

CLIMATE MUSEUM

Climate Museum: Climate Signals, Five-Borough Public Art Installation by Justin Brice Guariglia. Climate Museum Hub on Governors Island. September 21–October 31, 2018.
https://climatemuseum.org/climate-signals-release

Climate Museum: Climate Museum
https://climatemuseum.org

Climate Museum: Mission—Climate Museum
https://climatemuseum.org/mission

DOMINO PARK

Park website
https://www.dominopark.com/

James Corner Field Operations: Domino Park
https://www.fieldoperations.net/project-details/project/domino-park.html

Damian Holmes: Domino Park designed by James Corner Field Operations opens in New York
https://worldlandscapearchitect.com/domino-park-designed-by-james-corner-field-operations-opens-in-new-york/#.XyxYyMgzZVc

Domino Park—Sustainability
https://www.dominopark.com/footer/sustainability

Overstreet, K. (2020): Domino Park Turns 2: A Look Back on New York City's Game-Changing Development Site. *ArchDaily*, July 31, 2020.
https://www.archdaily.com/944413/domino-park-turns-2-a-look-back-on-new-york-citys-game-changing-development-site

Gibson, E. (2018): Six-Acre Park Opens at Williamsburg's Domino Sugar Factory. *Dezeen*, June 8, 2018.
https://www.dezeen.com/2018/06/08/domino-park-sugar-factory-james-corner-field-operations-williamsburg-brooklyn-new-york/#:~:text=New%20Yor%E2%80%A6%201

HUNTER'S POINT SOUTH PARK

Fazzare, E. (2018): Hunter's Point South Park Is a Model for Urban Flood Resiliency. *Architectural Digest*, June 27, 2018.
https://www.architecturaldigest.com/story/hunters-point-south-park-urban-flood-resiliency

Lerner, J. (2020): The Thin Green Line. *Landscape Architecture Magazine*, March 2020.
https://landscapearchitecturemagazine.org/2020/03/12/the-thin-green-line/

Young, M. (2018): 10 Fun Facts about the New Hunter's Point South Park in Long Island City. *Untapped New York*, August 24, 2018.
https://untappedcities.com/2018/08/24/10-fun-facts-about-the-new-hunters-point-south-park-in-long-island-city/1/17

Green, J. (2018): A Romantic Kind of Resilient Design. *The Dirt*, September 20, 2018.
https://dirt.asla.org/2018/09/20/a-romantic-approach-to-resilient-design/1/8

Doumar, K. (2018): A Storm-Resilient Park in Queens. *CityLab*, October 24, 2018.
https://www.citylab.com/design/2018/10/storm-resilient-park-queens/573661/

SWA/Balsley: Hunter's Point South Waterfront Park. Recreation, Respite, Art, and Resilience Find Harmonious Balance in New York's Newest Waterfront Park
https://swabalsley.com/projects/hunters-point-south-waterfront-park/

American Society of Landscape Architects: Hunter's Point South Waterfront Park – 2014 ASLA Professional Awards
https://www.asla.org/2014awards/467.html

DETROIT

Detroit Future City
https://detroitfuturecity.com/

Detroit Future City (2012): 2012 Detroit Strategic Framework Plan
https://detroitfuturecity.com/wp-content/uploads/2017/07/DFC_Full_2nd.pdf

CLIMATE CHANGE

Detroit Climate Action Plan (2017)
https://detroitenvironmentaljustice.org/wp-content/uploads/2017/10/CAP_WEB.pdf

GLISA: Historical Climatology: Detroit, Michigan
https://detroitenvironmentaljustice.org/wp-content/uploads/2017/10/2016-Detroit_MI_Climatology-3.pdf

Great Lakes Integrated Sciences & Assessments: The Potential Impacts of Climate Change on Detroit, Michigan
https://glisa.umich.edu/media/files/projects/DCAC/DCAC_Climate_Impacts.pdf

URBAN GARDENING

Keep Growing Detroit
http://detroitagriculture.net/

Detroit Food Policy Council (2019): Creating a Food Secure Detroit: Policy Review and Update
www.detroitfoodpc.org

Klett, M. (2019): Detroit – Transformation von der Autostadt zu Dorf-Archipelen. Oberster Stadtplaner Maurice Cox im Gespräch mit Stadt+Grün. *Stadt+Grün* 4/2019: 54–64.
https://stadtundgruen.de/artikel/detroit-transformation-von-der-autostadt-zu-dorf-archipelen-11203.html

Biba, A. (2019): In Detroit, A New Type of Agricultural Neighborhood Has Emerged. *YES magazine*, November 5, 2019.
https://www.yesmagazine.org/social-justice/2019/11/05/food-community-detroit-garden-agriculture/

Atkinson, R., Berry, M., Sheronick, T. (2017): Urban Farms, Green Infrastructure, and Storm Water Runoff. *Looking Glass*
https://glass.hfcc.edu/2017/05-01/urban-farms-green-infrastructure-and-storm-water-runoff

Beavers, A. W. et al. (2019): How Gardening and a Gardener Support Program in Detroit Influence Participants' Diet, Food Security, and Food Values. *Journal of Hunger & Environmental Nutrition* 15(2): 149–169. doi.org/10.1080/19320248.2019.1587332.

CAMPUS MARTIUS PARK

Rundell, Ernstberger Associates: Campus Martius Park
http://reasite.com/projects/campus-martius-park/

HOUSTON

CLIMATE CHANGE

City of Houston (2020): Resilient Houston
https://reduceflooding.com/wp-content/uploads/2020/02/Resilient-Houston-Reduced-Size.pdf

REFERENCES/SOURCES

City of Houston (2020): Climate Action Plan
http://greenhoustontx.gov/climate_actionplan/CAP-April2020.pdf

Combs, S. (2012): *The Impact of the 2011 Drought and Beyond*
https://texashistory.unt.edu/ark:/67531/metapth542095/m2/1/high_res_d/txcs-0790.pdf

Flavelle, C. (2019): In Houston, a Rash of Storms Tests the Limits of Coping With Climate Change. *New York Times*, October 2, 2019.
https://www.nytimes.com/2019/10/02/climate/hurricane-adaptation-houston.html

Project Drawdown (2020): The Drawdown Review: Climate Solutions for a New Decade
https://drawdown.org/sites/default/files/pdfs/TheDrawdownReview%E2%80%932020%E2%80%93Download.pdf

BUFFALO BAYOU PARK

SWA: Project Description
https://www.swagroup.com/projects/buffalo-bayou-park/

Urban Land Institute (2018): Buffalo Bayou Park. Developing Urban Resilience
https://developingresilience.uli.org/case/buffalo-bayou-park/

Bruner Foundation (2020): Buffalo Bayou Park: Houston, Texas.
http://www.rudybruneraward.org/wp-content/uploads/2020/09/RBA-Pub2019_BOOK_FINALhq_BuffaloBayouPark.pdf

LEVY PARK

Park website
https://www.levyparkhouston.org/

OJB Landscape Architecture (2017): Understanding Levy Park: Tour the Park.
https://www.ojb.com/project/levy-park,
https://www.ojb.com/news/tour-levy-park

MIDTOWN PARK

Park website
https://midtownhouston.com/midtown-park/

Design workshop: Midtown Park
https://www.designworkshop.com/projects/midtown-park.html

BOGOTÁ

CLIMATE CHANGE

Alcaldía Mayor de Bogotá D.C. (2018): Plan Distrital de Gestión del Riesgo de Desastres y del Cambio Climático para Bogotá D.C., 2018–2030
https://www.idiger.gov.co/documents/20182/71301/Plan+PDGRDCC+2018-2030.pdf

Secretaría Distrital de Ambiente Instituto Distrital de Gestión de Riesgos y Cambio Climático – IDIGER Bogotá D.C. (2015): Plan distrital de gestión de riesgos y cambio climático para Bogotá D.C., 2015–2050: Documento técnico de soporte
http://ambientebogota.gov.co/c/document_library/get_file?uuid=ac0bc27e-68f5-4739-926b-3f3c608eef29&groupId=3564131

McGregor, A., Roberts, C., Cousins, F. (2013): *Two Degrees: The built environment and our changing climate*. Abingdon: Routledge

National Geographic Resource Library: El Niño
https://www.nationalgeographic.org/encyclopedia/el-nino/print/

PARQUE 93, DEMOS

Grupo Verde: Parque 93
http://grupoverdeltda.com/portfolio/parque-93/

Grupo Verde: DEMOS Bogotá – Ciudad Caminante
http://grupoverdeltda.com/demos-bogota/

Obraestudio – Humedal Santa Barbara
http://www.obraestudio.com/portfolio/cesb/

Ott, C. (2019): Humedal Urbano Usaquén / CESB / Obraestudio, March 1, 2019.
https://www.archdaily.co/co/912453/humedal-urbano-usaquen-cesb-obraestudio

TOMINÉ

Grupo Verde: Parque Regional Embalse Tomine
https://grupoverdeltda.com/parque-regional-embalse-tomine/

MEDELLÍN

HISTORY AND SOCIAL SITUATION

Samper Escobar, J. J. (2010): The politics of peace process in cities in conflict: The Medellin case as a best practice. BArch thesis, MIT.
http://hdl.handle.net/1721.1/59768

Yolanda, earthlink (2019): Illegale Drogenproduktion verursacht massive Umweltschäden
http://www.drogenmachtweltschmerz.de/2019/07/illegale-drogenproduktion-verursacht-massive-umweltschaeden/

Wahler, M. (2018): Anzahl der Binnenflüchtlinge in Kolumbien auf Rekordhoch. *Amerika21*, June 26, 2018.
https://amerika21.de/2018/06/205090/binnenfluechtlinge-kolumbien-rekordhoch

Milton, L. (n.d.): Experiments in Social Urbanism
https://maptia.com/liannemilton/stories/social-urbanism

UNHCR The UN Refugee Agency
https://www.unhcr.org/figures-at-a-glance.html

Green, J. (2014): The Rebirth of Medellín. *The Dirt*, April 17, 2014.
https://dirt.asla.org/2014/04/17/medellins-metamorphosis/

Campos Garcia, A. et al. (2012): Analysis of Disaster Risk Management in Colombia: A Contribution to the Creation of Public Policies. Washington, D.C.: World Bank Group.
http://documents.worldbank.org/curated/en/648501468241191283/Analysis-of-disaster-risk-management-in-Colombia-a-contribution-to-the-creation-of-public-policies-executive-summary

Volckhausen, T. (2014): Colombia's climate change issues: 180,000 Medellín families in "high risk" of natural disaster. *Colombia Report*, January 27, 2014.
https://colombiareports.com/medellin-precarious-position-climate-change-increasing-natural-disasters/

Sociedad Colombiana de Arquitectos (2016): Grandes Proyectos Urbanos en Colombia
https://sociedadcolombianadearquitectos.org

REFERENCES/SOURCES

CLIMATE CHANGE

Área Metropolitana del Valle de Aburrá (2019): Informe de formulación del Plan de Acción ante el Cambio y la Variabilidad Climática del Área Metropolitana del Valle de Aburrá, 2019–2030.
https://www.metropol.gov.co/ambiental/Documents/Libro_PAC&VC_2019-2030.pdf

Instituto de Estudios Ambientales—IDEA (2018): Formulación del Plan de Acción para el Cambio y la Variabilidad Climática del Valle de Aburrá. Producto No. 1. Síntesis Preliminar Sobre Variabilidad y Cambio Climático en el Valle de Aburrá.
https://www.metropol.gov.co/ambiental/Documents/P4_Cap%C3%ADtulo_1_Sintesis_del_clima.pdf

UN Environment Programme (2019): Medellín shows how nature-based solutions can keep people and planet cool. July 17, 2019.
https://www.unep.org/news-and-stories/story/medellin-shows-how-nature-based-solutions-can-keep-people-and-planet-cool

Gerretsen, I. (2019): This is how cities around the world are adapting to soaring temperatures. Global Center on Adaptation, September 9, 2019.
https://gca.org/this-is-how-cities-around-the-world-are-adapting-to-soaring-temperatures/#:~:text=Medellin's%20'Green%20Corridors',nature%20as%20a%20cooling%20solution.&text=Trees%20and%20shrubs%20have%20reduced,Cities%20Network%20at%20C40%20Cities

Anguelovski, I. (2018): Case Study 6.3: Growth Control, Climate Risk Management, and Urban Equity: The Social Pitfalls of the Green Belt in Medellín. In: Reckien, D. et al. (2018): Chapter 6: Equity, environmental justice, and urban climate change. In: Rosenzweig, C. et al. (eds.): *Climate Change and Cities: Second Assessment Report of the Urban Climate Change Research Network*. New York: Cambridge University Press, 173–224.
https://uccrn.ei.columbia.edu/sites/default/files/content/pubs/ARC3.2-PDF-Chapter-6-Equity-and-Environmental-Justice-wecompress.com_.pdf

TRANSPORTATION INFRASTRUCTURE

Green, J. (2014): An Escalator to Opportunity.
The Dirt, April 22, 2014.
https://dirt.asla.org/2014/04/22/an-escalator-to-opportunity/

100 NEW PARKS

Alcaldía de Medellín: 100 Parques para vos
https://www.medellin.gov.co/irj/portal/medellin?NavigationTarget=navurl://2d28984d31d11b0e56a398afe70b89e3

Monsalve Gomez, S., Hoyos Taborda, J. D. (2018): Medellín River Parks. Medellín, Colombia. *World Landscape Architecture*, August 27, 2018.
https://worldlandscapearchitect.com/medellin-river-parks-medellin-colombia-sebastian-monsalve-gomez/#.X0PcucgzZVc

Landezine International Landscape Award: Medellín River Parks
https://landezine-award.com/medellin-river-parks-2/

Holmes, D. (2013): Urban Current[s] – Medellin Colombia – Land+Civilization Compositions, Taller 301 & openfabric. *World Landscape Architecture*, August 27, 2013.
https://worldlandscapearchitect.com/urban-currents-medellin-colombia-landcivilization-compositions-taller-301-openfabric/#.X0PclMgzZVc

Valencia, N. (2020): The Story of How Medellin Turned Its Water Reservoirs into Public Parks. *ArchDaily*, June 16, 2020.
https://www.archdaily.com/941465/the-story-of-how-medellin-turned-its-water-reservoirs-into-public-parks

Grupo EPM (2014): Diseño del Parque de lo Deseos gana mención de honor en premio latinoamericano
https://www.grupo-epm.com/site/home/sala-de-prensa/noticias/diseno-del-parque-de-lo-deseos-gana-mencion

+udeb Arquitectos: Parque de Los Deseos
https://www.udebarquitectos.com/intitusionales-y-civicas

+udeb Arquitectos: Parque de Los Pies Descalzos
https://www.udebarquitectos.com/parque-de-los-pies-descalzos

Mollard, M. (2015): Colombia's infrastructure reclaimed as public space. *Architectural Review*, June 10, 2015.
https://www.architectural-review.com/essays/colombias-infrastructure-reclaimed-as-public-space

MORAVIA

Unescosost (2018): Socio-Environmental Restoration in Moravia, Medellín, Colombia
https://www.unescosost.org/post/moravia

GREEN ARCHITECTURE

Ruta Medellín
https://www.rutanmedellin.org/es/

Ruta Medellín: Science, Technology, Innovation. Medellín, Latin America's Innovation Capital
https://www.rutanmedellin.org/images/rutan/brochure_ingles.pdf

Alejandro Echeverri, A., Valencia, G.: *Proyectos*.
https://www.alejandroecheverri-valencia.com/proyectos

Opus: Plaza de la Libertad. Memoria Síntesis
https://www.opusestudio.com/arqplaza-de-la-libertad

ArchDaily: Plaza de La Libertad Civic Center / OPUS + Toroposada Arquitectos
https://www.archdaily.com/556939/plaza-de-la-libertad-civic-center-opus-toroposada-arquitectos

RIO DE JANEIRO

CLIMATE CHANGE

Rio de Janeiro: Climate Change Adaptation Strategy for the City of Rio de Janeiro
http://www.centroclima.coppe.ufrj.br/images/Noticias/documentos/plano_de_adaptacao-ENG-FINAL.pdf

Rio de Janeiro: RioResiliente. Resilience Strategy of the City of Rio de Janeiro
https://resilientcitiesnetwork.org/downloadable_resources/Network/Rio-de-Janeiro-Resilience-Strategy-English.pdf

C40 Cities (2016): Case Study: City of Rio de Janeiro – Climate Change Planning through Direct Support
https://www.c40.org/case_studies/city_adviser_rio

Barata, M. M. L. et al. (2020): Use of Climate Change Projections for Resilience Planning in Rio de Janeiro, Brazil. *Frontiers in Sustainable Cities* 2: 28. doi.org/10.3389/frsc.2020.00028.

Lemos, M. F. (2019): Climate Adaptation in Rio, in: Gámez, J. L. S., Lin, Z., Nesbit, J. S., *Rio de Janeiro: Urban Expansion and Environment*. London: Routledge.

The World Bank (2013): The Rio de Janeiro Low Carbon City Development Program. Washington, D.C.: World Bank Group.
http://documents.worldbank.org/curated/en/339111468237587449/The-Rio-de-Janeiro-low-carbon-city-development-program-a-business-model-for-green-and-climate-friendly-growth-in-cities

SUPCLIM/SEA, GAEA, Centro Clima/COPPE/UFRJ (2018): Plano de Adaptação Climática do Estado do Rio de Janeiro. Relatório Final
http://centroclima.coppe.ufrj.br/images/documentos/Produto_11_PAERJ-Relat%C3%B3rio_Final.pdf

PORTO MARAVILHA

Schulz, O. (2016): Der Wunderhafen von Rio. *Bauwelt*, 27.2016.
https://www.bauwelt.de/themen/betrifft/Der-Wunderhafen-von-Rio-Olympia-Aufwertung-Porto-Maravilha-neue-Museen-Rafael-Cardoso-2614481.html

Randelhoff, M. (2013): Konzepte Urbane Mobilität. Rio de Janeiro: Umbau des Hafengebiets zum Porto Maravilha
https://www.zukunft-mobilitaet.net/17712/konzepte/stadtentwicklung-rio-de-janeiro-olympia/

Urban Hub (2016): Porto Maravilha in Brasilien: Wie aus einer alten Industrieruine ein Vorzeigeobjekt wurde [includes video simulation]
https://www.urban-hub.com/de/cities/porto-maravilha-ein-vorzeigeobjekt/

Urban Sustainability Exchange: Porto Maravilha Urban Operation
https://use.metropolis.org/case-studies/porto-maravilha-urban-operation

MUSEU DO AMANHÃ

Santiago Calatrava: Museu do Amanhã Rio de Janeiro
https://calatrava.com/projects/museu-do-amanha-rio-de-janeiro.html

CAIS DO VALONGO

President of the Republic (2016): Valongo Wharf Archaeological Site: Proposal for Inscription on the World Heritage List
http://portal.iphan.gov.br/uploads/ckfinder/arquivos/Dossie_cais_do_valongo_patrimonio_mundial_ingles.pdf

IPHAN—National Historic and Artistic Heritage Institute: Valongo Wharf—Rio de Janeiro
portal.iphan.gov.br/pagina/detalhes/1605/

WASTE DISPOSAL

Mendes, K. (2019): Rio de Janeiro hits the gas in push toward its zero carbon goal. *Reuters*, February 26, 2019.
https://www.reuters.com/article/us-brazil-climatechange-waste/rio-de-janeiro-hits-the-gas-in-push-toward-its-zero-carbon-goal-idUSKCN1QF09Z

Yeung, P. (2020): Umweltfreundliche Abfallentsorgung für Rio de Janeiro?
https://www.dw.com/de/umweltfreundliche-abfallentsorgung-f%C3%BCr-rio-de-janeiro/a-51897346

Oteng-Ababio, M. et al. (2018): Urban solid waste management. In: Rosenzweig, C. et al. (eds.), *Climate Change and Cities: Second Assessment Report of the Urban Climate Change Research Network*. New York: Cambridge University Press, 553–582.
https://uccrn.ei.columbia.edu/sites/default/files/content/pubs/ARC3.2-PDF-Chapter-15-Urban-Solid-Waste-wecompress.com_.pdf

NATURE-BASED SOLUTIONS

Embya: Corredor Verde Recreio
https://www.embya.com.br/case/corredor-verde-recreio-2

Federative Republic of Brazil (2016): Ecological Corridors: Brazilian Initiative and the Continental Perspective. Working Document.
file:///D:/ECOLOGICAL_CORRIDORS_-_WORKING_DOCUMENT.pdf

Cole, L. et al. (2017): Urban Green Infrastructure
https://www.academia.edu/34034745/Urban_Green_Infrastructure

Herzog, C. P., Antuña Rozado, C. (2019): The EU – Brazil Sector Dialogue on nature-based solutions: Contribution to a Brazilian roadmap on nature-based solutions for resilient cities. Brussels: European Commission.
https://op.europa.eu/en/publication-detail/-/publication/12818f2c-f545-11e9-8c1f-01aa75ed71a1/language-en/format-PDF/source-119406601

Herzog C. P., Finotti R. (2013): Local Assessment of Rio de Janeiro City: Two Case Studies of Urbanization Trends and Ecological Impacts. In: Elmqvist, T. et al. (eds.), *Urbanization, Biodiversity and Ecosystem Services: Challenges and Opportunities*. Dordrecht: Springer, 609–628. doi.org/10.1007/978-94-007-7088-1_29.

Herzog, C. P. (2016): A multifunctional green infrastructure design to protect and improve native biodiversity in Rio de Janeiro. *Landscape and Ecological Engineering* 12: 141–150.
doi.org/10.1007/s11355-013-0233-8.

Deutsche Gesellschaft für Internationale Zusammenarbeit (GIZ) GmbH (2019): Biodiversität und Klimawandel in der Mata Atlântica
https://www.giz.de/de/downloads/Mata%20Atlantica_BMU_2019_DE-2.pdf

MANAUS

CITY

IBGE | Cidades@ | Amazonas | Manaus | Panorama
https://cidades.ibge.gov.br/brasil/am/panorama

Garcia, E. (2012): *Manaus: referências da história*. Manaus: Norma editora.

MUSA: Botanischer Garten und Museum Amazoniens
http://museudaamazonia.org.br/pt/

Sotto, D. et al. (2019): Aligning Urban Policy with Climate Action in the Global South: Are Brazilian Cities Considering Climate Emergency in Local Planning Practice? *Energies* 12(18): 3418. doi.org/10.3390/en12183418

Espíndola, I., Ribeiro, W. (2020): Cidades e mudanças climáticas: Desafios para os planos diretores municipais brasileiros. *Cadernos Metrópole* 22(48): 365–396.
doi.org/10.1590/2236-9996.2020-4802.

AMAZONIA

Instituto Nacional de Pesquisas da Amazônia (INPA)
http://portal.inpa.gov.br/

Fatheuer, T. (2019): *Amazonien heute: Eine Region zwischen Entwicklung, Zerstörung und Klimaschutz*. Berlin: Heinrich-Böll-Stiftung.

WWF: Amazon: Facts
https://www.worldwildlife.org/places/amazon

Bader, F. (2017): Amazonien in der Welt. DocPlayer
https://docplayer.org/20877772-Amazonien-in-der-welt.html

INPA (2020): Cheia do Rio Negro em Manaus ficará nos limites normais, com média de 28,49 metros
http://portal.inpa.gov.br/index.php/ultimas-noticias/3715-cheia-do-rio-negro-em-manaus-ficara-nos-limites-normais-com-media-de-28-49-metros

Engelmann, D. (2019): Amazonien: Planet Wissen
https://www.planet-wissen.de/kultur/suedamerika/amazonien/index.html

ATTO (2019): Earth System Research in the Amazon Rainforest.
https://www.mpic.de/4554796/20190830_flyer_atto_de.pdf

ATTO Project
https://www.attoproject.org/de/ueber-atto/allgemeines/

Azevedo, S. G. et al. (2020): Climate change and sustainable development: the case of Amazonia and policy implications. *Environmental Science and Pollution Research* 27: 7745–7756. doi.org/10.1007/s11356-020-07725-4.

Rahnenführer, S. (2020): Alarmierende Bilanz zur Umweltzerstörung im Amazonasgebiet in Brasilien. *Amerika 21*, December, 2020.
https://amerika21.de/print/246086

Marengo, J. A. et al. (2016): Extreme Seasonal Climate Variations in the Amazon Basin: Droughts and Floods. In: Nagy, L., Forsberg, B. R., Artaxo, P. (eds.): *Interactions Between Biosphere, Atmosphere and Human Land Use in the Amazon Basin*. Berlin, Heidelberg: Springer.
https://www.researchgate.net/publication/310515436_Extreme_Seasonal_Climate_Variations_in_the_Amazon_Basin_Droughts_and_Floods

Lovejoy, T. E., Nobre, C. (2018): Amazon Tipping Point. *Science Advances* 4(2), eaat2340, February 21, 2018.
https://advances.sciencemag.org/content/4/2/eaat2340/tab-e-letters

Stang, M. (2019): Klimawandel am Amazonas. Gefahr für die Artenvielfalt. Deutschlandfunk Kultur – Zeitfragen
https://www.deutschlandfunkkultur.de/klimawandel-am-amazonas-gefahr-fuer-die-artenvielfalt.976.de.print?dram:article_id=457515

Deutsche Welle (2015): Cambio climático provoca caos en la Amazonía
https://www.dw.com/es/cambio-climático-provoca-caos-en-la-amazonía/a-18898377

BRASÍLIA

Administração Regional do Plano Piloto
www.planopiloto.df.gov.br

Governo do Distrito Federal, História
www.brasilia.df.gov.br/historia/

Governo do Distrito Federal, Geografia
www.df.gov.br/333/

Coat of Arms
http://www.df.gov.br/simbolos/

IPHAN (2017): Notícias: Brasília completa 30 anos como Patrimônio Mundial
http://portal.iphan.gov.br/noticias/detalhes/4481/brasilia-completa-30-anos-como-patrimonio-mundial

CLIMATE CHANGE

Governo do Distrito Federal (2016): Mudanças climáticas no DF e RIDE. Detecção e projeções das mudanças climáticas para o Distrito Federal e região integrada de desenvolvimento do DF e entorno
http://www.sema.df.gov.br/wp-conteudo/uploads/2017/09/Nota-T%C3%A9cnica-Mudan%C3%A7as-Clim%C3%A1ticas-no-DF-e-RIDE.pdf

Cunha, A. P. M. A. et al. (2019): Extreme Drought Events over Brazil from 2011 to 2019. *Atmosphere* 10(11): 642. doi.org/10.3390/atmos10110642.

Russau, C. (2017): "Das Ende der Fliegenden Flüsse": Wie die Wasserkrise in Brasilien mit der agrarindustriellen Inwertsetzung Amazoniens und der Cerrado-Trockensavanne zusammenhängt. In: *Der kritische Agrarbericht*. Lüneburg: ABL Verlag.

ECOVILA ALDEIA DO ALTIPLANO

CSA da Aldeia do Altiplano
http://mutiraoagroflorestal.org.br/conheca-o-csa-da-aldeia-do-altiplano/

Miccolis, A., Peneireiro, F. M. et al. (2019): *Agroforestry Systems for Ecological Restoration: How to reconcile conservation and production. Options for Brazil's Cerrado and Caatinga biomes.* Instituto Sociedade, População e Natureza—ISPN/Centro Internacional de Pesquisa Agorflorestal—ICRAF.

Miccolis, A. et al. (2017): Restoration through agroforestry: Options for reconciling livelihoods with conservation in the Cerrado and Caatinga biomes in Brazil. *Experimental Agriculture* 55 (S1): 208–225. doi.org/10.1017/S0014479717000138.

Peneireiro, F. M. et al. (2002): Apostila do Educador Agroflorestal. Introdução aos sistemas agroflorestais: Um guia técnico. Projeto Arboreto/Parque Zoobotânico/Universidade Federal do Acre
http://www.agrofloresta.net/static/mochila_do_educador_agroflorestal/apostila.htm

UNIVERSITY OF BRASÍLIA

Website of the University
https://unb.br

MONTEVIDEO

Website of the City Goverment
https://montevideo.gub.uy/

Apud, A. et al. (2020): Suitability Analysis and Planning of Green Infrastructure in Montevideo, Uruguay. *Sustainability* 12(22): 9683. doi.org/10.3390/su12229683.

CLIMATE CHANGE

Oriental Republic of Uruguay (2017): First Nationally Determined Contribution to the Paris Agreement (Unofficial translation)
https://www4.unfccc.int/sites/ndcstaging/PublishedDocuments/Uruguay%20First/Uruguay_First%20Nationally%20Determined%20Contribution.pdf

Intendencia de Montevideo, Desarrollo Ambiental (2014): Montevideo Frente al Cambio Climático. Políticas y Acciones de la Intendencia de Montevideo en Respuesta al Cambio Climático 2010–2014
https://montevideo.gub.uy/sites/default/files/montevideofrente-alcambioclimatico%5B1%5D.pdf

Ministerio de Vivienda y Ordenamiento Territorial: Entrevista al director de Cambio Climático Ignacio Lorenzo
https://www.gub.uy/ministerio-vivien-da-ordenamiento-territorial/comunicacion/publicaciones/nuestro-territorio-edicion-no9/nuestro-territorio-edicion-no9/territorio

REFERENCES/SOURCES

Ministerio de Ambiente (2012):
Plan nacional de Adaptación al
Cambio Climático en ciudades e
infraestructuras – NAP Ciudades
https://www.gub.uy/ministerio-
ambiente/politicas-y-gestion/planes/
plan-nacional-adaptacion-cambio-
climatico-ciudades-infraestructuras-
nap-ciudades

Plan Climático de la Región
Metropolitana de Uruguay (2012)
https://montevideo.gub.uy/sites/
default/files/plan_climatico_region_
metropolitana_uruguay.pdf

Intendencia de Montevideo (2018):
Montevideo Resilience Strategy
https://resilientcitiesnetwork.org/
downloadable_resources/Network/
Montevideo-Resilience-Strategy-
English.pdf

NATIONAL RESETTLEMENT PLAN

United Nations Climate Change:
Uruguay: National Resettlement Plan
https://unfccc.int/climate-action/
momentum-for-change/light-
house-activities/national-
resettlement-plan?normal=j&

Ministeriode Vivienda y Ordenamiento
Territorial: Relocalizaciones
https://www.gub.uy/ministerio-
vivienda-ordenamiento-territorial/
politicas-y-gestion/planes/
relocalizaciones

INSTITUTE OF DESIGN,
UNIVERSITY OF URUGUAY

Instituto de Diseño, Facultad de
Arquitectura, Diseño y Urbanismo,
Universidad de la República:
http://www.fadu.edu.uy/idd/
programas-de-investigacion-
permanente/paisaje-y-espacio-
publico/

INDEX

100 Resilient Cities Network 13, 14, 19, 163
2010 Winter Olympics 44
2016 Kigali Accord 100
2030 Agenda 13
Aburrá Valley 136, 138, 145
Acre 186
Adolpho Ducke Botanical Gardens, Manaus 191–193
Adolpho Lisboa market hall, Manaus 184
Agenda 21 162
Ahmed, Ashrafi 30
Aldeia see Ecovila Aldeia do Altiplano
Alphabet 32
Alves Pereira, Miguel 214
Amanda Burden Urban Open Space Award 94
Amapá 186
Amazon Basin 182, 183, 186, 189, 192, 195, 209
Amazon rainforest 186, 187, 189, 190, 191, 195, 196, 198
Amazon River 182, 183, 184, 186, 187, 189, 190, 192
Amazonas 182, 186
Amazonia 186, 187, 191, 196, 198, 209
Amorim, Cláudia Naves David 217
Anahuac National Wildlife Refuge 96
Andes 116, 117
Antioquia 136, 147, 153, 157
AquaRio, sea water aquarium, Rio de Janeiro 171
Argentina 189, 222, 230
Artifact Walk 72
Artscape 27, 29
Arví Regional Park 136
Ashden 140
Asociación Amigos del Parque 93 120, 122
Athens Charter 201
Atlantic 58, 59, 162, 163, 176, 178, 182, 183, 191, 200, 209, 222
ATTO Research Project 195
Augmented Reality 32
Award for Cooling by Nature 140
Baía de Guanabara, Guanabara Bay 162, 167, 169
Bayou Greenways 2020 114
Bedout, Felipe Uribe de 147, 148
Belém 182, 183
Bernardes Jacobsen Arquitectura 169
Best Innovative Green Building MIPIM Award 169
Bike Rio 163
Bioswale 60, 74, 88, 240
Black Creek Community Farm 29, 30, 31
Bloomberg, Michael 58
Bogotá 13, 115–134, 137, 238, 242
Bolivia 186
Bolsonaro, Jair 197
Brasília 199–220, 241
Brazil 162, 163, 166, 167, 168, 173, 174, 180, 182, 183, 186, 189, 190, 192, 197, 198, 200, 201, 205, 209, 210, 211, 217
British Columbia 38, 41, 43, 51, 56, 240

Brooklyn, New York City 58, 59, 63, 65, 67
Buenos Aires 222, 236
Buffalo Bayou Park, Houston 96, 100–106, 238, 239
Buffalo Bayou Partnership 101
Burle Marx, Roberto 201, 205
C40 cities 13, 163
Caatinga 208, 209, 211
Cais do Valongo, Valongo Wharf, Rio de Janeiro 173, 174
Calatrava, Santiago 169
CALP—Collaborative for Advanced Landscape Planning 51, 52, 53, 240
Campus Martius Plaza, Detroit 86, 92–94, 238
Canada 8, 18, 24, 29, 38, 40
Canelones, Uruguay 229
Cape, Geoff 24
Carbon Neutral Cities Alliance 163
Carioca Mosaic 176
Cariocas 162, 165
Carrot City 29, 30
Casa de la Música, Medellín 147
Casa Firjan, Rio de Janeiro 179
Cemetery of the New Blacks, Cemitério dos Pretos Novos, Rio de Janeiro 174
Central Park, New York City 58
Centre for Green Cities 26
Centro Clima 166
Cerrado 205, 208, 210, 211
Chen, Ying-Fang 120
Chico Mendes Municipal Natural Park, Rio de Janeiro 178
China 22, 38, 224
Cidade do Samba 173
Cidade Nova, Manaus 183
Citizen's Coolkit 53–55, 240
City of Ravines 18
Civic Center of the Department of Antioquia 153–155
Climate Action Plan (Detroit) 87, 88
Climate Action Plan (Houston) 97, 98
Climate Action Plan (Montevideo) 229
Climate adaptation plan 109, 186
Climate Change Adaptation Strategy (Vancouver) 41
Climate Change and Health Strategy (Toronto) 19
Climate Change and Land 11, 12
Climate Explorer 40
Climate Museum, New York 68–69
Climate Resiliency Design Guidelines (New York) 59, 60
Climate scenarios 40, 230
Climate Signals 68
Climate simulations 40
Climate-Resilient Development Pathways (CRDPs) 12, 13
Colciencias 148
Colombia 116, 124, 131, 136, 137, 144, 148, 160, 186
Complete Streets Program (Toronto) 20, 238, 242
Congrès Internationaux d' Architecture Moderne (CIAM) 201
Congresso Nacional, Brasília 205, 206
Conservation Authority 24
Copacabana, Rio de Janeiro 162
Cordilleras 116
Corredor Verde Recreio, Rio de Janeiro 176–180
Corredores verdes 140
Costa, Lúcio 200, 201, 202, 205
COVID-19 pandemic 32
De Melo Zimbres, Paulo 214

INDEX

Dearborn, Michigan 87
Delta, Canada 51
Design Workshop 111
Detroit 83–94, 238
Detroit Agriculture Network (DAN) 91
Detroit Future City 85
Detroit Model 89
Detroit Thrift Gardens 91
Distrito Capital de Bogotá 119
Distrito Especial de Mejoramiento y Organización Sectorial (DEMOS P 93) 120–123
Distrito Federal do Brasil 200
Domino Park, New York City 59, 69–72, 73
Domino Sugar Refinery 69
Don River 18, 24, 34
Don Valley 24, 27
Drawdown 99, 100
DTAH 23
Ducke, Adolpho 191
Durante Kreuk 48, 49
East River 58, 59, 60, 71, 72, 73, 74, 75, 81
East River Tunnel 81
Ecovila Aldeia do Altiplano 211–214
Ecuador 186, 233
Edible Cities Solutions Network 230
Eiffel, Gustave 183
El Dorado 131
El Niño 116, 117, 118, 138, 191
El Niño Southern Oscillation (ENSO) 117
Embalse de Tominé, reservoir 131, 133
Empresas Públicas de Medellín (EPM) 137, 145, 148, 156
EPM Building, Medellín 156
EPM Foundation 148
Equator 116, 182, 189
Escobar, Pablo 136
Estratégia de Adaptação às Mudanças Climáticas da Cidade do Rio de Janeiro 164
Estructura Ecológica Principal 117
Estudio Transversal 157
Ethnicities 171
Europe 20, 29, 38, 89, 180, 184, 224
Evergreen Brick Works 24–27
Evergreen Canada 24, 26
Fairford Avenue, Toronto 243
Fajardo, Martha 120
False Creek, Vancouver 38, 42, 44–49
False Creek Coastal Adaptation Plan, Vancouver 42
Farm-A-Lot Program 91
Field maple 22, 23
First National Report on Climate Change (Primeiro Relatório de Avaliação Nacional sobre Mudanças Climáticas – RAN1) 209
Ford Motor Company 84
Ford Rouge Company, Dearborn 87
Ford, Henry 84, 87
Fragrant sumac 65
French Guiana 186
Fuerzas Armadas Revolucionarias de Colombia (FARC) 136
Future Delta 2.0 52–53, 240
Galveston Bay 96
Galveston Island 98
Garden Resource Program (GRP) 91
Gay, Dixie Friend 111
Geneva 11
Global Resilient Cities Network 98
Global Warming of 1.5 °C 11, 13
Goiás 200

Golden Horseshoe 18
Gonçalves, André 162
Google 32, 55
Gorgolewski, Mark 29
Governors Island Park, New York City 63–67
Great Lakes Integrated Sciences and Assessments (GLISA) 86
Greater Toronto Area 18
Greater Vancouver 38
Green Building Resource Center, Houston 99
Green City 43
Green infrastructure 7, 8, 9, 10, 15, 18, 20, 21, 38, 41, 43, 49, 60, 85, 88, 98, 120, 122, 123, 140, 142, 143, 176, 180, 198, 210, 220, 230, 235, 236, 237, 238, 241
Green Infrastructure Plan (New York) 60
Green Streets Program 20, 21, 242
Greenest City Action Plan (Vancouver) 42
Greiff, León de 144
Grupo Verde 120
Guaraní 222
Guariglia, Justin Brice 68
Guatavita 131, 133
Gulf Coast 96, 98, 100
Gulf of Mexico 96, 98, 111
Gutiérrez, Andrés Ibañez 128
Guyana 186
Harvey, Hurricane 97, 104, 105, 239
Hazel, Hurricane 20
Heat island effect 10, 20, 55, 63, 87, 88, 119, 128, 143, 153, 164, 195, 231, 237
High Line, New York City 58
Hong Kong 38
Houston 13, 14, 95–114, 238, 239, 240
Houston Parks and Recreation Department 100
Houston Ship Channel 96
Houston, Sam 96
Hoyos, Juan David 142
Hudson River 58, 60
Humedal Santa Barbara, Bogotá 124–127
Hunter's Point South Park, New York City 59, 73–81, 238, 239
Imelda, Hurricane 97
Institute for Research and Remembrance 174
Institute of Hydrology, Meteorology and Environmental Research (IDEAM) 118
Interstate 495 81
IPCC, Intergovernmental Panel on Climate Change 11, 12, 13, 15, 209, 235
James Corner Field Operations 72
Johnson Space Center 96
Kawashima, Noboru 120
Keep Growing Detroit (KGD) 88–92
Kebony technology 75
Kigali Cooling Efficiency Program 140
Kobra, Eduardo 169, 171
Komisar, June 29
Kreuk, Peter 49
Kubitschek, Juscelino 200
La Ciclovía 130–131
La Niña 116, 118, 119, 191
Laboratório de Controle Ambiental (LACAM) 217
Lago Paranoá 202, 208
Laguna de Guatavita 131, 132
Lake Erie 84

Lake Huron 84
Lake Ontario 18, 32, 34
Lake St. Clair 84
Lápiz de Acero Azul 148
Largo de São Sebastião, Manaus 184
Latin America 132, 136
Latin American Biennial 233
Le Corbusier 201
Lèbre La Rovere, Emilio 166
LEED 26, 29, 49, 99, 156, 160, 239
Lei Áurea 183
Levy Park, Houston 107–109, 111, 240
Lima, André 210
Livingstone, David 7
Lobko, Joe 23
London 7
Loudon, John Claudius 7
Lovejoy, Thomas E. 190
Lower East Side, Manhattan 59
Main Street, Houston 114
Manaus 181–198
Manhattan, New York City 58, 60, 63, 65, 67, 69, 72, 73, 75, 79, 81
Manufacturing Belt 84
Maranhão 186
Mato Grosso 186
Max Planck Institutes for Chemistry and Biogeochemistry 195
McFaddin National Wildlife Refuge 96
Medellín 13, 14, 135–160, 237, 238, 240, 241, 242
Medellín Cartel 136
Melo, Juan 124
Mertens, Eva 9–16, 235–243
Mexican Biennial of Landscape Architecture 233
Miami 18
Michigan State University 86
Midtown Park, Houston 111–114, 240
Millennium Water Olympic Village, Vancouver 38, 44–49
Minas Gerais 200
Mitigation of Climate Change 11
Moll, Gary 22, 23
Monsalve Gómez, Sebastián 142
Montevideo 8, 221–233, 236, 237, 238, 242
Montevideo Program on Climate Change 229
Monumento à Abertura dos Portos às Nações Amigas 184
Moravia, Medellín 150–152
Morro da Conceição, Rio de Janeiro 174
Mud Creek 24
Muiscas 131
Murphy, Frank 91
Museu de Arte de Rio (MAR) 170
Museu do Amanhã, Rio de Janeiro 170
Nagasawa, Nobuhu 74, 79
NASA 96
Nasr, Joe 29, 30
National Adaptation Plan to Climate Change in Cities and Infrastructures 228
National Historic and Artistic Heritage Institute 173
National Historic and Artistic Heritage Institute (IPHAN) 183
National Institute for Space Research 164
National Institute of Amazonian Research (INPA) 191, 195
National Plan on Climate Change 209
National Resettlement Plan 231–232
Nature 32
New York Bay 58, 60

New York City 13, 14, 20, 57–82, 238, 239, 242
New York Panel on Climate Change (NPCC) 59, 60
New York Times 81
Newtown Creek 59, 73
Niemeyer, Oscar 201, 205, 214
Niterói 168
Nobre, Carlos 190
Obraestudio 124
OJB Landscape Architecture 107
Olmsted, Frederick Law 58
Olympic Village, Vancouver 240, 241
OPUS 153
Pacific 38, 40, 116, 117, 191
Pacific Climate Impacts Consortium (PCIC) 40, 41
Pacific Institute of Climate Solutions, PICS 51, 56
Paes, Eduardo 163
Palácio Itamaraty, Brasília 205
Palácio Rio Negro, Manaus 184, 198
Pampas 209
Panel on Climate Change (PBMC) 209
Pantanal 209
Pará 186
Páramo 117, 118
Paris 12, 13, 97, 183, 190, 201, 210, 235
Paris Climate Agreement 12, 13, 14, 210
Parque 93, Bogotá 120–122, 238
Parque Biblioteca España, Medellín 144
Parque Biblioteca León de Greiff, Medellín 144
Parque de la Imaginación, Medellín 146
Parque de los Deseos, Medellín 146–147, 157, 240
Parque de los Pies Descalzos, Medellín 148–149
Parque del Río, Medellín 142–143, 238
Parque Metropolitano Simón Bolívar, Bogotá 117
Parque Nacional Natural Sumapaz 117
Parque Regional de Tominé 131–134
Parque Senador Jefferson Péres, Manaus 198
Pau Brasil (*Caesalpina echinata*) 200
Paulistas 190
Pedro II. 182
Peneireiro, Fabiana 211, 213
People-first Streets 36
Perimetral 168, 169
Peru 136, 186
Philadelphia 22
Pingree, Hazen S. 89, 91
Pitt, William "the Elder" 7
Plan Colombia 136
Plan de ordenamiento territorial, Bogotá 117
Plan Distrital de Gestión del Riesgo de Desastres y del Cambio Climático para Bogotá D.C., 2018–2030 119
Plan2Adapt 41
Plano Piloto, Brasília 200, 205
Plaza de la Libertad, Medellín 153
Plaza Independencia, Montevideo 236
Pontifical Xaveriana University 128
Porto Maravilha, Rio de Janeiro 163, 166–176, 238
Praça Mauá, Rio de Janeiro 169, 171
Pro-cicla civic organization 130
Quayside, Toronto 32–36
Queens, New York City 59, 81
Queens-Midtown Tunnel 81
Quercus virginiana 104, 114
Quito 233

Rain gardens 15, 49, 60, 61, 88, 100, 107, 108, 110, 111, 113, 114, 230, 238, 240, 242
Regent Park Community Food Centre 29
Rei, Luís 174
Resilience strategy 14, 19, 98, 163, 230
Resilience Strategy (Toronto) 19
Rhus aromatica 65
Ribeiro, Darcy 214
Río Bogotá 131, 132
Rio de Janeiro 13, 14, 161–180, 189, 238
Rio de Janeiro State University 166
Río de la Plata 222
Rio Declaration 162
Río Medellín 136, 143, 150, 160
Rio Negro 182, 183, 184, 185, 187, 198
Río Paraná 222
Rio Solimões 183, 185
Río Tominé 131
Río Uruguay 222, 232
Rockefeller Foundation 13, 14, 19, 97, 163
Rocky Mountains 38
Roman, Lara A. 22
Rondônia 186
Roraima 186
Rubber tree (*Hevea brasiliensis*) 183
Rundell Ernstberger Associates 92
Ruta N 148, 157–160, 241
Ryerson Avenue, Toronto 243
Sambódromo, Rio de Janeiro 173
San Jacinto 96
San José, Uruguay 229
San Rafael reservoir 132
Sandy, Hurricane 59, 68, 74, 81
São Paulo 174, 189, 190
São Sebastião do Rio de Janeiro 162
Saraiva dos Santos, Nelson 214
Sea Rim State Park 96
SEA2CITY 42
Shell Oil Company 97
Sheppard, Stephen 51
Sidewalk Labs 32–36
Smart city 32
South America 10, 15, 116, 117, 131, 134, 162, 171, 173, 189, 198, 208, 222, 224, 236
Space Center Houston 96
St. Clair River 84
Stanley Park, Vancouver 38, 42, 238
Statue of Liberty 58, 63
Stiles, Richard 7–8
Stormwater management 20, 21, 41, 49, 85, 87, 88, 101, 109, 114, 180, 220, 230
Strait of Georgia 38, 50
Street trees 20, 22, 23, 42, 60, 237, 238
Supercuadras 200, 202, 205, 220, 241
Suriname 186
Sustainable Development Goals, SDGs 12, 13
Sustainable Energy for All 140
SWA Group 103
Swiss Alps 51
Teatro Amazonas, Manaus 184
Teixeira, Anísio 214
Texas 96, 97, 98, 100, 106, 114
Texas Point National Wildlife Refuge 96
The Stop Community Food Centre 27
Times Square, New York City 60, 62, 242
Tocantins 186
Toronto 13, 14, 17–36, 237, 238, 242, 243
Toroposada Arquitectos 153
TransformTO 19
Tropics 12, 153, 183

Two Trees Management 69
UN Conference on Environment and Development 162
UN Framework Convention on Climate Change 11, 230
UN Refugee Agency 137
UNESCO 173, 205
Unidades de Vida Articulada (UVA) 145, 147
United Nations 11, 12, 13, 100, 229, 230
United Nations Environment Programme (UNEP) 11, 229
Universidad de la República de Uruguay 232
University of Amazonia (UEA) 195
University of Antioquia 147, 157
University of Brasília 215–219
University of British Columbia 51, 56, 240
University of Michigan 86
University of Victoria 40, 56
Upper Kirby District, Houston 107
Urban Land Institute 94
Uruguay, Oriental Republic of Uruguay 8, 222, 224, 228, 230, 231, 232, 233
USA 22, 38, 136
Usaquén, Bogotá 124
Valongo Hanging Garden, Rio de Janeiro 174–175
Vancouver 8, 13, 14, 37–56, 237, 238, 240, 241
Vancouver Island 38
Vancouver Organizing Committee 44
Vancouver Plan 42
Vancouver, George 38
Venezuela 137, 186
Victoria amazonica (regia), Giant water lilies 189, 191, 192
Victoria Falls 7
Villa Hermosa, Medellín 146
Wagner, Martin 7
Washington D.C. 86
Waterfront, Toronto 32
West Vancouver 50
Wild Wonderland 111
Williamsburg Bridge 59, 72
Williamsburg, New York City 59
World Earth Day (April 22) 99
World Meteorological Organization 11
Wychwood Barns, Toronto 27–29
XIV Pan-American Architecture Biennial 233
Young, Coleman A. 91

253

INDEX

ILLUSTRATION CREDITS

The owner of the rights to all photos and illustrations not listed separately in the illustration credits is Elke Mertens.

TORONTO

2 Courtesy of WEISS/MANFREDI
23 Sidewalk Labs
24 DroneBoy for Sidewalk Labs
25–27 Picture Plane for Heatherwick Studio for Sidewalk Labs

VANCOUVER

5, 8–11, 13–15, 17 Courtesy of DURANTE KREUK LTD.
12 Canadian Society of Landscape Architects
20–25 CALP (Collaborative for Advanced Landscape Planning), UBC

NEW YORK CITY

7 Photo: Iwan Baan
8–16 ©West 8
22 Eight and a Half, courtesy of the Climate Museum
31, 43 ©Bill Tatham/SWA, courtesy of SWA/Balsley and WEISS/MANFREDI
32–36, 40 Courtesy of SWA/Balsley and WEISS/MANFREDI
38, 39, 41, 46 ©Albert Vecerka/Esto, courtesy of SWA/Balsley and WEISS/MANFREDI
42 ©David Lloyd/SWA, courtesy of SWA/Balsley and WEISS/MANFREDI

HOUSTON

1, 4, 5 ©Singleton/SWA
3 Courtesy SWA
6 Houston First
7 Photo by Geoffrey Lyon of G. Lyon Photography, Inc.
11–16 Courtesy of OJB Landscape Architecture
17 Morris Malakoff

BOGOTÁ

2, 3, 5, 6, 8–11 Grupo Verde/Asociación Amigos del Parque 93
12 Courtesy of OBRAESTUDIO, photographer Andres Valbuena
13 Courtesy of OBRAESTUDIO, photographer Daniel Segura
15 Courtesy of OBRAESTUDIO, photographer Jairo Llano
16–18 Courtesy of OBRAESTUDIO

MEDELLÍN

31 Courtesy of OPUS, paisaje arquitectura territorio
32 Sergio Gómez, courtesy of OPUS, paisaje arquitectura territorio
38, 39 Alejandro Echeverri + Valencia arquitectos
Rio de Janeiro
21–24 Embyá Paisagens & Ecossistemas

BRASÍLIA

2 http://www.df.gov.br/simbolos/
5–10 Thiago dos Santos Nascimento
21–23 Courtesy of Fabiana M. Peneireiro, published in: *Agroforestry Systems for Ecological Restoration: How to reconcile conservation and production. Options for Brazil's Cerrado and Caatinga biomes*
25, 26 Fabiana M. Peneireiro

LANDSCAPE ARCHITECTURE AND THE RESILIENCE OF CITIES IN TIMES OF CLIMATE CHANGE

6, 9 Kristina Hausmanis
7, 8 Maili Sedore

ABOUT THE AUTHOR

After completing school in Germany and the USA, Elke Mertens trained initially as a gardener, specializing in the cultivation of trees. She went on to study landscape architecture at the Technical University of Berlin, spent a semester as an intern in Cameroon, and wrote her diploma thesis on an urban planning project with a strong focus on bioclimate. After a period working in practice, she returned to research at the intersection of landscape architecture and bioclimatology, writing her doctoral thesis on the bioclimate of urban building structures. In 1998, she was appointed a professor at Neubrandenburg University of Applied Sciences in the field of garden architecture and open space maintenance as part of the landscape architecture program. Over the years, her work has continued to focus on the dual aspects of landscape architecture and climatology. A research trip in 2018/19 to North, Central, and South America provided the opportunity to explore this topic in detail, and ultimately formed the basis for this book.

THANK YOU!

This book would not have come about without the fantastic support of many colleagues, friends, and experts of all kinds and the energy they invested in assisting me. Some of the friendships and contacts who have helped me research this important topic—one that has always been close to my heart—go back decades. This book is therefore a heartfelt thank you to all who have time and again helped and assisted me with knowledge and information.

I would also like to thank everyone who offered information and guidance before, during, and after our six-month journey through North, Central, and South America. Our various professional discussions helped make connections and clarify ideas, while the many additional conversations we had and tips we received on our journey provided valuable contextual information that helped us better understand the respective circumstances.

Similarly, I must also thank the numerous landscape architecture offices, urban design and architecture practices, municipal authorities and government ministries, as well as colleagues at various universities who generously provided pictures, documents and more in-depth information on projects, planning strategies, and procedures. The knowledge we gained was enormously helpful when visiting sites and reviewing literature, allowing me to see more and to better comprehend the rationale behind certain planning initiatives.

Yasmim, Arthur, Thiago, Carla, and also Juanita accompanied us for parts of our journey, providing friendly and professional assistance, as well as smoothing our path. Your help in understanding the respective contexts, and in clearing up occasional linguistic misunderstandings, was invaluable. Thank you for your hospitality, friendship, and the wonderful experiences we had together!

And finally, last but not least, a heartfelt "thank you" to Lutz for taking the time to accompany me on this trip, for your valuable input on all aspects, for sharing all the beautiful experiences with me, for being there in the occasional less pleasant moments, and for working out the best, most detailed travel plan one could wish for!

IMPRINT

Translation:
Julian Reisenberger

Layout, typography and cover design:
Birkhäuser

Editors for the publisher:
Michael Wachholz
and Andreas Müller, Berlin

Production:
Heike Strempel

Printing:
Grafisches Centrum Cuno
GmbH & Co. KG, Calbe (Saale)

Paper:
120 g/m² Amber Graphic

This publication is also available as an e-book PDF (ISBN 978-3-0356-2265-2) and in a German language edition (ISBN 978-3-0356-2233-1, e-book PDF: ISBN 978-3-0356-2235-5).

© 2021 Birkhäuser Verlag GmbH, Basel
P.O. Box 44, 4009 Basel, Switzerland
Part of Walter de Gruyter GmbH,
Berlin/Boston

Printed on acid-free paper produced from chlorine-free pulp. TCF ∞

Printed in Germany

ISBN 978-3-0356-2234-8

9 8 7 6 5 4 3 2 1

www.birkhauser.com

Bibliographic information published by the German National Library

The German National Library lists this publication in the Deutsche Nationalbibliografie; detailed bibliographic data are available on the Internet
at http://dnb.dnb.de.

This work is subject to copyright. All rights are reserved, whether the whole or part of the material is concerned, specifically the rights of translation, reprinting, reuse of illustrations, recitation, broadcasting, reproduction on microfilms or in other ways, and storage in databases. For any kind of use, permission of the copyright owner must be obtained.

Library of Congress Control Number:
2021947372

This book is published in cooperation with the Heinrich Böll Foundation (www.boell.de).

SPONSORS

COMPUTERWORKS GMBH

VESTRE

Vectorworks: the software for BIM in landscape

www.vectorworks.de

Vectorworks supports landscape architects and planners from the competition through design to implementation planning. Our tools are developed specifically for landscape architecture. Vectorworks Landscape is therefore the ideal CAD and BIM software for implementing projects from start to finish.

Break new ground and successfully implement BIM projects:

With its integrated functions for landscape architecture and Building Information Modeling (BIM), Vectorworks meets the individual requirements and specifications that each BIM project entails. Digital structures and outdoor facilities can be created using components and geometries to which object information such as material descriptions are integrated. A wide range of import/export functions as well as support for openBIM and IFC enable exchange and collaboration with other architects.

Sustainable street furniture

www.vestre.com

Norwegian street furniture manufacturer Vestre has been creating sustainable social gathering places for over 70 years. Its product range includes a wide variety of seating elements, tables, litter bins, bicycle racks and planter boxes.

The company stands out above all for the extreme durability of its products. All products are designed for long-term use in outdoor areas. Among other things, Vestre offers a lifetime warranty against rust and a 15-year warranty against wood rot.

In addition to the appealing Scandinavian design, Vestre sets clear standards in the area of sustainability: all furniture is manufactured with sustainable regional raw materials and the focus of production is to minimize the environmental footprint.

1
©Vectorworks Inc./McGregor Coxall

2
©Vestre